TEXT ME WHEN YOU GET HOME

TEXT ME WHEN YOU GET HOME

THE EVOLUTION AND TRIUMPH
OF MODERN FEMALE FRIENDSHIP

KAYLEEN SCHAEFER

DUTTON

DUTTON

An imprint of Penguin Random House LLC
375 Hudson Street
New York, New York 10014

LIBRARY OF CONGRESS CATALOGING-IN-PUBLICATION DATA
has been applied for.

ISBN 9781101986127

Printed in the United States of America
3   5   7   9   10   8   6   4   2

BOOK DESIGN BY CASSANDRA GARRUZZO

For my mom

CONTENTS

TEXT ME WHEN YOU GET HOME

Why Women Tell Each Other, "Text Me When You Get Home"

Well, female friendships are fucking extraordinary.

—Keira Knightley, actress

Text me when you get home. Usually it's late when women say this to each other, the end of a night that at some point felt thrilling. We might have been at dinner, a concert, or a cocktail bar. We might have been just hanging out talking even though we knew we'd be tired the next day. Maybe we shared secrets or surprise compliments (or both). Maybe we danced. Maybe we hugged with total joy. Maybe we were buoyed by booze or maybe we just felt light because of our love for each other.

My best friend, Ruthie, who lives a few blocks from me in Brooklyn, and I say it to each other after these kinds of nights. "I love you," one of us will say. "Text me when you get home," the other will say. We're saying the same thing.

I hear it on the street sometimes, like the other night when

I passed a woman walking away from her group of girlfriends and into a rowdy crowd. "Text me when you get home," one of her friends called after her. I hear it on television, too, on the HBO show *Insecure,* which is more about the star, Issa (Issa Rae), and her best friend, Molly (Yvonne Orji), than anything else. "Text me when you get home," Issa tells Molly after Molly drops her off at her apartment just after two A.M.

Men do not tell their friends to text them when they get home. Some guy somewhere must have been worried about his buddy finding his way back okay at the end of a night, but he probably just said, "Get home safe," or didn't say anything at all.

This is because women who say, "Text me when you get home," aren't just asking for reassurance that you've made it to your bed unharmed. It's not only about safety. It's about solidarity. It's about us knowing how unsettling it can feel when you've been surrounded by friends and then are suddenly by yourself again. It's about us understanding that women who are alone get unwanted attention and scrutiny. *Should I hold my keys in my hand? Why is this driver talking so much? Is this guy following me? Am I too drunk? Is that guy who just said, "Hey, gorgeous," going to say anything else? My place feels so empty.*

Blythe Baird, a poet in her early twenties in Saint Paul, Minnesota, wrote, in a poem called "Pocket-Sized Feminism":

> *We accept this state of constant fear*
> *as just another part of being a girl.*
> *We text each other when we get home*

The words, and the corresponding texts we send when we do get home, are a web connecting us, winding through the many moments we spend together and apart, helping us understand that whenever we're unmoored or terrified or irate or heartbroken or just bored, we're not by ourselves. It's a way for women to tell each other, *I'm always with you. I won't forget about you when you walk away. I am here when I'm standing in front of you or any other time you need me, no matter what.*

"Text me when you get home" is not an aggressive rallying cry like the anti–Donald Trump, pro-woman "This pussy grabs back," but it does mark a sea change. It's a way women are saying, through our care for each other, that our friendships are not what society says they are. We're reclaiming them. We're taking them back from the shitty words they've been smothered by for way too long:

> *Women can't get along.*
> *They're probably lesbians.*
> *Women who say they like each other are lying.*
> *What a bunch of catty bitches.*
> *Women ditch their friends when they meet a guy.*

What we're doing by holding each other close in whatever ways we can is lifting our friendships out of those stereotypes. We're not going to let the kinds of relationships we want to have be undermined any longer.

We won't accept that we're mean girls or that our friends should be also-rans compared to our romantic partners or children or anyone else tied to us with an official title. It isn't

true. Our friendships—the ones we're living every day—can stand on their own. They are supportive, enthralling, entirely wonderful, and, often, all we need.

I wasn't raised to rely on women. Men were supposed to be my heroes and protectors. I grew up in a Texas town where the boys were football players and the girls were cheerleaders, and while there were many kids who were neither (including me), the caste system was set by those two types. Male athletes could do whatever they wanted. The quarterback used to sit behind me in history class and spit chewing tobacco into a soda can for the entire hour. A lot of the boys at school wore cowboy hats and boots, which I think, looking back, is a pretty good metaphor for how I grew up seeing men. There was a general vibe that the guys were capable in a way the girls were not.

This didn't bother me. I didn't know any different. My mom wouldn't have called herself a feminist then, and she wasn't trying to teach me to be one either. She would often say, "Thank goodness for that nice man," when a male stranger would swoop in to help her. She would never tell me, "You should never be dependent on a man."

I had female friends. They were fun to pinball through social events with, but I also always felt as though I was competing with them, for boys or grades or who looked the prettiest in group pictures.

I never thought much about whether all of this jockeying was necessary. It seemed like what I was supposed to be

doing. And for a decade after I'd left my hometown, through college and my first job, I held on to this behavior. For the most part, I saw other women as either enemies or superfluous. My vision of female friendship was fueled by popular girl-fight television shows and movies like *Ally McBeal* and *Mean Girls*. I also worked in a male-dominated office, where, as in high school, I saw the men as the stars. Women went to step classes or, worse, book clubs. The idea of leaning on them was as alien to me as hiring someone to do my laundry.

I didn't expect to end up where I am now, making female friendship the center of my story. But when I decided I wasn't ready to marry my long-term boyfriend in my early thirties, I looked around, and instead of being unsure, I was inspired. Surrounding me were a bunch of women who were doing exactly what I wanted to do: striving to do good work, setting themselves apart, and aligning themselves with other amazing people. They were also really fun. I wanted to spend whatever time I could with them. This crew, these women who I think are the coolest, became essential to my identity and psyche. Someone once described female friendship to me as a soft place to land, and it was.

I wish I'd understood sooner what women can give each other. I look to my friends for the kind of support that comes from wanting only to be good to each other. The women I love are like a life raft I didn't know I was looking for before I got on it. But my friendships are not just about being nice. My people push me to do better. They listen, but not in a quiet, passive way. They're always on point for correcting me when I put myself down or fall into the trap of thinking things are my fault when they aren't. My friends are brilliant, funny, fearless, wise, and generous. We champion each other in e-mails, in texts, in congratulatory flowers, or simply by saying how much we trust each other.

It feels like I'm part of a team, even if some of the women on it don't know each other. When I'm with my friends, no matter if we're gossiping or analyzing something serious, we're always tripping over each other trying to express how much we empathize with what the other person is saying. No matter if I'm hanging out with one friend or five, we tend to be so hyped to be in the same place, it feels like we're vibrating a little.

These friendships are marked by all of the signposts of romantic relationships, except they're platonic. But they are love stories, complete with lingering dinners, lots of talk about how wonderful we think one another is, and an understanding that this is a continuing courtship—we're not letting the other person go.

But what could be looked at as cute (like how female friendship is represented on greeting cards with pictures of stilettos or glasses of wine) is more than that. What's happening now goes beyond women raving about their girlfriends. We're reshaping the idea of what our public support systems are supposed to look like and what they can be. Women who might have assumed they could find care, kindness, and deep conversations only in romantic relationships are no longer limited to that plotline. Whether women marry or not, whether they have children or not, their friends are fundamental parts of their lives that they won't be giving up. "I just can't imagine not having friendships be a priority," says Briallen Hopper, a lecturer at Yale. "I might end up having a romantic life partner. I might have a child. That's unclear, but either way I can't imagine not having friends that I've had going on fourteen to fifteen years where we've just been through everything together. It's hard to imagine what could break us up."

There just isn't only one love story in our lives. "Whether through our whole lives, or through decades at the beginning of them—and, often, at the end of them, after divorces or deaths—it's our friends who move us into new homes, friends with whom we buy or care for pets, friends with whom we mourn death and experience illness, friends alongside whom some us may raise children and see them into adulthood," Rebecca Traister wrote in her book *All the Single Ladies: Unmarried Women and the Rise of an Independent Nation.*

I am not alone in lifting up my friendships. "The most consistent, central relationships of my life thus far have been with my female friends," Julie Beck wrote in *The Atlantic.* "More than the men I've dated, often more than my family, they have nourished and challenged me, pushed me to take positive risks, shown me the depth of compassion people are capable of."

"A woman will always be my best friend," star of the HBO show *Girls* Jemima Kirke told *GQ.* "I'll never have a best friend who is a man. It just doesn't work that way. So many times young girls will be like, 'I'm a guy's girl.' And I'm like, 'No, you're not. There's no way a man can understand you like a woman, and you're a guy's girl because you're threatened by other women.' I was like that. I was only men. But that's because I felt special around men, and with a woman I can really be put in my place, and I'm on the same level as them. That's the way it's changed, is that I love women now, and I didn't before. Because I was scared of them, because they understood me."

Modern television shows and movies are putting female friendship at the center of their stories, too. On NBC's *Parks and Recreation,* star Leslie Knope (Amy Poehler) was aggressively and sometimes nonsensically complimentary of her BFF, Ann Perkins (Rashida Jones). "You are a beautiful, talented, brilliant powerful musk-ox," she once told her. On another episode she said, "Ann, you're a genius! Your brain is almost as perfect as your face."

HBO's *Big Little Lies* was about playground skirmishes, angry mothers, and dark secrets, but in the end, its female stars—Madeline (Reese Witherspoon), Celeste (Nicole Kidman), Jane (Shailene Woodley), Renata (Laura Dern), and Bonnie (Zoë Kravitz)—didn't turn against each other. Instead, they came together in a protective, empowering clutch. "I read a quote once that said, 'Friendships are the masterpieces of nature,'" Jane tells Madeline at one point. "I know it's cheesy but you're totally my masterpiece." The final shots of the show are of the women on the beach with their children, with no men in sight.

My friends took me out of the way I was taught to be and turned me into something better. This book wouldn't exist without them, but it's also an echo of what I see everywhere right now. Naratives about female friendships—from celebrities, on television, in film—are the ones we want to consume.

And yet, the idea of relying on friendship is in tension with the fact that these relationships are unrecognized and unstructured. There are no licenses or certificates that make them legit or guide how we conduct them. We could lose each other at any moment.

"We don't have external structures in place to keep us close," Hopper says, "and it's still true that if I text a friend and don't hear back in a certain amount of time there's anxiety, and it could be anxiety about the friendship or about them."

Alexander Nehamas, a professor in the humanities at Princeton University, compares our friendships to art in his book *On Friendship;* we value them because they're beautiful. "My thinking about friendship is abstract," he says. "There are relationships where we know what we want from the other person, like how I know what I want from a waiter or a salesperson. That relationship doesn't really change us at all. I have a particular desire or value and I expect you to supply it, whereas with friends I don't know what to expect, either from them or for them. Friendship or a relationship that is more than an instrumental relationship is always leading into an uncertain future. It makes it both exhilarating and also dangerous. The worst thing I can expect from a waiter is a bad meal, whereas with a friend it can be total destruction."

I think this is a striking way to describe our friendships.

When I see my girlfriends, I don't love them because of any trade of services I expect to get from them. I love them because they're there.

But this thinking underscores how tenuous our friendships can feel, depending on what supposedly more legitimate relationships they're being compared to. We have to keep pressing for them to be recognized. If we just treat them as something heady because they exist and are heart filling, they won't last. They'll be diminished by a culture that, at best, is extremely critical of most of the things women say they love. We have to continue acknowledging how necessary these relationships are, whether it's making friends our emergency contacts at the doctor, our yearly Thanksgiving companions, or the people we reach for first whenever anything good, awful, or irritating happens.

"I'm constantly sort of stressing that the world is a really hard place," says Julie Klam, who wrote *Friendkeeping,* a book about how to keep your buddies close. "It's a hard place for men, but it's a really hard place for women. We do so much and we really need to be a good network for each other. We're mostly all doing everything, all of the different jobs. So that is something I feel like is important to remember and is important to remind people. That's survival. No one understands the things that you are doing or the things that you're balancing the way your women friends do."

This book is about the validation—and celebration—of our friendships, but it's also only a start. The conversation about how important other women can be in our lives has just begun.

———————

ext me when you get home. When women say this to each other, they're also saying, *Let's keep talking.* It's my favorite possibility, that when we get home we're probably going to send each other at least half a dozen more texts before the night is officially over. For me, these are the love-drunk, sometimes actually drunk, near-exhausted thoughts I have to send out before I fall asleep. They could be the name of some cultural reference we couldn't remember, a belated compliment ("your skin looked so great tonight"), or another twist in the same joke we'd been making all evening. It all feels important to say right then, and I think that's because of both how happy I feel after I've seen my friends and the fear—rational or not—that these times we have together may disappear at any moment. So we say:

> *Text me when you get home.*
> *Tell me you're safe.*
> *I'm always here for you.*
> *Let's keep talking.*

CHAPTER 1

The Friendships That Shaped Our Own

As I've gotten older, I've understood more the
importance of friendships, and so, I really make an
effort to reach out and make play dates, not let too
much time go by.

—Jane Fonda, actress, writer, political activist

I n 1969, a year and a half after my parents married, my dad, who was a civil engineer in the Air Force, was sent to the war in Vietnam. My mom stayed by herself in an apartment near the military base in Omaha, Nebraska. She had a job teaching Spanish to high school students, so during the day she went to work and at night she came home and wrote my dad a letter. "I made a promise that I would write every night," she says. A couple she and my dad had been friendly with looked after her, taking her to the movies or out to dinner, but "not weekly," she is quick to add.

She didn't have any other friends, or want any, which is inconceivable to me. It's not that I know my mom as someone who surrounded herself with girlfriends. I don't. But I assumed that at this point in her life, in her mid-twenties, by herself, states away from her parents and siblings, she'd at least have looked to other women for companionship and commiseration. Weren't there other women on the base whose husbands were in Vietnam? But she didn't.

"I never even thought of it," she says. "I didn't desire it. I concentrated on my teaching and wrote your dad letters. This was my way to support the effort in Vietnam. I had to be tough, and withstand anything; I couldn't be sad, or unhappy. I was just busy."

This is partly just my mom's personality. Being introspective, especially if that might turn into feeling depressed, is as unnatural to her as texting with her thumbs instead of her index fingers.

But her view on female friendships isn't unique among women of her generation. She's in her seventies now, and no longer feels like she has to soldier on being devoted only to her family. When she was a young wife and mother, she thought of friendships as an indulgence. They were nice, but not essential. What she was responsible for was taking care of her family, so she restrained herself from being interested in anything that would get in the way of that.

This was the contemporary view of how to live, at least if you were white and in the professional class, according to Judith E. Smith, a professor of American Studies at the University of Massachusetts Boston. "Heterosexual romance and the focus on the heterosexual couple is one of the hallmarks of being modern," she says. Men and women who had once looked for support from their friendships and extended families, even after they were married, now turned inward toward each other. My parents, who are white and upper-middle class, did exactly this. They believed the family unit superseded other relationships, and my early thinking that female friendships were superfluous came directly from their example and that of other families like ours in my hometown.

Some women, though, have always moved through the world together. In the mid-twentieth century, the professional class focused on their immediate families, but poorer, working-class women, who were white and non-white, continued to depend on larger networks, including relatives and female friends. They leaned on each other for help with childcare and finding jobs, and for companionship needs not met by sexual relationships. "People who were living from hand to mouth totally needed those additional relationships," Smith says.

At least in part because they couldn't afford not to, these women raised their friendships to the same level as other relationships in their lives. They took care of each other because it was necessary for survival.

My mom says she never felt lonely when she was a new wife, even though she didn't have any girlfriends. It never quite made sense to me because she had friends before she got married, in childhood and college, and in her early twenties she shared a two-bedroom apartment in West Covina, California, with three other women who were also teachers. They became a foursome; everyone at school knew their group. "I think they noticed us because we were young, attractive, and single," my mom says. My mom and one of her roommates carpooled together in the mornings. There was only one bathroom and never enough time, so every night before they went to sleep, the roommate yelled at my mom, "Are you shaving your legs tomorrow?" They went out to bars (my mom drank vodka gimlets) and on trips together, to San Francisco, Bear Mountain, and Honolulu, where they always shared one hotel room for the four of them, partly because they didn't have much money and partly because it was more fun. "We were always talking late into the night," she says. After three years, they all moved out. At first they sent a few letters back and forth, but eventually their only communication was through annual Christmas cards.

The writer Judy Blume, who is in her seventies, also moved away from her friends when she married, at twenty-one. She and her new husband lived on a cul-de-sac in New Jersey, where she "made this new life, at least that's what I thought we were doing, a life centered around my husband," she says. "That's what we did then. It may not have been true for everyone, but it was true for me."

But unlike my mom, Blume reports, "I was very lonely. I missed my girlfriends terribly, my women friends." She soon had two children to take care of, and her female neighbors were raising their own kids, which they did inside their own homes. Today when she's at her apartment in New York, she sees moms together, pushing strollers in the park or eating together at the kinds of lunch places that specialize in jam.

"I think, *Wow, that's so different from anything we did,*" she says. "Because we didn't go out."

One of the friends she missed was her best friend, Mary, whom she met in seventh grade, when they were twelve. In ninth grade, they dated the same guy. "We were both mad about this boy," Blume says. Instead of ruining their friendship, it gave them more in common. "We'd talk on the phone, like after she was out with him, after I was out with him," she says. "It was like, 'How many times did he kiss you?'"

When Blume lived in New Jersey with her husband, Mary lived in New York with hers, and the couples didn't socialize. "We'd married such different guys," Blume says. "Our husbands were never going to be friends."

She desperately wanted to find a friend like Mary in New Jersey. Whenever she saw a moving truck on the cul-de-sac, she'd think, *This is going to be the one. I'm going to make a friend.* She never did. "It just didn't turn out to be, and I can't tell you how lonely I was without my female friendships," Blume says.

Instead, she started to write fiction. Her first book, *The One in the Middle Is the Green Kangaroo,* was published in 1969, and Blume went on to write many beloved children's and young adult books, including *Blubber, Deenie,* and *Are You There, God? It's Me, Margaret.* "Writing saved my life," she says.

But her new career made it even harder for her to make friends with her neighbors. "I think it was more of the times than the women themselves," she says, "but there was something there in that neighborhood that, you know, there was a lot of, 'Who does she think she is, writing? What makes her think she can do this?' There was a lack of support that I had to get back in my life."

Throughout history, women have seen their bonds dismissed, picked apart, or outright mocked. Men from classical philosophers to religious leaders told women they had weak morals, which made it impossible for them to engage in friendship. Because of this, women may have been close, but they didn't dare call themselves friends. "In the texts we have, you don't find the word 'friend' connected to women," says Marilyn Sandidge, who coedited *Friendship in the Middle Ages and Early Modern Age* with Albrecht Classen. "There aren't any women saying 'my friend so and so.'"

Only men used the word "friend" and only to talk about other men. Critics have said this means that women didn't rely on each other during this time, but "that's just absurd," according to Sandidge. Women were friends, but it's hard to find proof for two reasons, both having to do with how marginalized women were. First, they never wrote about themselves—men did the writing—so the documentation of their private lives was paltry. Men wrote what they thought about women or translated their thoughts. Catherine M. Mooney writes in *Gendered Voices: Medieval Saints and Their Interpreters* that women's words "almost invariably reach us only after having passed through the filters of their male confessors, patrons, and scribes." But Sandidge says when you look closely at how the men writing these books and documents describe what women are saying and doing, you can see that they do have close relationships with each other.

The second reason it's hard to point to these ties is that even if women suspected they were friends, men told them that was impossible. Women were too deceitful to relate to one another in the pure, selfless way men did.

Men believed their friendships helped them grow spiritually—they were based on being good to one another, behavior they assumed would bring them closer to God. Women, on the other hand, could never be so virtuous. "Only men were strong enough to maintain a serene, mostly rational, idealistic friendship with another person," Sandidge says.

All women could do, according to men, was mess up men's lives. Ever since Eve ate the forbidden fruit in the Garden of Eden, which got Adam and her kicked out, women have been cast as sex-crazed, evil-seeking troublemakers. If it weren't for us, men would never be tempted with sex, fight each other, or do anything else regrettable. Aristotle's breakdown of the elements in the human body, from about 330 BCE, continued this demonization of women. He saw females as cold and wet, categorizations that meant women were unstable and sexually threatening (males were the opposite, warm and dry). This thinking continued to resonate through the Middle Ages. "We have a lot of liquids coming out of us," Sandidge says. "Men thought that was gross. That is the heart of this misogyny and the reason we were seen as so sexual and dangerous."

In the Middle Ages, the single way it was acceptable for women to be friends was if they were cloistered in a monastery. "There they would be trained by the church and have their sex drive contained," Sandidge says. Those women could then maybe have the same kind of wholesome friendships men did.

As time went on, most men still didn't accept the concept of female friendship. In the seventeenth century, Katherine Philips, a poet who was known by the pseudonym Orinda, formed what she called "the Society of Friendship" anyway. Historians debate whether the group ever had formal meetings, but they did share poems, and most of what Philips wrote about was friendship between women.

One of her poems, "To My Excellent Lucasia, on Our Friendship," read in part:

> But never had Orinda found
> A soul till she found thine;
>
> Which now inspires, cures and supplies,
> And guides my darkened breast:
> For thou art all that I can prize,
> My joy, my life, my rest.

Some scholars have said Philips's work was about lesbianism, but others, like Sandidge, see platonic affection. In 1657, Philips wanted to clear up her confusion about why she seemed to have achieved these deep friendships even though men told her she couldn't. She wrote Jeremy Taylor, a religious leader, asking if he could help her understand what was going on. She felt like a true friend. Could she be one?

Taylor wrote back and published his response: "A Discourse of the Nature, Offices, and Measures of Friendship, with

Rules of Conducting It, in a Letter to the Most Ingenious and Excellent Mrs. Katharine [*sic*] Philips."

His answer, summarized, was that unlike many other men, he was okay with women having friends. He writes, "Madam, you may see how much I differ from the morosity of those cynics, who would not admit your sex into the communities of a noble friendship." He goes on to talk about how devoted women can be. "A woman can love as passionately, and converse as pleasantly, and retain a secret as faithfully, and be useful in her proper ministries, and she can die for her friend as well as the bravest Roman knight," he writes.

Still, despite this, he concludes that Philips and all other women aren't as skilled at friendships as men are, simply because they're women. "I cannot say that women are capable of all of those excellences, by which men can oblige the world; and therefore a female friend in some cases is not so good a counsellor as a wise man," he writes.

This history helps explain how the idea that women can't trust each other, that we're better off forgoing friendship because eventually we're going to fail at it, became so intractable. Men told us not to rely on our own sex—and turn to them instead.

In my grandmother's and mother's generations, female friends met mostly through their husbands and children. What time they spent together was usually alongside a family member, if they joined a couples' group or dragged a toddler to afternoon tea. If they had a hobby in common, they might get together for it. In the 1950s in Sheboygan, Wisconsin, when my grandmother, Christine (my mom's mother) was in her forties, she played the card game canasta with three other women every month. Other than that my mom doesn't remember her having many friends. She had a husband and four children and was busy caring for them, cooking—every day, she made breakfast, lunch, and dinner—and doing laundry. On Mondays, she washed the clothes and then spent the rest of the week ironing them. "There was no such thing as not ironing then," my mom says. "Whenever I came home from school, I usually found her ironing." The women whom she talked with most regularly were other relatives, like her nephew's wife, Betty, who would come by once in a while, or her sister-in-law Elaine, who called sometimes. On canasta nights, though, she'd have dinner with the family and then leave to join her friends, in a nice dress and heels. "I liked seeing my mom go out by herself," my mom recalls. When the women came over to her house, my mom remembers them talking and laughing around a card table set up in the living room. "She seemed relaxed," my mom says.

Even so, friends weren't likely to sit around discussing their feelings about anything, especially their friendships. The chef Julia Child and her friend Avis DeVoto wrote more than four hundred letters to each other, beginning in 1952 when they were both in their forties, a portion of which Joan Reardon compiled in her book, *As Always, Julia: The Letters of Julia Child and Avis DeVoto*. But they mostly discussed food and Julia's cookbook, not how much they valued finding each other. "The letters weren't emotional," Reardon says. "They were professional."

They became friends because they were both enthusiastic

chefs. "People who love to eat are always the best people," Julia writes to Avis in an early letter, and the two go on to praise everything from braised endive to calves' hearts. The correspondence began after Avis's husband, Bernard DeVoto, a journalist and historian, wrote a column in *Harper's Magazine* complaining about the quality of American knives. Julia, who was living in Paris with her husband, Paul, mailed him a gift of one made in France. Avis, who worked as her husband's secretary, wrote to thank her.

Their letters start near the beginning of Julia's work on the cookbook that would become *Mastering the Art of French Cooking,* which she wrote along with Simone Beck and Louisette Bertholle. Avis championed what she was sure would be a "profound book." She was an early recipe tester (about Julia's eggs *pipérade,* Avis writes, "I found there was a little too much fat in it") and eventually introduced Julia to not one but two publishers, after the first fell through.

They traded kitchen equipment (omelet pans, lemon zesters, spatulas) and exotic ingredients (truffles, dried chives) through the mail. Julia would send Avis searching for ingredients she wasn't sure Americans could find in the supermarket, like shallots or fennel. Fennel was stocked only in drugstores at the time, Avis told her, in dried form used for poultices. When Avis mailed her the dried chives, Julia was horrified by them: "Taste like hay with onion flavor."

Avis read many drafts of *Mastering* and offered her opinions: "Page 5—cleaning eggs. Wire wool—what do you mean? First place we never have eggs that dirty. Second place there's steel wool only nobody uses it in kitchens any more— only for stripping paint and so on. Death on the hands."

Both women were married, and Avis had two sons, but they didn't mention their families much, other than to say they'd traveled somewhere with them. Sometimes Julia would talk about what Paul, an avid photographer, was taking pictures of. More personal comments on their relationships were almost nonexistent, although Julia once wrote about sex. "Before marriage I was wildly interested in sex," she writes to Avis, "but since joining up with my old goat, it has taken its proper position in my life." Avis confided in Julia about aging. "I like every part of growing older except what happens to your feet," she writes.

They wrote a little about politics; they were both liberal, and Julia was passionate about wanting to toss out the values of what she called "Old Guard Republicans of the blackest and most violently Neanderthal stripe." Avis sent her news about Senator Joseph McCarthy's hearings hunting for communists in the federal government and beyond, which "Julia thought were just deplorable," Reardon says.

Mostly, though, their letters were about food, cooking, and what became a joint project to make *Mastering* a success. Their shared interests made them "kindred spirits in a way," Reardon says. But even as they had a huge respect and affection for each other, their husbands and families were "really the core of their emotional lives," she says.

Shasta Nelson, the author of *Frientimacy: How to Deepen Friendships for Lifelong Health and Happiness*, gives lectures and runs workshops around the country to teach women how important it is to have friends and to go out with them regularly.

Nelson says there are many women, of all ages, who still think that friendship shouldn't be as much of a priority as their families. "If women are feeling like they're not spending enough time with their kids, they'd feel guilty going out with a friend," she says.

This is learned guilt. At her workshops, Nelson often does an exercise where she asks the audience members to write down memories they have of their moms' friendships. *Do you remember her going out? Or heading off to girls' nights? Or talking on the phone?*

Nelson says usually sixty to seventy percent of the women there have a hard time recalling their moms having friends. Typically, this isn't because their moms didn't have friends, but because they hid them from their children so they didn't feel slighted. "They think they're doing their kids a favor by not taking away from time with them," she says.

When I was a kid, my mom did exactly this. She had a friend she saw five days a week, for forty-five minutes, when I was asleep. She met Anna one morning shortly after we'd moved to town while they were both out walking around the neighborhood. After enough mornings passing each other, they decided to exercise together.

Anna lived on the same street we did, maybe fifteen houses down, so every weekday, they'd meet at five A.M., either in the middle or "she'd wait outside my house or I'd wait outside hers," my mom says. Then they'd walk and talk together, mostly in darkness.

Anna had a daughter my age, and we were friends too, but it was the opposite of how my other friendships worked, where I brought my mom into the equation. In those cases, my mom would pick me up from a playdate and talk with the other mom at the front door for what I felt was way too long, but my mom would never see her otherwise if I wasn't around. With Anna, their friendship existed apart from me. They had similar personalities, in that they were reluctant to talk too much about their personal problems. "She was real hesitant to tell me everything," my mom says, "and I liked that because I'm not going to tell everybody everything right away either." Eventually they got closer and did confide in each other. Anna told my mom she was getting a divorce; my mom told Anna how angry she was when my dad wanted her to quit her job teaching because it was taking her away from the family. "Being with Anna made the walking so much nicer, and we developed a strong bond," my mom says.

Even so, if Anna hadn't wanted to walk with her in the predawn hours, my mom says they wouldn't have been close. "I would not have made the time to see her," she says. "I felt family and marriage came first. Any desires, needs I might have had, were secondary. Girls' night out was unheard of, unthinkable at that time, at least to me."

Other women do remember their moms having friends, who they made clear were important to them. The memoirist Emily Rapp Black, whose mom, Mary, is in her seventies, recalls that whenever her mom's best friend would call, she would disappear for two hours. "I remember seeing the phone cord going down the hall," Emily says. "She was in her bedroom with the door closed. We were given express instructions not to bug her."

She also always saw her mom sending cards and presents to friends, and if her friends in town needed to talk about something that was upsetting them, they'd come over. "It was very apparent to me by the way in which they talked to one another, there was an intimacy there that I really didn't even see between my parents, who have a perfectly fine marriage," Emily says. "That was like their private thing. The friendship intimacy was very much on display."

Mary says that she didn't do this so that Emily would want to have the same kinds of friendships when she got older, but that's what happened, even if she didn't intend it. "I saw my mom have friendships when I was growing up that were incredibly important to her," Emily says, "people who were treated like family and loved like family, and I think that's probably where I got some of the motivation to be a really good friend."

"I didn't say, 'I want her doing that,'" Mary says. "I was touched that she did. You never know what your kids pick up, but this kind of felt, if I don't leave her with anything else and she does have a lot of friends, that's a good thing."

Some of my favorite movies and television shows about friendship as a kid were written by women my mom's age, not that I knew that then. *Beaches,* which was written by Mary Agnes Donoghue, is about a girlhood friendship between scrappy CC Bloom and coddled Hillary Whitney that turns into a grown-up lifeline and forever connection for both women.

My aunt played it for me on video one July. We both cried and, for the rest of the summer, listened to the soundtrack whenever we were in her car.

At the time the movie was released in 1988, there weren't many films about women at all. Male buddy comedies were the biggest moneymakers, including *48 Hrs.*, the first two *Lethal Weapon* movies, *Dragnet*, and *Spies Like Us*. There wasn't a directive to write more movies about women or give audiences anything besides another *Lethal Weapon* where Danny Glover says to Mel Gibson, "I'm too old for this shit." No studio thought a film about female friendship was going to be a surefire hit.

The movie got made only because the singer and movie star (and goddamn legend) Bette Midler wanted to star in it. She had a contract with Walt Disney Pictures and had starred in several hits produced by its Touchstone Pictures division, including the comedies *Down and Out in Beverly Hills* and *Ruthless People*. "Touchstone wanted to make the movie because Bette was Bette," Donoghue says.

Donoghue didn't care what the reason was; she was grateful she was getting to write about female friendship at all. "It was hardly the flavor of the month," she says. The actress Barbara Hershey, who played Hillary, has also acknowledged how unlikely it was for the film to have gotten made. "I knew it was a rare thing to have a film about the friendship between women," she told *Parade* in 2013.

Many of the movies and television shows in the 1980s that had two female characters showed them not getting along. They were usually rivals, often fighting over a man.

Before *Beaches,* Midler starred in a movie called *Outrageous Fortune* with Shelley Long (it was released in 1987). The two women realize they're sharing the same lover and "all they do is fight and hate each other," Donoghue says.

When women have tension between them, and especially when they raise their voices about their disagreement, it brings up a hissing word that is practically dripping with male anticipation: catfight.

In 2014, the actress Rosie Perez, who was then co-hosting the all-female talk show *The View,* got angry about the panel's on-air disagreements always being labeled catfights. "It's pure sexism at play," she told *Huff Post Live,* the Internet-based video network run by news website *The Huffington Post.* "Because listen, you look at one of my favorite shows, *Hardball,* you see the spit coming out of Chris [Matthews]'s mouth at times when he gets really passionate. Even on *Meet the Press*—remember [Rudy] Giuliani and Mike Eric Dyson? Oh my gosh, I thought they were going to go to fisticuffs. They didn't call that a catfight. They didn't even call it a brawl. They called it a debate. But when we do it, it's a catfight . . . and [people say] we hate each other, and that is just not the case."

In its earliest uses, a catfight meant an actual physical altercation between women. One of the first citings of the term, according to the *Oxford English Dictionary,* was in 1854 by writer Benjamin G. Ferris to describe scuffles between Mormon wives in his book *Utah and the Mormons: The History, Government, Doctrines, Customs, and Prospects of the Latter-day Saints.* After he spent six months observing the community, Ferris wrote about the Mormon men practicing polygamy, or having more than one wife, and described the styles of the houses they lived in, which were designed in order to "keep the women . . . as much as possible, apart, and prevent those terrible cat-fights which sometimes occur, with all the accompaniments of Billingsgate [vulgar and coarse language], torn caps, and broken broom-sticks."

A hundred years later, in the 1950s and 1960s, catfights were a staple of fetish films and low-budget B movies, often with a blonde facing off against a brunette. One of the first men to put catfights on-screen, Irving Klaw, liked this pairing in his matchups. Klaw started his career in the 1940s selling photographs of women being bound and gagged in their underwear. In the 1950s, he decided to film the women in these outfits and make them wrestle. "Pin-Up Beauties Fight" stars Bettie Page and June King, dressed in bras, underwear, stockings, garters, and high heels, attack each other on a tile floor. Page is in black lingerie, while King is in white. They spend the entire five-minute movie shoving and spanking each other—at one point, they also try to crush each other with their legs. It ends with them collapsing in a pile, one on top of the other.

In the 1980s, catfights were lifted out of pornography and put on network television, most notably on the nighttime soap opera *Dynasty*. In 1981, the first season of *Dynasty* was getting low ratings compared to *Dallas,* another nighttime soap and *Dynasty*'s main competitor. So producers hired Joan Collins to play Alexis Carrington Colby, a brunette, who'd fight with Linda Evans's character, Krystle Carrington, a blonde. The two fought mostly over oil tycoon Blake Carrington, Krystle's current husband and Alexis's ex. As the network hoped, their dramatic blowups—Krystle slopped a glob of cold cream in Alexis's face; Alexis threw pond scum down Krystle's blouse—boosted the series' ratings.

"*Dynasty* upped the ante," wrote Susan J. Douglas in *Where the Girls Are: Growing Up Female with the Mass Media.* "On one side was blond stay-at-home Krystle Carrington, the Mother Teresa of soaps, endlessly empathetic and supportive, always willing to listen and care, beloved by her servants. . . . In the other corner was the most delicious bitch ever seen on television, the dark haired, scheming, duplicitous, supremely self-centered and self-assured career vixen, Alexis Carrington Colby. Krystle just wanted to make her husband happy; Alexis wanted to control the world. How could you not love a catfight between these two?"

With *Beaches,* Donoghue stepped into this history of women scrapping and making spectacles of themselves and, instead, wanted to show that that wasn't the norm. Women could interact in ways other than fighting over a man. *Beaches* is based on the novel by Iris Rainer Dart, but Donoghue's script differs from it; before she got the job she says, "I went in and told them what I'd do with it, which was basically to leave the book behind and start again." A friend of hers had died at age thirty-nine from leukemia less than a year after the birth of her first child, so she wanted to write about that (in the movie, Hillary has a heart disease and dies when her daughter is about eleven). "That was a huge thing that drove me," she says. The scene where Hillary goes to the library and plows through every book and bit of research she can find about her illness was a direct copy of what her friend did.

Donoghue is still close to her friend's daughter, who's now married and has children of her own, and continues to tell her—and send her letters about—what she remembers about her mom. "I felt like I had to keep her alive in a way forever," she says.

One of Donoghue's favorite exchanges in *Beaches* happens when CC and Hillary are playing cards at Hillary's beach house when she's very ill. CC says to Hillary, after Hillary knows she won't live, "I know everything there is to know about you and my memory is long. My memory is very, very long." After CC walks away, Hillary says to herself, "I'm counting on it."

The movie was also personal for Midler. "I had a girlfriend who really changed my life," she told *Entertainment Tonight* in 1989. "I was kind of a wallflower when I met this girl and she made me laugh so much that I really just bloomed into a whole other person. She died my first year in college. I still think of her. She had a great profound effect on me."

Donoghue wanted to make the movie a platform for showing that women do get along and that friendships can be as essential and enduring as any other relationships in our lives. "I just loved my girlfriends," she says. "That was mainly it. There's so little you see about the subject, and it is powerful. My experience in life is that the longer those relationships go on, the more you can say, and be trusted that you have no other agenda other than your affection for your friend."

But the director Garry Marshall, who was known at the time for creating the sitcoms *Happy Days, Laverne & Shirley,* and *Mork & Mindy,* wanted to go the same old route that had worked for stories about women in the past. He wanted a catfight.

Beaches begins with CC racing to visit Hillary in the hospital, where she's close to death, before flashing back to the beginning of their friendship: Hillary and CC meeting in Atlantic City, New Jersey, in the 1950s when they're both eleven. Hillary is lost on the beach, and CC is under the boardwalk, smoking a cigarette and hiding from her mom. (She offers Hillary a drag. "A drag . . . ?" Hillary says.) They take pictures in a photo booth, sticking their tongues out and pressing their cheeks together when they hug. Hillary splits the strip of four photos in half, writes her address on the back of the section she gives to CC, and they become pen pals.

In one letter to CC, Hillary writes,

> *Dear CC,*
>
> *We're spending the summer at our beach house. It's very peaceful here. I get to ride horses and think a lot. I miss you. It's fun to have somebody to be silly with.*

"Ride?" CC responds. "All I ride is the subway."

Later, in their twenties, they've both moved to New York, where they share an apartment and a crush on the same guy, named John. This is where Marshall wanted to bring in the catfight. Their friendship would end over John. Donoghue tried to tell him that this didn't make sense; women's big fights aren't about men.

"I kept saying, 'Women don't fight about that, they just don't,'" Donoghue says. "You might not be happy with the way certain things go, but it's not going to make or break a friendship. It's one thing if you're married to somebody and your best friend's been sleeping with him for five years and you find it out. That might cause a rupture. But not two women being attracted to the same guy and he ends up with one of them."

Marshall kept insisting, and Donoghue kept refusing. "I'm not running Gary down, but he was a guy of a certain generation," she says. "He didn't have a clue about what made women tick. I dug in and wouldn't write it. I just knew it wasn't true."

What she did write was a scene in which, after Hillary and John have sex, she and CC talk about it the next morning. There's tension, but there's no shouting or slapping. "It's so real," Donoghue says. "It's not full of hatred. It's kind of defeated and sad, but CC accepted it. It's not two women ripping each other's hair out."

Marshall still wanted a catfight and hired a group of writers to add one and make other changes to the script. When the new script came in, the head of the studio hated it and insisted Marshall reinstate Donoghue's version.

A writers' strike that began around the time *Beaches* started filming also helped save her work. "Any movies that were in production or being shot were very closely monitored to make sure people weren't writing in spite of the strike," says Donoghue, who was on a picket line while *Beaches* was being shot. "It was great. They couldn't screw around with the script."

They did make one change Donoghue didn't agree with. She wanted to have CC arrive at the hospital at the end of the story to find that Hillary had already died, but in the movie, Hillary and CC leave the hospital together for one last stay at Hillary's beach house. "In spite of the strike, they changed it," Donoghue says. "As you may notice there's almost no dialogue in those scenes. Someone that sick doesn't leave the hospital, they just don't. So that part of it seemed sentimental and weird to me. But it might have been too rough to have her friend already be gone."

In the middle of the movie, Hillary and CC do have a fight so crushing that they don't speak to each other for years, but it's not about John or any other man. Hillary envies that CC became a famous singer, like she said she was going to, while Hillary gave up her career as a civil rights lawyer for her marriage. "The big fights are about jealousy and seeing that your friend has done all of the stuff that you never managed to pull off and all of the competitiveness that's been going on," Donoghue says. "I think that's much closer to what happens between two women."

Afterward, CC asks her husband, "What will I do without a best friend?"

"You have me," he says.

"It's not the same," she says.

I tell Donoghue that, now that I've watched the movie again as an adult, these are some of my favorite lines. "It truly isn't the same," she says, laughing. "I think no one knows you to the extent your best girlfriend does. There's just a really deep bond that I don't think you would ever have with a guy. As much as you love each other and as close as you are, that similarity isn't there. He means well, but it ain't the same."

The movie wasn't a hit immediately. In the current age, in

which a film needs to be a big draw the instant it opens, *Beaches* wouldn't have made it. Most critics didn't like it. "*Beaches*—which has a couple of key scenes at the beach but otherwise never justifies that title except perhaps with the vague view that we are all life's driftwood—is pure soap from beginning to end," Janet Maslin wrote in *The New York Times*. But after a few weeks, "blam, this thing took off," Donoghue says. "It took word of mouth."

No doubt Midler's version of the song "Wind Beneath My Wings," which plays at the end of the movie, helped it soar. Even if you've never seen *Beaches,* you've most likely heard Midler sing: "Did you ever know that you're my hero? / And everything I would like to be." It was a number one single in the United States, a worldwide hit, and Record of the Year and Song of the Year at the 1990 Grammys. Donoghue remembers being on Fifth Avenue in New York and "all you could hear coming out of every single store was 'Wind Beneath My Wings,'" she says.

She also recalls being on a flight in business class while the movie was playing and seeing the men around her watching it start to cry. "All of these serious-looking men pretended they were wiping their glasses, but they were weeping," she says. "It was great."

The last lines of the film are heard over a flashback to young CC and Hillary in the photo booth in Atlantic City. Hillary says, "Be sure to keep in touch, CC, OK?"

"Well, sure, we're friends, aren't we?" CC says.

"I love my girlfriends," Donoghue says. "I mean I love them. They are critical to my life. If anything happens to one of them, it's a terrible loss, as much of a loss of anything, anyone. They're family."

Sitcoms in the 1980s, unlike movies and nighttime soaps, were telling a few stories about women beyond them fighting over a man. The women tended to be strong and funny, which led to *Murphy Brown* and *Roseanne* at the end of the decade, but two of my favorite childhood shows about female friends, *The Golden Girls* and *Designing Women*, came before that. Both were loose adaptations of what sitcoms were usually about at the time—a family or a workplace—but done with protagonists who weren't often featured on television.

The Golden Girls debuted on NBC in 1985 and ran until 1992. It was created by Susan Harris, who'd been a writer on 1970s shows *All in the Family* and *Maude*. NBC pitched her (through her husband and producing partner Paul Junger Witt) a show about "older women in Miami." "I said, 'Of course. Yes,'" Harris told *Out* magazine. The network thought "older" meant women in their forties, "which was astonishing to me because I think that's what I was at the time," Harris said. "We managed to compromise at the women hovering around late 50, early 60s. But ultimately, their ages were never expressly mentioned." The cast was Bea Arthur as Dorothy, Betty White as Rose, and Rue McClanahan as Blanche (Estelle Getty as Dorothy's mom, Sophia, was a last-minute edition). From the theme song ("Thank You for Being a Friend") to the final line ("You will always be my sisters, always," Dorothy says), the show was about the women propping up each other.

With *Designing Women,* which premiered on CBS in 1986 and ran until 1993, creator Linda Bloodworth Thomason, who'd been a writer on *M*A*S*H,* also "wanted to elevate the concept of female friendship," she says. "I wanted to show the kind of bonds that women can have that stand up to the cultural stereotypes that women's friendships are rife with jealousy and resentment. I wanted to show that women have friendships, not only like men do, but they have the same kind of camaraderie, and probably even a deeper kind of friendship than men because women are willing to go deeper."

Executives at NBC immediately ordered twelve episodes of *The Golden Girls* after seeing the pilot, but the same thing didn't happen at CBS with *Designing Women.* Before the head of programming at CBS previewed the pilot episode to media and advertisers, he apologized. He wasn't sure if he wanted to include it in the network's lineup for the fall season and told the crowd about his uncertainty. "I want to caution you that this is going to be quite different from anything you've seen," he said, "and we still don't know what to do with it."

Some of the television critics in the crowd, who'd already seen the show, starting booing. "No, we like it," they yelled.

"The press fell in love with it," Bloodworth Thomason says. "I mean, in love. They just overruled him, and he was shocked he was so off base."

The four *Designing Women,* with Dixie Carter as Julia, Delta Burke as Suzanne, Annie Potts as Mary Jo, and Jean Smart as Charlene, worked together at an interior design firm in Atlanta called Sugarbaker & Associates, but the business was not the point. Bloodworth Thomason just needed a place where the smart southern female characters she envisioned could have conversations. "The initial thing was the excitement of them intellectually," she says. "I didn't want to write women who were talking about their boyfriends and their hair and all that."

The Golden Girls also spent a lot of time in the same space: the kitchen table in their shared home, late at night, where they'd discuss the same worries that were keeping women who weren't on television awake (and they'd eat cheesecake).

"We liked to tackle—not outrageous issues—but important issues," Harris said. "Things that I knew that people went through that hadn't been addressed on television." This included gay rights, age discrimination, and the history of racism in America.

Bloodworth Thomason was exposed to this kind of debate during her childhood in Poplar Bluff, Missouri, where she often sat on the front porch listening to her grandfather, father, and three uncles. "They were a loud, cantankerous, well-read, very articulate bunch of men," she says. "They argued about everything."

With *Designing Women,* she wanted to get that back, but with women instead of men. "I wanted to have a little penisectomy and have these women be like that," Bloodworth Thomason says. "They weren't exactly like the men, of course, but I wanted that kind of, bam, when they're all together you know something big is going to happen. There's going to be a big argument, or there's going to a big psychological, intellectual, or political dilemma."

Like *The Golden Girls, Designing Women* was feminist and politically liberal. "I wanted to be funny as hell," Bloodworth Thomason says, "but I definitely had an agenda." She wrote episodes about women being shamed for gaining weight ("They Shoot Fat Women, Don't They?") and being judged harshly for accusing men of sexual harassment, based on the reaction to Anita Hill's testimony about Clarence Thomas at his Supreme Court confirmation hearings ("The Strange Case of Clarence and Anita").

This kind of debate and discussion meant that the women didn't always get along, although there wasn't any shaving-cream or pond-scum throwing. There was discomfort and disagreement, and sometimes they were personally hurtful to each other. Dorothy's barbs on *The Golden Girls,* in particular, were legendary. When Rose says, "Can I ask a dumb question?" Dorothy answers, "Better than anyone I know."

But, no matter what, they supported each other, and these shows were about women's solidarity and their ability to care for one another. "It's so interesting to me that it doesn't change, the things women need, the things that women have to overcome, the things that women do for each other, and the reason that we stand on each other's shoulders," Bloodworth Thomason says. "Those things really haven't changed. It starts over with every generation."

Women who are in their fifties today were among the first to tilt away from thinking that their friends couldn't take time away from their families, and they made a point of focusing on their friendships even when they were newlyweds. Dawn Carlson, who's fifty-five and lives in Brandon, Florida, has five friends she's been close with since they all started hanging out together in high school (some she met in middle school). They were on the dance team, went to prom in a big group, and spent their weekends on the beach. All of them except one married in their early twenties, and while they were all going to each other's wedding showers, one of them said, "Gosh, we only get together at these things. Let's do something else." They started having monthly girls' nights. Dawn hosted the first one at her house, a poker party, even though none of them had played before. She had her husband print out the rules of the game, and "we all drank pink wine back then, but I got longneck bottles of beer," she says. "We didn't know what we were doing but we were trying to be badass."

"We laughed a lot and we still do," Dawn says. "They all have such a smart, quirky sense of humor. We can poke fun at each other and really laugh and we're okay."

They went on weekends away together too, even as most of them had infants to take care of. Dawn remembers one trip to nearby Longboat Key, when they stayed in her grand-mother's mobile home. "None of us had any money," she says. "It needed to be cheap." They wanted to lie on the beach like they did when they were teenagers, but now they had babies to bring along too, so they dragged full-size playpens across the road and set them up on the sand. "We still laugh about that," Dawn says.

Other times they asked their husbands to watch the kids, which could be as tricky as hauling playpens across a high-way. "We did have to justify it some," she says. "All of us had really great husbands, but we still had some trouble. It could get testy at times. They'd say, 'You're gone for the weekend, what about my golf?' But they still did it."

Dawn and her friends talk a lot about how their moms didn't—and couldn't—do anything like this. Like with my grandma, her mom saw more relatives than friends. "It was more acceptable," she says. "They were strapped to their babies. Just a few decades later, we could have a life. I got to say to my husband, 'I'm going to go for a weekend with my girlfriends. They're really important to me.'"

As with any good group, other women wanted to join, which Dawn says her friends found funny. "You're in your thirties and people want to join your friend group," she says. But it also underscored how special what they had was. "We're not the norm," she says. "We had to really work at this, had to get the husbands on board, had to be dedicated and say we're going to do this."

When Judy Blume was writing what turned out to be her bestselling book ever, *Summer Sisters*, she'd moved away from the cul-de-sac in New Jersey. But what she'd learned there about how necessary friendships are, and how devastated one can be when they're gone, stayed with her.

The book, which was published in 1998, is the story of Vix and Caitlin, best friends who meet when they're twelve and spend every summer together on Martha's Vineyard. It starts with Caitlin shocking Vix by telling her she's marrying Vix's first love and asking her to be the maid of honor.

Despite this soap opera beginning, the book was the rare piece of fiction at the time that showed the kind of completely absorbing friendship many young women, myself included, could relate to: Caitlin and Vix's relationship was intense and intimate, and wonderful and awful. When Lena Dunham interviewed Blume for *The Believer,* she told her *Summer Sisters* influenced her HBO show, *Girls.* "It was the first thing I ever consumed that looked at the way female friendship can be glorious and can be complicated and a worse betrayal than something romantic," Dunham said. *Summer Sisters* comes up again and again as the book young women say they've read the most times. Some reach for it every summer. My best friend, Ruthie, has read it six times, but "I have read the sex scenes at least twice that," she says, laughing.

"It's my least autobiographical book," Blume says. "My least. But I knew how important a friend was because I was longing for one."

By the time she wrote *Summer Sisters,* she had divorced her first husband and reconnected with Mary in New York, where they lived in apartments around the corner from each other. She dedicated the book to Mary:

> To Mary Weaver
> my "summer sister"

They're still best friends today. "We're talking sixty-something years," Blume says, "and we're never going to lose that now. We're way too old."

In part, *Summer Sisters* is about finding that friend who

feels like magic to you, as if you can't believe she picked you to share secrets with. "What I'm talking about is how girls fall in love with their best friends," Blume says. "I mean it's not a sexual thing, but it's, I don't know if Mary would say this, but it was like falling in love. It was just like being together was so much fun, and again it might be very different for her. But that's how it was. It was always great, just spending time together, being together, our crazy senses of humor."

Today, Blume spends most of her time in Key West, Florida, but she and Mary talk on the phone every week. They still talk about their ninth-grade crush. When they read in the paper that his daughter was getting married, Mary tried to get Blume to spy on the wedding with her. "Let's go stand outside and get a look at him," she said.

They see each other when Blume's in New York; they have the same apartments near each other. They often go out with Blume's husband, too, but on a recent trip Blume and Mary had dinner, just the two of them, something they hadn't done in a long time. Afterward they hugged good-bye on the sidewalk and reflected on their friendship. "We said, 'Oh, we just love being together,'" Blume says. "We have such a good time, through all of what's happened to us and all of the directions that our lives have taken."

Blume watched her mom rely on her female friends as she got older too. While her dad was alive, she remembers them socializing only with other couples. "They had a Sunday night club," she says. "I remember the couples who came to our house," she says.

But when her dad died, her mom was in her mid-fifties

and "she went out and made new women friends," Blume says. "Those friends were so important to her for the next thirty years." As the years went on, they all became widows and looked out for each other. "They were maybe neurotic," Blume says. "They had a little thing, a little round-robin. They called each other every morning to make sure they were still alive. One would call one and then call the other and call the other. Now that I'm getting up there, I think, Well that's great that they did that. They checked on each other every day."

My mom is retired now and making new friends. She had two women, whom she knows from the gym, over to her house recently for wine, pizza, and cookies. "We quickly went through one bottle of wine and followed that one with another," she says. They talked about recent surgeries and raising their children, trashed one of their ex-husbands, and laughed about how one of them keeps getting in trouble for talking during exercise class. "We laughed and laughed," my mom says.

I like hearing my mom talk about her friends. When she tells me about them, she sounds happy. And in her descriptions of these women and the time they spend together, I hear an echo of how I feel about my own friends. Even though for decades my mom thought that friendships would take her away from her family, what's happened now that I'm a grown-up is that having our friends be important to us is something we share.

The other day she told me about going over to a friend's house to hang out on her backyard deck on the first nice day of summer, where they talked about their plans for the next few months and drank mojitos. That friend is trying to convince my mom to go on a kayaking adventure in Alaska with her, even though my mom would prefer an amenity-heavy hotel.

"I don't know about kayaking," my mom told her. "I'm seventy-five."

"So am I!" her friend said. "We'll do it together."

CHAPTER 2

Mean Girls and Nice Girls

Gretchen, I'm sorry I laughed at you that time you got
diarrhea at Barnes & Noble. And I'm sorry I told
everyone about it. And I'm sorry for repeating it now.

—Karen in *Mean Girls*

How do I even begin to explain Renée Tarwater?

She was tiny and delicate, about four foot ten, and mostly limbs. Her ponytail and giant bow, the required hairstyle in middle school, were always perfect. She had big eyes and the kind of confidence that I could only muster in front of my bathroom mirror, alone and in flattering lighting. Her wardrobe was made up of the most stylish clothes anyone could wear then, mostly Hypercolor T-shirts and Girbaud and Z. Cavaricci jeans. Even the accent in her name was cool.

If I close my eyes and imagine her back then—I met her in elementary school and we graduated from high school together—I see her being carried by a crowd, high above the rest of us. This is probably because she was actually being lifted up a lot. As the smallest cheerleader, she was the one on top of the human pyramid the cheerleaders formed at pep rallies and on the sidelines at football games. And in the halls, the many guys who had crushes on her were always picking her up and swinging her around as a way of flirting with her.

I went to high school before *Mean Girls,* the 2004 movie written by Tina Fey and based on the book *Queen Bees and Wannabes* by Rosalind Wiseman, but as soon as I saw Regina George, the Queen Bee of the film, blowing air kisses at her classmates as she's puppeteering the whole social scene at North Shore High School, I remembered Renée. In the movie, there's a scene where Regina's classmates describe their obsession with her. They say:

> *Regina George is flawless.*
> *She has two Fendi purses and a silver Lexus.*
> *I hear her hair's insured for ten thousand dollars.*
> *I hear she does car commercials . . . in Japan.*
> *Her favorite movie is* Varsity Blues.
> *One time, she met John Stamos on a plane.*
> *And he told her she was pretty.*
> *One time, she punched me in the face. It was awesome.*

In the same way, I saw Renée as the center of our school, the most popular girl in a class of six hundred. Especially in middle school, I spent a lot of time observing her and her three best friends, who were always with her. They were so at ease with the mundane requirements of being an adolescent girl that I never had a clue about, like knowing you needed spray-on deodorant for after gym class. I was fascinated by Renée in particular, in part because I really did feel like she was the person we all orbited around; any social blessing or curse I received would come from her. Early on in middle school, she asked me to spend the night at her house. I thought we had fun. She'd had some professional modeling pictures taken, and I remember being impressed as we flipped through the album while sitting cross-legged on her bedroom floor. But I must have failed whatever friendship test took place during our sleepover, since we never spoke at school after that.

I always felt like I was alone. I remember being on the fringes of the yard where everyone gathered before school started, going from one circle of girls to the next trying to find one that would let me stand there. I was finally feeling comfortable hovering around one cluster when one of the girls asked me to leave. "Um, Kayleen, could you go somewhere else?" she said. "I need to talk to my friends."

I walked away, stunned and humiliated. I didn't know what I'd done wrong, but I assumed that after Renée decided I wasn't worth being friends with, no one else wanted to hang out with me either. It was hard for me not to think that every social ding I got in school started with Renée, as if her judgment fragmented into small flying rocks that I had to dodge.

Another time, a new guy at school—whom I had crush on—told some girls that he wanted to ask me out. They filled him in since he was new and didn't know; I wasn't on the top of anyone's list to date. He should ask out someone else. I'm not sure why he repeated this to me, but he did. I felt stuck. I didn't know why my middle school classmates were so sure I wasn't worth hanging out with, and why they seemed certain I'd never be, but instead of trying to change their minds, I gave up.

For the rest of middle school, I spent most of my time by myself. I was happiest when I was lying on the carpet in my bedroom with the latest issue of *Sassy* magazine, a feminist alternative to *Seventeen*. It let me into a place that was more political, sarcastic, and stylish than the one I existed in every day. When I was reading the magazine, I had smart, funny friends who wanted to talk about poetry, whether to be pro-choice or pro-life, or the cutest knee socks to wear with sandals. Outside *Sassy*, there wasn't anyone around who wanted to let me in on their inner angst or even weigh in on if they thought I could get away with ripping my tights like Courtney Love did.

I remember giving a presentation in eighth-grade English class that was a wholesale rip-off of a story I'd read in *Sassy* where a writer kept a diary of all of the times she'd been hollered at on the street by guys. I stood in front of the class and listed the instances when I'd been catcalled ("in the park while I was running"). I think now that even though I was telling myself that I didn't care if I had friends or not, this was a blind shot to find someone else who could relate, a friend who could empathize with how threatened and embarrassed street harassment made me feel. My English class presentation was the biggest platform I had at the time. But when I finished, the rest of the students had no comment. They only looked relieved I'd stopped talking. Their silence made me regret talking, too, and the disappointment I felt going back to my seat made me realize how much I'd wanted the opposite reaction: someone to say they understood me.

Elaine Welteroth, who is in her early thirties and the editor in chief of *Teen Vogue,* told me she felt the same way about *Essence* as I did about *Sassy* when she was younger. It gave her a whole community to identify with that didn't exist in her physical world. "I grew up in a primarily white neighborhood with a black mother and a white dad and I felt like *Essence* was this place for me to get fed, to connect with that part of my identity because I didn't have black friends," she says.

After a while, the part of me that just wanted to fit in somewhere pushed the part of me that wanted friends I could totally relate to out of the way, and I tried to make any friends I could. This meant figuring out which group I could belong to in the arena Wiseman later called Girl World. In high school there were more kids to make friends with—three middle schools fed into the high school—and people were divided into clusters according to generalizations, like if they were band geeks, druggies, or ropers (the kids who wore Western wear and took agricultural classes). I had a lot of classes with the girls everyone would have called "goody-goodies" and became friends with them. We were smart and sweet, known for never getting in trouble—and proud of that fact. We never talked about anything we couldn't also bring up in front of our moms, which meant I was in a lot of conversations about cheerleading routines and lipstick. We wanted to be model girls.

But with them, even as we tried to radiate goodness, I

found myself doing exactly what I'd been on the receiving end of when I didn't have any friends: judging and competing with other girls.

Part of this was because I wanted to go along with my friends; if they wanted to say someone was bad because they skipped class or smoked cigarettes, then I thought that person was terrible too. The other part, though, was looking out for myself. I'd learned that my default position was supposed to be to see other girls as enemies as we jockeyed for status and popularity at school. I had a sense that I had to be competitive with them, and even with my new friends. There was a feeling, a frisson as we passed each other in the halls, that what we coveted—cute boys, good grades, votes for student council—was limited. If some other girl got those things, then we wouldn't. I don't think I realized that this was what I was doing, that I was constantly competing for something. I just thought I was doing what I was supposed to. I was spending hours on how my hair looked, flirting with the guy I knew my friend liked, or not telling another friend when I was invited to a party without her because I didn't know any other way. That's just what we did. Our general operating principle was that it's fine, and expected, to knock other girls down.

Before Nancy Jo Sales's *American Girls: Social Media and the Secret Lives of Teenagers* was published, she would tell adults what she was working on and their first response was often about how *mean* girls are. "I'd say I'm doing a book about girls," Sales says, "and one of the first things that I heard from so many people over time, just talking anecdotally about my book was, 'Aren't girls mean?'; 'They're so mean, aren't they?'; or 'Why are girls so mean?'"

For something so widely believed, the idea that girls are mean is relatively new. Sales points out that Rachel Simmons's book *Odd Girl Out: The Hidden Culture of Aggression in Girls,* which was published in 2002, was one of the first publications to make the point that girls are bullies. Simmons used anecdotal examples of girls being tormented by other girls and cited studies that came out in the early nineties on "relational aggression." The term, used by researchers led by Finnish professor, Kaj Björkqvist, describes indirect aggression that's meant to covertly diminish a person's reputation or social status. Girls weren't likely to have fistfights or slam anyone's head against a locker, the researchers found, but they would shut out a friend who'd displeased them or say nasty things about her behind her back.

Wiseman's book *Queen Bees and Wannabes* came out the same year as Simmons's book. *The New York Times* ran a story in its Sunday magazine, mostly about Wiseman's work, called "Girls Just Want to Be Mean." In her twenties, Wiseman was working as a self-defense teacher for teens—she has a second-degree black belt in a style of Karate—when she realized that what the girls in her seminars really wanted to talk about was the hell they were going through at school at the hands of other girls. They told her about the cutthroat cliques, the emotional bullying, and the pressure to fit in—and how they couldn't make their parents comprehend what they had to do to survive Girl World. Her book is supposed to be a hand-book for parents to help them decode what their daughters were experiencing in adolescence. "Parents didn't understand the world of their daughters," Wiseman says. "I wrote the book because of a lot of parents asking me to explain it to them. I really felt like I was caught in the middle. Being in my twenties while this was happening was important. The girls who wanted to be able to communicate to their parents were frustrated, and I had moms who were remembering what it was like to be that age, what their friendships had been like, but they didn't have the words to put with it."

Part of what Wiseman did was label the girls according to how they behaved among their friend groups, with names such as "The Queen Bee," "The Sidekick," "The Messenger," "The Pleaser/Wannabe," among others. The Queen Bee is described, in part, like this: "Think of a combination of the Queen of Hearts in *Alice in Wonderland* and Barbie. She's the Queen Bee, the epitome of teen girl perfection. Through a combination of charisma, force, money, looks, will, and so-cial intelligence, this girl reigns supreme over the other girls and weakens their friendships with others, thereby strength-ening her own power and influence."

Wiseman hoped that by doing this she was giving parents and their daughters a common lingo so they could start breaking down how the girls saw themselves and what was going on in their friendships, but in many cases, it didn't work out like that. She was dismayed to see that for some girls and their parents the labels simply became typecasting that no one bothered to look past. Figuring out who was the Queen

Bee and the players who filled out the rest of her court was the beginning and end of what there was to talk about. "It's important for people to have a language because it's a starting place for discussion," Wiseman says, "but I have increasingly thought about the double-edged sword about labeling behavior and labeling people. I knew it from the beginning but I didn't realize how much people would struggle to see themselves and others beyond labels."

The movie *Mean Girls* opened in 2004, with the antics of the popular clique the Plastics, led by Regina George, cementing the thinking that girls can't have genuine friendships. "The weird thing about hanging out with Regina was that I could hate her, and at the same time, I still wanted her to like me," the new girl at school, Cady Heron, says in the movie.

This leads to the trait that has been slapped on teen girls for the last two decades: They're mean. Fraught, often outright cruel, friendships are thought of as "normal, if regrettable, girl behavior," Sales writes in *American Girls*.

Until recently, I am embarrassed to say that I didn't question this idea or claim. I really believed it was true, as if there were a gene that caused us to be hateful and spiteful to each other while we were in school. I thought that being stuck in Girl World meant that at least some kind of subterfuge was unavoidable: Constantly spreading rumors about one another, changing alliances, and only indirectly letting a friend know she'd upset you by doing something to her that you hoped would hurt her just as much was just how young women had to come of age, I assumed. It was the way I'd grown up.

Even though I hung out with "goody-goodies," we weren't immune to being cruel. We had our own Queen Bee, and rallying around her led to the most vicious thing I ever did to another girl in high school—and I hope it's the low point of my entire life as far as girl-on-girl crime goes. It happened one night near graduation. My Queen Bee had wanted to be prom queen, and she was convinced the girl who won had rigged the election (it only made the whole deal worse that this same girl had beaten her to be the class president, too). We were having a slumber party and got to talking about how this girl shouldn't have won. She was horrible and someone needed to stop her from being so stuck-up. A recurring feature of Girl World is the need to not let any one girl have too much self-confidence. ("You think you're really pretty?" Regina asks Cady in *Mean Girls*. "Oh . . . I don't know," Cady says.)

I don't know whose idea it was to make the paper crowns to put on the prom queen's lawn, but I don't remember questioning it. In the suburbs of Dallas, where I grew up, decorating someone's lawn with toilet paper isn't uncommon and it isn't always mean. More often how frequently your yard was TP'd was a marker of popularity—I lived in the same neighborhood as Renée, and the trees in her front yard on weekend mornings were often heavy with toilet paper streamers. But what we did with the crowns wasn't a compliment. It was flat-out horrible. At the slumber party, we cut dozens of paper crowns out of construction paper, like we were in a demented art class, and wrote on them, our brutal messages to the suspect queen. I don't remember exactly what we said, but I remember the spirit. We made fun of how she looked, called her a fake and a cheater—the overall message was that if she'd wanted to win so badly that she'd stolen the election from my Queen Bee, then she could have all of these crowns that said nasty things about her too.

I started to feel bad when I was actually at her house, near dawn—it had taken a while to make all of the crowns. I hid behind a car as some of the other girls placed our handiwork around her yard. After my friends who'd been doling out the crowns rushed back to the car and we drove away, they were exuberant, congratulating each other on how brave they'd been to go as close to the house as they did. But the car got quieter as we returned to the slumber-party house. Whatever had fueled the crown-creating frenzy—insecurity, loyalty—was wearing off, and we were left with what we'd actually done. No one said much when we finally lay down to go to sleep.

I don't know if our target ever saw the crowns. I thought maybe her parents might find them first and throw them away, which is also the cowardly reason I've never apologized to her for what we did—I hope she doesn't know it happened.

This wasn't friendship. The girls I was with weren't relating to each other. We were simply moving en masse, stuck together and unwilling to question what we were doing at the moment because we had nowhere else to go, unless we wanted to leave the group. For me, at least, this was unthinkable. I wouldn't have been able to articulate this at the time, but I can see now that I was afraid that if I didn't go along with my Queen Bee I'd be right back where I started, without any friends, dancing from group to group to find one that would let me in. In school, my friends acted together. It was textbook groupthink. We were all always watching each other to make sure we were doing the same thing. Consequently, there were only two ways to be: with your friends or against them. There was no in-between.

But it also wasn't proof that girls as a whole are mean, like I thought it was for a long time.

Megan Abbott is a crime novelist who often writes about consuming, sometimes appalling, teenage girl friendships, like the best friends in *Dare Me*, a thriller about high school cheerleaders that was published in 2012. The characters Addy Hanlon and Beth Cassidy are an unbalanced pair, with Addy enacting whatever Beth commands, which is mainly to humiliate other girls. "By and large, what's true when I write about female friendships," Abbott says, "is that they're often made up of the girl who is more troubled and adventurous, and more active and possibly more dangerous, and the one who's more the observer. This is a classic structure of friendships in books, but it also seems to be true in real life. At that age, if you are a shy or introverted teen, you're drawn to the energy of the complicated girl, and if you're a complicated girl, you're drawn to the stability of the introvert."

What Abbott captures with these friendships—and what's earned her the devotion of teen girls and young women—is how tricky and twisty, but also how rich and fundamental, they are. There are many Tumblr pages and music playlists dedicated to Addy and Beth.

But critics often sum up the friendships in her books by saying that she writes about "mean girls," a label Abbott hates. "In some ways I think it's code for complicated girls, or girls who are real girls," she says. "I think it's a way to minimize and make cute something that people don't really want to look at, which is girls do have feelings of aggression and desire at that age, and they're not always behaving as they should be. They're filled with yearning and anger and all of these things. It seems diminishing to me. If you look at those two words, 'mean,' which is sort of a very light term. It's not saying 'evil' or 'dark' or 'wild.' It's almost sweet. And then 'girls' of course, not young women. I think it's the whole package. It feels like a pat on the head like, 'Oh, you mean girl.'"

Movies before *Mean Girls* have shown girls not being nice, including perhaps most famously *Heathers*, the 1988 dark comedy about high school cliques in which one member of the popular group of girls—called the Heathers—wishes the Queen Bee dead. Played by Winona Ryder, Veronica Sawyer is the only one of the four girls in the group not named Heather. She loathes her Queen Bee but still feels tied to her; it's similar to how Cady thinks about Regina. "She's my best friend," Veronica says. "God, I hate her."

"One of the things I loved about the script was that there was an honesty about the characters," says Michael Lehmann, who directed *Heathers*. "It didn't judge them in simple terms. Veronica knew what she was doing and hated what she was doing, but couldn't stop herself at the same time."

Unlike *Mean Girls*, *Heathers* was made in an age when adults seemed content to leave their daughters' worlds to their daughters. "In certain ways parents have become progressively more involved in their kids' lives," Lehmann says. "That didn't happen then. There was little attempt on the part of the parents to try to understand what the kids were doing during the *Heathers* period."

"I approach 'Heathers' as a traveler in an unknown country," Roger Ebert wrote in his review in the *Chicago Sun-Times*, "one who does not speak the language or know the customs and can judge the natives only by taking them at their word."

The film was a commercial failure, in that it made only 1.1 million dollars in the five weeks it was in theaters, but it was well reviewed and had a big life in home video. "People saw it and they talked about it," Lehmann says. "It wasn't promoted. It just seeped into the culture."

Teens could relate to the injustice that popular kids can make anything cool (in *Heathers* suicide is what becomes trendy). Abbott was in high school in Grosse Pointe, Michigan, when she saw *Heathers* and remembers it fondly. "It's frightening and dark so I always loved it for that," she says, "but it felt like my high school. You had to have a tribe."

But as much as *Heathers* was relatable, it was never seen as proof that all girls were mean. "I think it reflected experiences I'd had and people I knew," Lehmann says, "but the phrase 'mean girls' wasn't heard during that time."

Taking people who have a superficial trait in common and labeling them anything is stereotyping, but it took me forever to see that the idea of "mean girls" was actually a classic example of this kind of a generalization. I really did think it was true, as if our double X chromosomes made us mean, too. I didn't recoil when I heard anyone say, "Girls are so mean." I accepted it as a fact, no more irritating or able to be disproved than other things we believe about girls, such as that they like glitter or sugar. I never thought, *How is it possible that girls can be meaner than anyone else?*

Sales, on the other hand, saw this fallacy long before she even began working on *American Girls*. "When I started to notice people saying that, it was shocking to me," she says. "I just thought this is nonsense. It's a ridiculous statement. We've become so conditioned to thinking that it's 'true' in a very short time, and we don't even question it. If you look at it, it's absurd to say that one whole group of people is anything. It's sort of the hallmark of bias. The hallmark of prejudice is to say that any group is something negative."

The studies that first gave "mean girls" their scientific basis in "relational aggression," the ones done by Björkqvist's research team in the nineties, in fact, Sales points out, don't say that girls are more aggressive than boys. "What they said was only that they showed some kind of aggression equal to that of boys in different ways," she says.

In 2015, StopBullying.gov, a website managed by the US Department of Health & Human Services that provides education on everything from defining bullying to preventing it, published an article called "The Myth of 'Mean Girls,'" saying that there was no proof that girls were any more vicious than boys.

"In the past two decades," the article said, "relational

aggression has received an abundance of media attention. Books, movies and websites have portrayed girls as being cruel to one another, thus creating and reinforcing the stereotype of 'mean girls.' However, this popular perception of girls being meaner than boys is not always supported by research . . . Several large cross-cultural studies and meta-analyses have found no gender differences in relational aggression."

So how did girls become mean, and boys just become, well, boys?

Sales believes that the notion of "mean girls" came about as a backlash to the feminist movement in the 1990s. Then, in pop culture, opinionated, independent, and vocal women were on-screen and onstage—and inspiring other women to test what they'd been told about how they should behave, too.

Thelma & Louise, a film released in 1991 starring Geena Davis and Susan Sarandon, and written by Callie Khouri, was about a duo who runs from the law after one of them kills a man who is attempting to rape the other. During their often exhilarating journey, they become more empowered and bonded than they thought they could be.

"Something's, like, crossed over in me and I can't go back. I mean I just couldn't live," Thelma says to Louise.

"I know what you mean," Louise says. "Anyway, don't wanna end up on the damn *Geraldo* show."

Khouri, who won an Academy Award for her screenplay, told *Dazed Magazine* that she wrote it because she wasn't seeing women represented in a way that "made me want to be one."

Elsewhere, the Riot Grrrl movement, in the Pacific Northwest and Washington, DC, was propelled in part by hardcore punk bands dedicated to exposing the patriarchy and inspiring female empowerment, such as Bikini Kill, Bratmobile, and Heavens to Betsy. One of the hits from the time is the 1993 song "Rebel Girl" by Bikini Kill, which subverts the idea that other women are our enemies. It forcefully lifts up sisterhood, with lead singer Kathleen Hanna declaring, midway through the song, "That girl thinks she's the queen of the neighborhood / I got news for you, she is!"

There was also an academic focus on what girls were going through while growing up, specifically the emotional and educational problems they were having. In 1991, the American Association of University Women, a nonprofit that advances equity for women and girls through advocacy, education, and research, published a nationwide study of girls ages nine to fifteen showing that they weren't being called on in class or encouraged as much as boys, leading them to have lower self-esteem and believe their opinions and ideas weren't as valuable. In 1994's *Reviving Ophelia: Saving the Selves of Adolescent Girls,* Mary Pipher, a clinical psychologist in Lincoln, Nebraska, used her conversations with hundreds of girls to argue that their confidence was also being decimated by the sexism and sexual violence they experienced.

"On the part of the educational system, there was a momentary awakening," Sales says, "and initiatives to do something about it. Then came the backlash. It's not surprising. Waves of feminism are always followed by these backlashes, as Susan Faludi noted in her landmark book *Backlash.* So we had this wave suddenly saying, 'Oh, by the way, guess what? Girls are mean.'"

I thought I was. Here's another thing I did in my past mean-girl days. I went to prom with a guy my friend had a crush on. I spent most of my time with this friend, usually driving around our suburb after school listening to the oldies station, sometimes stopping for snacks. It was the classic kind of relationship Abbott describes; she was dramatic and I was chill. She cried all of the time, because she got a bad grade or because we'd seen the movie *Philadelphia,* and I mostly observed and consoled her. It was out of character for me to do something she didn't want me to, but when this guy asked me to prom, I never even considered saying no. I didn't even like him. All I saw was prom and my opportunity to go. The dance had been built up in my mind mostly through movies like *Pretty in Pink* as a way to show you were accepted—kids who belonged went to the prom. Andie (Molly Ringwald) in *Pretty in Pink* starts the movie as an outcast at her high school but ends up at the prom kissing the popular guy.

After my friend found out (from someone else; I couldn't even tell her myself I was going with the guy she liked), she wrote me a note: "I don't understand why this had to happen. I feel like a complete idiot."

Now I wouldn't even look at a guy one of my friends was into, but that doesn't change the fact that back then I pushed aside any regret I was feeling and went ahead with the date. I wrote my friend a note apologizing: "I would never do anything that would hurt you." But that was at best insincere and at worst a total lie. I knew I was hurting her, but I went to prom with him anyway, and our friendship was never the same.

I used to think I was a mean girl who grew out of it. That was the line our moms gave us most of the time, no matter if we were complaining in a group about Renée or pretending we didn't know why one of our friends wasn't speaking to us. "Wait it out. Time will take you past this," they said. "Popularity doesn't matter after high school."

But if you dig a little deeper, the stereotypes fall apart: Not all mean girls are popular, and not all popular girls are mean. The truth is, girls are no meaner or nicer than anyone else. I wasn't the only person caught up in acting how the rest of my friends were because I was afraid of being rejected by them. I wasn't the only one who thought prom was the only fancy party I'd ever get invited to and was willing to do anything to go. I wasn't the only one just trying to make it through adolescence.

It's easy for me to look back now and realize what I should have done differently. Instead of scrapping with the other girls, I wish I had tried to figure out how to be friends with them. I should have learned how to tell another girl she'd hurt my feelings or understand I'd hurt hers. I should have been able to figure out how to say that I didn't know how to turn down a boy's attention, or that I'd rather not come along, but that doesn't mean I'm not still your friend.

But I didn't.

With the rise of the term "mean girls," we're strangling teens with the notion that they are all mean and should keep busy doing the backstabbing that they were born to do. "If you tell somebody enough times that they're this or they're that, it's not surprising that this seeps into their own identities or assessment of what's going on around them," Sales says. "We say, 'This is happening because girls are mean,' not because we have a knee-jerk culture that's telling them that these are these stereotypes of themselves. They're children. They're vulnerable. They're impressionable. They listen to what's going on all around them and they hear these things and they begin to believe them. It would be surprising if they didn't to some extent."

We have to take teen girls out of this frame that they're mean. Dismissing every social skirmish because of this stereotype isn't helping their friendships and how they feel about themselves. We can't just tell them they have to be nice all the time either. That's just as problematic as calling them mean. My mom used to have a framed print of a nursery rhyme on the wall that said, in part:

> *What are little girls made of?*
> *Sugar and spice*
> *And all things nice*

Whenever I stopped to read it, I remember rolling my eyes.

"People are mean," Sales says. "People are bad. People are kind. People are good. We're all humans, and this is a stereotype. I think it's been very damaging and we have to dismantle it because it's not helping girls to have anyone care about them or their problems."

Wiseman, too, for her part, regrets anything she had to do

with contributing to the stereotype. "Every time I see a T-shirt on a five-year-old that says 'I'm a Queen Bee' it kills me inside," she says. "It's the opposite of what I wanted."

In a way that shows how hard it is to forget the hierarchy of school, I was nervous when I wrote Renée. I wanted to ask her, long after we'd graduated, what her friendships had been like back then. I wanted to know if she remembered her middle and high school experience the same way I imagined it. I hesitated before sending her a note, stopped by the same feeling I had as a kid; Renée wouldn't want to talk to me. I remembered the uncertainty and the stress that comes with worrying that the girls around you are measuring everything you do.

Her response surprised me. It was warm, even deferential. "I will help you in any way possible," Renée wrote. "Let me know what you need. I'm thrilled and honored to help you."

We met in Los Angeles, where we both happened to be visiting. Renée was on a business trip there for her job as a senior vice president at a financial services firm. She was as cute and effervescent as the person I'd known in high school, turned out in the way Texas women tend to be, in a short skirt, high heels, and lots of mascara. A few minutes into our conversation, I realized that we had a lot in common. We were both single, devoted to our careers, and thankful for our girlfriends. Anyone who walked by us wouldn't think it was strange that we were sitting there together, drinking sparkling wine and sharing flatbread pizzas. Whereas if we'd been at a high school reunion, I pointed out, people would have wondered, *Why are they talking?*

"It's so dumb," Renée says. "Think about it today. Had we never had any history together and we met each other, and we're both women who work, who are single, we'd have a totally different dynamic than the dynamic we have right now."

After she and her husband divorced five years ago, Renée became what she calls "purposefully single," with her sons, who are eleven and nine, and her girlfriends as the priorities in her life.

"I went through a host of dating sites and Match and all that," she says, "and I decided I really love my life. The right thing will come or it won't, and the time that I have away from my kids, I have to make the highest and best use of and it's never wasted on my girlfriends.

"I don't know that I would get up and go without the encouragement of my friends," she continues. "Life is hard. No one ever tells you that."

"But high school wasn't hard for you?" I ask. "It seemed to me like you had all of these girlfriends kind of effortlessly. Everyone liked you."

"I think 'effortlessly' is probably not the right word," she says. "I think I'm a people pleaser in so much of my life, so I really wanted people to like me so I worked really hard at it. I don't know really if people just saw me as something different from afar. I'll meet people from high school who will say something like you, like, 'Oh, didn't you know what I thought?' But I didn't know. I didn't have a clue. I had my own people who weren't including me, so I had that side of it."

It turns out that our high school friendships and the way we behaved within them were pretty much the same. Like I can, she can pull up all of the crappy things she did back then. She was territorial about her female friends, once telling a new girl at school whom she could be friends with. "You have a decision to make," she told her. "You can either be friends with me or you can be friends with her, but you can't be friends with us both."

"That was awful, but so true," Renée says.

She and her friends would sometimes call other girls and tell them lies about their boyfriends. "I mean, we'd say bad stuff and none of it was true," she says, "just because another girl liked him and didn't want his girlfriend to like him anymore."

She can also recall what friends did to her. At one point, when she broke her ankle and didn't make the cheerleading squad, she was surprised that some of her friends ditched her; she didn't realize that was why they'd been hanging around her in the first place. "When people stopped talking to me because I wasn't a cheerleader, it was surprising to me because I wasn't prepared for it," she says.

There were parties she wasn't invited to that her friends weren't supposed to tell her about. When she found out about them anyway, she was heartbroken to have been excluded. And one of Renée's friends did the same thing to her that I did to my friend: She went to prom with Renée's first love. "I mean, she'd been my best friend since sixth grade," she says. "My very best friend. You know the first girl you call and say, 'Oh my gosh, I slept with him.' She's the one. I didn't talk to her for like a year. I didn't have anything to say to her."

They're friends again today; she apologized "probably seventeen hundred times," Renée says. "My high school friendships were fleeting. They were so come and go, like they'd be mad at me and I wouldn't be invited to some party, or this would happen or that would happen, and we'd be in a fight. But now with some of these girls, we're actually real friends. All of these years later, I'd just do anything for them. Like right now if they called and needed anything, I would do anything possible that I could to make their lives better."

With other girls, though, some hurt lingers, or at least Renée suspects it does. On Facebook, she tried to friend an old classmate, but she won't accept the request. "If you would have asked me, I would have said we'd been friends since fifth grade," she said, "but the fact that she hasn't accepted my friend request, and I've sent her messages with no response, makes me hypersensitive. Chances are very good that I did something shitty. I'm not going to lie about that. I'm certain right now whatever it is that I'm sincerely sorry about it."

She's trying to make up for her juvenile behavior in other ways. When another classmate wrote on Facebook that her young daughter is having a hard time at school with cliques and bullies, Renée messaged her, wondering if she'd ever made the woman who posted feel that way. They'd both been cheerleaders, but she'd never been invited to any of the parties Renée had at her house.

"I read your sweet post about your daughter," Renée wrote to her. "If I was ever someone who made you feel not included, I'm sorry. If there was an invitation I didn't extend that hurt in any way, please forgive me."

In Los Angeles, we finished our drinks and walked outside, where I waited for Renée to get an Uber. We hugged, made plans to meet again in New York or Texas, and by the time I got back to where I was staying, she'd texted me: "It was great to see you! Made it back! Let me know that you did too!" In other words, *text me when you get home.*

CHAPTER 3

All About the Boys

No man is capable of being your best friend.
A best friend is someone who goes to get their nails
done with you.

—Chelsea Handler, comedian

I n college, I joined a sorority. I rushed in part because my high school Queen Bee did—we both went to The University of Texas at Austin. The same desire that made me want to go to prom made me want to join a sorority. I thought that being part of one would be proof that I was accepted. I was also fairly career-minded and had heard that joining one would give me a professional network after I graduated.

I didn't rush to meet guys. That sounds like a lie, but I didn't. When a guy I started dating at freshman orientation, who was in the process of pledging a fraternity, asked me during rush which sororities I was considering, I told him, and he was pleased. "Good, we mix with all of those," he said.

I did not understand at that point that he meant that if I joined a sorority his fraternity didn't have mixers with, we

72

wouldn't be dating anymore. I didn't think the sorority was going to have anything to do with whom I dated.

At UT, rush is held the week before classes start. The summer after I graduated from high school, I watched my high school Queen Bee's mom take pictures of her in their front yard to send to the sororities (with a résumé and recommendation letters) and thought, *I want to try this too.*

Rush is not chill. There's a schedule (two days of open houses, followed by Philanthropy Day, then Skit Night, and finally Pref Night) and a suggested dress code. I needed khaki shorts (with at least a three-inch inseam) to pair with the T-shirt all the rushees were given for the open houses, bright sundresses and sandals for the midweek activities, and a black cocktail dress and heels for Pref Night. In addition, this all happens in August, when the temperature is always in the nineties, and UT's campus is giant, so the whole event is basically a weeklong slog through a sauna the size of four hundred football fields while trying to look nice.

Even so, I *loved* rush. When I was having my picture taken and packing my exactingly specific outfits, I'd been a little unsure. I wasn't ready to reject my high school friend group completely, but I knew that I wasn't my truest self with them. I was hoping that in college I'd meet people whom I wanted to befriend for better reasons than not wanting to be alone.

But feeling like people want you around is powerful. I shook off any uncertainty I had about joining a sorority as soon as I started going to the houses, which were mostly southern-style mansions with white columns and ornate brass door knockers. Everyone was so nice! It was overwhelming.

I'd just gotten to school and all of these girls, who I thought were strangers, were freaking out about me being there. They actually said stuff like, "We've been waiting for you all summer!" Inside the houses, I was passed from one girl to the next; there was a lot of hugging and bouncing. Once, I saw a sorority member tackle one of my fellow rushees because she was so thrilled to see her.

A video of the girls in the sorority I eventually joined, Alpha Delta Pi, opening the door of their house to a group of rushees was posted online in 2016. (It's unclear when the video was taken.) The sorority sisters are crowded into the doorway in what's called a "door stack." They look like they're crouched on top of one another, but because I used to be one of them, I know they're on bleachers. I remember practicing this pose and being told to scrunch together so it would look like there were twice as many of us than there actually were. The women in the video scream, hold their arms out, and wiggle their fingers before starting to clap and chant, "Boom-boom, I wanna go A-D-Pi. Don't you?" Some Twitter users thought it was terrifying and questioned why the sorority was made up of only white girls. "They really did just open the gates of hell," @poeticgf tweeted.

I see their point. The women do seem possessed (they probably are; during rush you work all day and night on the business of getting girls to join) and they are all white (most everyone was white when I was a member too). But back then, when the sororities at every house opened their doors (they all did door stacks) I didn't think about much beyond that all of these girls were cheering—*cheering!*—because I had ended up on their doorstep. It didn't occur to me to question why.

Some women make lifelong friends with their sorority sisters. I've been to weddings, well past college, where the bride and her sorority sisters get out on the dance floor and sing one of their group's songs. Women also use the sorority for networking after college (like I'd once hoped to). Sarah Berkes, who's in her mid-twenties and works in fashion, had been a Delta Gamma at the University of Washington in Seattle, and when she moved to New York to find her first job, she immediately joined her sorority's alumnae group. Through different women in it, she got a job, found a place to live, and made friends in her new city.

I never even came close to lifelong friendships. I didn't have any friends in my sorority, mostly because of my own actions. After rush, I learned that on ordinary days there was not a ticker-tape parade every time I arrived at the sorority house. On Mondays we could eat at the house for free before the weekly meeting we were required to go to, and I often sat on the fringes of a group, which reminded me of middle school. Barely anyone said hello to me, and I was too shy to say hi to them first. I felt stupid for thinking I'd had all these new friends. I should have thought it was weird during rush that all of these girls were embracing me like someone they'd met in a past life, even though all they knew about me was what I looked like, where I was from, and what my high school GPA was. But I didn't because I liked the attention. I didn't consider that after they'd accomplished getting me to join the sorority their work might be done. But after Bid Day, the insta-love was gone, and even though I hadn't joined the sorority to meet guys, I found myself using the group to do just that. (My orientation dude and I had stopped dating in the first weeks of the semester.) We were supposed to invite men to most of the parties and other events, and this worked great for me. It gave me a more seemingly legit reason to spend time with guys I liked than just to tell them it was a Tuesday.

The "crush parties" were my favorite. That's when you invited two guys—anonymously—to a bar by sending them a sorority T-shirt. There were also date parties, where you got to invite only one guy, and the mixers with fraternities, which my orientation boyfriend had filled me in on.

It never occurred to me that the effort I put into scheming how to approach a guy about a date party or get him that crush T-shirt in secret could have been used to get to know my sisters better—and I'm not sure they thought about this either. Men were a really important part of the sorority, and we all took this seriously. There was a little bit of a feeling that the sorority cared about *who* you dated—when we didn't pick one girl's boyfriend's fraternity to mix with one semester, I remember her crying—but what mattered more was just that you were dating *someone*.

I went to college during a period that was a boom time for romantic comedies (roughly from the beginning of the 1990s to the mid-2000s). I adore some of these movies. I will stand slack-jawed in front of *When Harry Met Sally . . .*

whenever I see it on a screen, and I hope there's another golden era of rom-coms that gives me more of them. But for decades, they were the main way women saw themselves in stories—and the main way we saw women relate to each other. All these movie women seemed to do was look for their own mates or help their friends find them.

In 1985, even before the boom began, to make a point about how distorted women on-screen were, cartoonist Alison Bechdel wrote "The Rule," a comic strip in her book *Dykes to Watch Out For.*

In it two women on a date are trying to figure out what movie to watch.

"Well, I dunno. I have this rule, see," one says. "I only go to a movie if it satisfies three basic requirements. One, it has to have at least two women in it, who, two, talk to each other about, three, something besides a man."

"Pretty strict," her date answers, "but a good idea."

"No kidding," the rule maker says. "Last movie I was able to see was *Alien.*"

"The Rule" became known as the Bechdel Test. Bechdel has said the idea was inspired by Virginia Woolf's 1929 essay "A Room of One's Own," where she writes about her shock in reading about two female characters who actually like each other instead of being jealous of each other as they vie for men's attention. "All these relationships between women, I thought, rapidly recalling the splendid gallery of fictitious women, are too simple," Woolf writes. "So much has been left out, unattempted. And I tried to remember any case in the course of my reading where two women are represented as friends . . . They are now and then mothers and daughters. But almost without exception they are shown in their relation to men. It was strange to think that all the great women of fiction were, until Jane Austen's day, not only seen by the other sex, but seen only in relation to the other sex. And how small a part of a woman's life is that."

I'm not sure whether the focus on guys in my sorority came more from popular culture or from Texas sorority culture, but either way the structure of sorority life revolved around them. I personally was using the group to live out my romantic exploits, but I wasn't alone. My sisters were better friends with each other than I was with them, but they were trying to meet men too—and support each other doing so. And if a sister found one she wanted to marry (and who wanted to marry her), that was cause for an official sorority ceremony.

It was called "candlelight." At the Monday night meeting, the president would hold up a candle that had been left on her bed by a mystery sorority member and shout, "Candlelight tonight!" After the meeting, we'd all stand in a circle singing a song in which part of the lyrics was about "pining for you" while passing around the lit candle. The girl who put it on the president's bed was supposed to blow it out. If she let it go around once, it meant she'd gotten "pinned" by a fraternity member (a sign he'd ask her to marry him someday), but twice—and there was always a gasp when the candle started its second turn—meant she'd gotten engaged.

Some women start fantasizing about their own candlelight as soon as they experience their first one. The first time

I saw it, I had no idea what was going on, and when I realized we were in this hushed atmosphere to hear about one of my sisters getting engaged, I marveled at the ceremony. Unlike some of the rituals in the sorority, like the induction one, which I thought seemed a little half-hearted, this ceremony captivated everyone. It has great elements: the secrecy, the anticipation of who's going to blow out the candle, her retelling in a dark room the story of how it happened. It feels special.

Sometimes a girl who gets engaged while school isn't in session will keep it a secret until the break is over so that she can have a candlelight. At the University of Alabama in Tuscaloosa, an Alpha Chi Omega named Kaci didn't tell her sorority friends about her engagement for an entire month because it happened over the winter break. "This may sound crazy," she wrote on her blog in 2011, "but every girl dreams of having a candlelight." There's genuine excitement over these ceremonies. One sorority member wrote on Twitter, "the fact that we have a candlelight tonight is the only thing getting me through my 8 hour class today. #sisterhood."

I quit the sorority two years after joining. I quit because I met a guy I really liked. We both went with mutual friends on a trip to a swimming hole off campus, and by the next day, I wanted him to be my boyfriend. He wanted this too, so I didn't need the sorority to help me find a guy anymore. He wasn't in a fraternity and wasn't a big fan of the Greek system in general, which gave me all the more reason to drop out of the sorority.

I started to hang out with him all the time, but we didn't completely isolate ourselves, like some starry-eyed new couples do. I'm sure we did this to some degree, but I had friends who weren't in my sorority whom I thought were awesome and was conscious of not shutting them out.

These were mostly women I met in my freshman dorm. They were funny, independent, and opinionated, more comfortable with who they were and confident than I was then. I liked that about them. One of these girls was named Ellie. Her real name is Ellen, but she hates being called that.

Ellie is a party in a person. She has long blond hair that's always snarled, a thick Texas accent, and a wardrobe that takes equal cues from Wonder Woman and teen girls with attitude. When I saw her recently she was wearing a sweatshirt I'd given her back in college that said "smelly" under a sticker of cherries that you could scratch and sniff. In college she introduced me to what we called "fancy pants," colorful leggings we wore out dancing, and today she still has blue and red patent-leather pairs in her closet. We lived together for three years during college, and at one house, she used to mow the lawn while drinking a margarita. "That happened maybe twice because we didn't mow that often," she says. She decorated her room with fabrics printed with Dalmatian spots or neon planets, and when she wanted to expand this look to the living room, I tolerated it. "You said, 'All right,' and gave a little shoulder shrug," Ellie says.

With these friends, like with the girls in the sorority, we were consumed by guys. We were always talking about which ones we liked, gauging if they liked us too, and dealing with the fallout after either hooking up with one of them or learning that he was interested in someone else. It was the backdrop of our college life.

But in a way that wasn't like the sorority for me, it felt like these friendships were more permanent. They weren't a holding pattern until a man took us away. The "candlelight" ceremony in the sorority seemed to mark a transition from being with your sisters to going off with a guy. With my friends, guys were in the background always, but we loved being alone together too. Ellie and I would always go driving in search of a pool, Mexican food, or a store that sold the tacky candles she liked, and she remembers getting lost all of the time with me. This was before cell phones had GPS. "We'd always be in some neighborhood," she said. "Just me and you in your car with no idea where we were. I'd be like, 'Kayleen, we could just die out here.'"

Other afternoons, during a stretch of free time that's hard for me to fathom now, we'd have a dance party. One of us would come home to find the other grooving by herself and soon we'd both be moving like maniacs to "Walking on Sunshine" or "California Love."

College was the first time I realized that a group of women could look out for and take care of each other—my friends did just that. We were always at parties and bars, usually because some guy was maybe going to be there too, but we never ditched each other. When one of us left the group and went somewhere in the crowd, we always kept watch, as if our friend was a celebrity moving around the club. One of my roommates once shoved a guy off Ellie after he licked her leg at a bar (she was dancing on a table). "Did you just *lick* her leg?" she said in disbelief. Ellie would force men to step back when we were out. She'd throw her arms back and yell, "Give us some space."

This isn't to say that we always had some magical all-for-one attitude that no male could puncture—sometimes guys did come between us. Freshman year, one friend and I both had a crush on the same guy. I didn't have the guts to tell her when I hooked up with him, which makes me disappointed in myself even now. When she found out, she was sad, and I was too. We stayed friends while we were both infatuated with him, even though there were some moments when we both thought the other one was being a jerk. I think there was an understanding between us that having each other—to watch *Grosse Pointe Blank* with for the billionth time, make late-night ice cream runs, or plot the best way to convince Ellie not to have a toga party—was the most important thing, and we'd deal with the ups and downs with the guy as best as we could.

Later on, Ellie and another roommate had intense—and back-to-back—relationships with the same guy while we were all living together. This led to some fierce fights I witnessed and wished hadn't gone down like they did. Ellie feels the same way. "I still feel bad," she says. "I wish I'd been a little more mature."

At times our romantic dramas were all consuming, but there were more stretches where they weren't, where we were studying, writing papers or stories, making films, or otherwise fantasizing about the future selves we would be when we graduated in ways that didn't involve men at all.

The star of the rom-com usually had a best friend, but un-like BFFs in the real world, these two never talked about much but the guy the star had fallen for. All the best friend did was listen while the lead pined for—and sometimes panicked about—her romantic interest. The character was underdeveloped but often funny (especially in the nineties).

Becky (Rosie O'Donnell) in 1993's *Sleepless in Seattle* gets good lines: "Verbal ability is a highly overrated thing in a guy," she says to Annie (Meg Ryan), "and it's our pathetic need for it that gets us into so much trouble." But she exists to prod Annie into ending up on top of the Empire State Building with Sam (Tom Hanks).

Usually the best friend was supportive of the relationship. In 1990's *Pretty Woman,* when Vivian (Julia Roberts) is unsure if she should continue seeing Edward (Richard Gere), the rich guy who hired her as a prostitute for a week, her best friend, Kit (Laura San Giacomo), says, "Hey, he asked you, right? Maybe you guys could, like, um, you know, get a house together and, like, buy some diamonds and a horse. I don't know." (In my opinion, this is the best best-friend line of all time.)

Sometimes, however, the funny best friend discouraged the pairing, at least at the start of the movie. "Dorothy, this guy would go home with a gardening tool if it showed interest," Laurel (Bonnie Hunt) warns her sister and best friend, Dorothy (Renée Zellweger), about a shattered Jerry (Tom Cruise) in 1996's *Jerry Maguire.*

In 2001's *Bridget Jones's Diary,* Bridget (Zellweger again) gets cautioned by her best friend, Shazza (Sally Phillips), about the reserved Mark Darcy (Colin Firth). "I mean there's been all these bloody hints and stuff, but has he ever actually stuck his fucking tongue down your fucking throat?" Shazza asks.

But by the end, the best friend has come around to the guy and is usually gone from the movie. Judy Greer, who played the best friend in *13 Going on 30, 27 Dresses,* and *The Wedding Planner,* parodied the limits of the role in a Funny or Die video: "Judy Greer Is the Best Friend." In it, over a lunch of salads and water, she insists that her best friend run to the airport to tell a guy how she feels. "Do you know how hard it is to find love in this crazy world?" she says. "His plane doesn't take off for fifteen minutes. You can make it."

After she leaves, the other woman at the table asks Greer, "So, what have you been up to lately?"

"Oh gosh, um, hmm, well I have, um, just been really spending a lot of time with Sarah and helping her through her relationship with Dan," Greer says. "I don't really have a lot going on, except being Sarah's best friend."

There is one movie where the star and the friend who's been her confidant have the final scene together, 1997's *My Best Friend's Wedding,* but that friend is a gay man. A dejected Julianne (Julia Roberts) is at the reception for the wedding she tried—and failed—to break up when George (Rupert Everett) arrives. The song "I Say a Little Prayer" starts playing, the crowd parts, and he's there saying, "Maybe there won't be marriage. Maybe there won't be sex. But, by God, there'll be dancing." The movie ends with them dancing together.

Originally the filmmakers had Julianne dancing with a different guy, a man she'd just met at the wedding who, it was implied, would help her get over her now-married love. The test audience hated it. "The cards basically said, 'Who is this guy that she's dancing with at the end? What's she doing with him?'" Ron Bass, the screenwriter, said.

It was a victory for the best friend, but not for female friendship. Our best friends, according to Hollywood, were only there to support us while we found love and let us go after that.

I graduated from college having fallen in love, but I also left school impressed and charmed by other women for the first time. The women I was drawn to were funny, bold, and as ambitious as hell. I admired Ellie then and still do today. Ellie was in a sorority too—she'd joined because her mom had been in one—but she quit after a year, for a more principled reason than I did. A friend of hers couldn't afford to pay the money she was supposed to for the sorority's philanthropy and the other women were giving her a hard time and upsetting her, so Ellie wrote a check for her friend and then quit. "I think I threw a check at them and said, 'Here's your money. Fuck off,'" she says. How smart, centered, and sure of who she was at eighteen has only intensified. Today she's an aerospace engineer with a husband and a little girl, who admits she's stressed out all the time, even as she tries to temper that by continuing to decorate parts of her home as if it's a Spencer's Gifts store.

I see her only about once a year, but when we do hang out, our friendship still feels strong. When we saw each other recently we talked about what's going on with both of us and were amused to find out that we have matching anxiety-induced eye twitches. We sympathized over the struggles of our very different lives and, even though we were eating sushi and not having a dance party, we were making each other feel better again. "We never talk," Ellie says. "We never see each other, but our eye twitches will bring us together."

But when I moved to New York City to try to get a job as a magazine writer, I stopped looking for female friends. I had a few girlfriends already in the city, and it felt like enough. I wanted to focus on my career.

This was during an era of reality television shows in which contestants competed to be the last person on the island or marry the millionaire, and a common trope about the stars reflected the way I felt about starting my working life: I didn't come here to make friends.

All I wanted was to be a magazine writer, and I was single-minded about wanting it.

I thought making friends with women would interfere with my career in more ways than just distracting me from work. I thought if I wanted to be a writer, I had to look to men. That's because real writers were men. No one told me this. They didn't have to. It was just something I knew, the same way I knew I had to pretend to hate Times Square now that I lived in New York.

Of course this isn't true. Your gender has nothing to do with your ability to put words in order. But at the time, I was always conscious of being a woman, in a way that I hadn't been in high school or college, when I wasn't so convinced that my sex might be holding me back. J. E. Buntin wrote about constantly thinking about the fact that she's female in an essay for *The Rumpus,* an online literary magazine. "For me, it's I am a woman I am a woman I am a woman while buying groceries, I am a woman I am a woman riding a bike, I am a woman peeing, I am a woman I am a woman turning the light on, I am a woman turning it off I am a woman," she wrote. "My femininity is my white noise, the creaks and groans of the house that is my body."

That's how I felt for the first few years of my professional life too, and I spent a lot of time making Herculean efforts to strangle my femininity. I'd done this before in middle school when I also felt uncomfortable being a girl. I'd grown breasts and gotten my period in the span of a few months, so to pretend this wasn't happening, I wore a black leotard under my clothes that flattened my boobs. If I couldn't see what was there to separate me from the boys, then I didn't have to deal with being a girl in a world that I suspected hated girls.

I ditched the leotard back in middle school, but my mindset when I moved to New York was similar. If I could make the fact that I was a woman disappear, then I wouldn't have to deal with a professional world that I was pretty sure didn't take women seriously.

First, I ruled out working for a women's magazine. I wanted to be a writer long after 1950, when Sylvia Plath's first short story, "And Summer Will Not Come Again," ran in *Seventeen,* or 1956 when Joan Didion started working at *Vogue.* If you had told me, when I was sending out résumés to get my first job, that they had written for women's magazines, I wouldn't have believed you.

Years after *Sassy* shut down, I thought women's magazines

were fluff. I got mad when I flipped through them and saw stories about how to tame my frizzy hair or have sex while I had my period. Part of the problem was that reading stuff like that made it feel impossible to escape my female body. But I also didn't think those subjects were worthy of my literary ambitions. Superficial, silly girls cared about those things, but I didn't.

At the time so-called shopping magazines were popular, and I remember rolling my eyes at a girl who said *Lucky* was her favorite magazine. It looked like a catalog, with pages of shoes captioned with descriptions like "these flat calfskin boots have a sophisticated cut." "There's, like, no words in it," I told her.

I wanted people to look at me and see a writer. If I spent my days writing about frizz, periods, or shoes, I might as well put a neon sign over my head that said "girly girl." The only option was to try to get a job at a men's magazine. I thought that's where the legitimate literary scene was, where the employees got to care only about the words they plucked out of their brains, not the way their bodies might be malfunctioning. That's where I had to work if I wanted to join their brilliant, rumpled ranks.

I wasn't alone in thinking that I couldn't be a serious writer if I worked at a women's magazine. Janet Reitman, who writes for *Rolling Stone*, *GQ*, and *Men's Journal*, has said she refuses to write for women's magazines. "I was never going to be a 'chick,' you know, doing 'chick stories,'" she said in 2012 when she was on the Longform Podcast, which features conversations with nonfiction writers about how they got their start. "The reality is, and continues to be, that the women who write those stories are ghettoized into the women's magazine ghetto." In an interview with *The Rumpus*, bestselling author Elizabeth Gilbert, who was a contributing writer for *GQ* before she wrote *Eat, Pray, Love,* recalled wrinkling her nose at these magazines too. "I gave a lot of speeches in bars about how much better the men's magazines were than the women's magazines," she said.

I moved to New York toward the end of the television show *Sex and the City*'s run. The HBO series that set out to subvert romantic comedies premiered in 1998 and had its final episode in 2004. It gave the rom-com best friend heft, intelligence, and opinions that she'd never had before.

There were four friends on the show: Carrie (Sarah Jessica Parker), Miranda (Cynthia Nixon), Samantha (Kim Cattrall), and Charlotte (Kristin Davis). The characters (except Charlotte) were acerbic and sometimes bitter, in a way that women who forced themselves to be nice when they really wanted to tell someone to go fuck themselves could thrill at.

Carrie was the narrator and star, but the other women were given substantial enough story lines that viewers started identifying with one or another of them, at least until their avatar did something awful. When Carrie got angry at Charlotte for refusing to lend her money for the down payment on an apartment Carrie wanted to buy, self-appointed Carries cringed.

The foursome did what friends in rom-coms do—had

brunch, went shopping, drank cocktails, talked about sex, and linked arms while walking down the street—but unlike in the movies, their main goal wasn't to see their friend end up with the guy and then step out of the way. When one of the women was dating someone who seemed to be controlling or callous or noncommittal, they were concerned or actually angry, like when Miranda and Carrie fight over Mr. Big, Carrie's love interest for most of the series. Carrie tells Miranda she's going to lunch with him, after they had dated, broken up several times, and had an affair while he was married.

"You know what?" Miranda says. "I'm not holding your hand through this again."

"I'm not asking you to hold my anything," Carrie says. "We're just having lunch."

"It's a huge mistake," Miranda says.

"It is not a huge mistake. It's lunch," Carrie says.

"Wake up, Carrie," Miranda says. "How many more times are you gonna go through this? He is bad for you. Jesus, every time you get near him, you turn into this pathetic, needy, insecure victim. And the thing that pisses me off the most is that you're more than willing to go right back for more."

They argue more about her starting up with Big again, which Carrie swears she's not going to do.

"Well, if you do, I don't wanna know anything about it," Miranda says. "I mean it, Carrie. No calls. No crying."

Carrie and Miranda fight again when Carrie tells her she quit her job to move to Paris to live with her wealthy, megalomaniac Russian boyfriend Aleksandr (Mikhail Baryshnikov).

"Why can't you be happy for me?" Carrie says.

"I'm sorry but . . . I don't understand why you have to move away and give up your life," Miranda says.

"I can't stay in New York and be single for you," Carrie says.

But, in the end, in the last episode of the series, after Carrie regrets moving to Paris, it's Big, and not her friends, who rushes there to rescue her. "Carrie, you're the one," he tells her on a bridge overlooking the Seine, which might be why the series now seems less subversive than it started out to be. "Endings count in television, maybe too much," Emily Nussbaum wrote in an essay about *Sex and the City* for *The New Yorker.* She praised the show for refusing to make the women cute, plucky creatures who wanted nothing more than to be likable, but wished that the writers had been brave enough not to wrap up Carrie's story with a "girl gets guy" happy ending. "I can't help but wonder: What would the show look like without that finale?" she wrote. "What if it were the story of a woman who lost herself in her thirties, who was changed by a poisonous, powerful love affair, and who emerged, finally, surrounded by her friends?"

The way the women in *Sex and the City* looked out for each other was not the way I was living in New York. I was still happily dating my college boyfriend and wasn't interested in helping any other women through their lives, romantic or otherwise, or letting them help me through mine. I'd forgotten the way my college friends and I had comforted and encouraged each other. Instead, I spent most of my time pointed toward men.

I did get hired at a men's magazine called *Details*. My job there was to assist the managing editor, which meant I sent writers and photographers their contracts and got them paid after they did their work. *Details* was for men, but these guys didn't want to read about going on wilderness adventures or convincing your girlfriend to have a threesome. Instead, they were interested in how to wear jewelry or what it was like to get a chin implant. We ran photos of sweaters with shawl collars and screeds about how men should never have on flip-flops anywhere but the beach. In 2003, an article in *The New York Times* by Warren St. John identified these guys as "metrosexuals": "straight urban men willing, even eager, to embrace their feminine sides." St. John wrote that *Details* was "a kind of metrosexual bible" and interviewed my editor in chief, Dan Peres, who said that the reader was comfortable with others questioning if he was gay because he liked white jeans or face cream. "Wanting them to wonder and having them wonder is a wonderful thing," he said in the piece. "It gives you an air of mystery: could he be? It makes you stand out."

I loved *Details* as soon as I was assigned a cubicle. (Like *Sassy*, *Details* no longer exists. The magazine's last issue was in December of 2015.) The guys around me every day (most of the staff was male) acted like what we were doing was smart and valuable, so I treated it like very important work too.

Years removed from working there I can see the content of the magazine was just as frivolous and reductive as that of the women's magazines I'd been repulsed by. But at the time,

I never thought *Details* was silly. What women cared about, I thought, was embarrassing and bad. What men cared about mattered. Any interests they had should be taken seriously.

It wasn't part of my job to come up with stories for the magazine, but that didn't stop me from being preoccupied with "our guy," as everyone on staff called the tender fellow we imagined was buying each issue. What would he want to read about? Whenever someone had what Dan thought was a good idea, he hopped with anticipation, like when an assistant editor suggested a story about straight guys entering into domestic partnerships with other straight guys to get insurance benefits. "Yes!" he said. "I want that. Make that happen for me."

I wanted to be a part of that, to have my ideas accepted or rejected, to help create this magazine. It all felt crucial, as if being able to divine what these men wanted was all I really needed to do at this moment in my life. I'd dream up possible stories even when I wasn't at work, while I was running, in the shower, or commuting.

I was spending all my time doing what the writer Claire Vaye Watkins calls "watching boys do stuff." "Nearly all of my life has been arranged around this activity," she wrote in an essay for the literary magazine *Tin House*.

> I've filled my days doing this, spent all my free time and a great amount of time that was not free doing it. I've watched boys play the drums, guitar, sing, watched them play football, baseball, soccer, pool, Dungeons and Dragons and Magic:

The Gathering. I've watched them golf. Just the other day I watched them play a kind of sweaty, book-nerd version of basketball. I've watched them work on their trucks and work on their master's theses. I've watched boys build things: half-pipes, bookshelves, screenplays, careers. I've watched boys skateboard, snowboard, act, bike, box, paint, fight, and drink. I could probably write my own series of six virtuosic autobiographical novels based solely on the years I spent watching boys play Resident Evil and Tony Hawk's ProSkater.

I've watched boys do stuff my whole life too. When I was little I watched them play video games and baseball. In high school, I watched them drive around and listen to rap music. In college, I watched them play guitar and sing or play rugby and drink beer. But I never watched boys do stuff as much or as intently as I did in my early twenties.

This went beyond *Details*. I lived with my brother and another rotating roommate who was usually a dude, and there were a bunch of other guys around. They all considered themselves artists, even if they were spending more time at their menial jobs than on anything creative. I watched them work on screenplays, sculptures, paintings, and cartoons. One Saturday, a few of the guys took acid and I watched them walk around the Metropolitan Museum of Art for hours as they tripped and geeked out about Neo Rauch's bright paintings with ominous undercurrents.

We had a weekly poker game at the apartment that I was invited to because I lived there. I was often the only girl. There I watched them bet, bluff, and barter. I watched them get mad, storm off, and return. I watched them go broke and gamble some more.

I called these guys my friends, and they were; in part these were simple relationships: I liked them and they liked me back. But what I also liked was the notion of being around them, perhaps more than I did actually talking about their art or playing poker. If you have convinced yourself, like I did, that what men like are the smartest and most interesting things to like, then being allowed to hang around them— being one of the guys—is heady. I felt intelligent and edgy when I was with them, in no danger of being just another empty-headed girl.

B etsy Thomas created the sitcom *My Boys*, which ran for four seasons on TBS, from 2006 to 2010, specifically about this kind of friendship. The main character, P. J. Franklin (Jordana Spiro), a sportswriter for the *Chicago Sun-Times*, spends the series with her group of guy friends: playing poker or pickup softball, watching sports, and hanging out at a favorite bar. Thomas conceived the show because it reflected her life in Los Angeles at the time. She lived with four male roommates in a house, was the only woman at her weekly poker game, and loved watching Cubs games and playing video games with her guy friends. She also wrote it "as a little bit in reaction to *Sex and the City*," she says. "At the time, I was like, I don't do this. I don't care about shoes and talking about dicks. I felt like there were girls and then there were boys and what I didn't see was that crossover."

What she wanted to bring to television was the easy camaraderie that she felt with her male friends, to show that P.J. could be an equal in the group, even if she was a girl. "I wanted to show a woman being treated the same way a guy friend would be," she says. "She gets the same amount of shit. She flops on the couch the same. The relationship is the same."

Elaine Benes on *Seinfeld*, played by Julia Louis-Dreyfus, is perhaps the first modern example on television of a girl who is one of the guys. She dated the protagonist, Jerry Seinfeld, and they remained good friends after they broke up. Elaine was added to the show only after NBC executives felt the show was too male-centric and emphatically requested that cocreators Seinfeld and Larry David cast a woman in a significant part, according to Jennifer Keishin Armstrong in *Seinfeldia: How a Show About Nothing Changed Everything.* But throughout the show, her gender was unremarkable—she was a proportionate part of the foursome of friends that also included George Costanza (Jason Alexander) and Cosmo Kramer (Michael Richards). "It didn't have to be made a point of whether she was girly or not girly," Thomas says. "She was just one of the guys. They didn't separate her out. It wasn't a novelty that she was involved. It just was."

On *My Boys,* P.J.'s sex was the point—Thomas wanted to show that men and women weren't from different planets; they could be friends. But, at least in the earlier seasons of the show, apparently men and women couldn't be friends if the girl was too feminine. P.J.'s foil on the show was Stephanie Layne (Kellee Stewart), the author of a bestselling book about relationships, *You're a Great Guy, but . . .* ; she worked as a journalist, couldn't stand the boys P.J. was friends with, and rolled her eyes a lot. It was important to shout out that P.J. wasn't like this; she was the anti-Stephanie.

B ack then, I judged and criticized women in ways I never did with men. That sounds severe, and it was. In general, I thought girls—especially the ones who I'd decided were too into hearts and flowers—were not worth my time. I was so focused on the boys and being the kind of woman they wanted around that I dismissed any woman who wasn't as into guy stuff as I was, which, as I saw it, was most women. I mocked girls for doing anything that seemed like it was ripped from the pages of chick lit, like agonizing over what jeans to buy or not being able to just get over an ex already. I would have yanked out all of my eyelashes before I'd go to a girls' night. Like in high school, I still wanted to belong, but this time I wanted to be one of the guys.

My friend Greg used to say, "Kayleen doesn't like other women." I might have protested a little when he said this—"*I have friends who are girls*"—but it didn't really bother me. I didn't think it was an insult to not like other women. Instead, I'd tuck that statement away, as if it were an affirmation. What I heard wasn't "Kayleen doesn't like other women." I heard "Kayleen isn't like other women."

Greg remembers being at a party with me when I was

interacting with another woman whom "you were sniping at all night long," he says. "It wasn't anything like outright aggression on your part. It was more like classic undermining comments coming from you."

He also recalled a female roommate I once had, a woman who was the opposite of the woman I was trying to be. She was highly feminine. If she had a rough day at work, she'd treat herself to a cupcake. She owned multiple low-cut "going out" shirts that she wore to meet guys at bars. When she woke up hungover, she'd clean the kitchen. Her group of girlfriends mystified me. She called them her best friends, even though it felt to me as if they didn't actually like one another very much.

When I would bring her up to my male friends, I thought they'd be entertained by my stories. But Greg remembers feeling bad for her. "It seemed like maybe you were tougher on other women than you were on men," he says.

"It's immaturity," *My Boys* creator Thomas says about the tendency of girls who are one of the guys to demonize other women. "When you're insecure about something, you can project that this person who's not like you is somehow the enemy. Because if you can compartmentalize them that way, if you can make them that way, that validates who you are."

At *Details,* I refused to befriend any of the other women who were also in junior positions on the staff. I lumped them together as the kinds of girls I did not want to be. They didn't seem to care how the office full of men judged them. They were not calm. They often got upset over what I thought were unremarkable incidents. They cried at their desks. They were always whispering in the women's bathroom. They were loud about whatever drama they were having with their boyfriends. On Mondays, they brought in what they'd baked over the weekend. They did not think it was a joke when a male editor said something crude.

I isolated myself to send a message: I am not like them.

Even so, we were often stuck together, like when we had to stay late at the office while the rest of our coworkers went to the staff party. One night, I remember walking over to a bar our colleagues were at already with one of the women, whom I'll call Ann. Ann did not try to fit in with the guys. At the time, I would have said she whined and complained a lot. I would have said she was annoying.

On this night, even though we'd already missed an hour or so of the gathering, she said that she didn't think her deodorant was working and that she wanted to stop and buy some more. "Who cares?" I said.

But she insisted, and I remember waiting outside the store for her, literally tapping my foot on the sidewalk because I wanted to hurry to the party so I could get away from her and mingle with the male editors I could spare all of the time in the world for. She didn't seem to notice and made me wait longer while she applied her new deodorant right there in front of the store.

Looking back on it, I can see she probably felt as awkward at the magazine as I did and was trying to do everything she could not to make a misstep in the male-infested office politics too. I didn't want to giggle or be too emotional; she didn't want to smell. But I didn't see this, or I didn't care. I should have reassured her that we'd get through this party and, eventually, these entry-level jobs. We could have worked to-gether to make ourselves feel more comfortable at work in-stead of constantly zigging and zagging to conform to what the boys wanted us to be. Instead, I didn't want to be any-where near her. I didn't want her to drag me down.

What I was doing was similar, though not identical, to being a bully at work—and like in school, women who are bullies in the office are often called "mean girls." They do what they can to undercut other women, such as shutting them out of meet-ings or spreading rumors about them to other colleagues. This behavior, I think, comes from the same place my refusing to befriend other women at the office did: the fear that only one woman can be promoted. We're made to believe that it's impos-sible to rise together. The only way up is to be the one woman who's worthy, whether that's by ingratiating yourself with the guys, like I did, or by cutting off all other female contenders.

"I've definitely worked with women who've used the fear factor to push others down and push themselves up," says Devin Tomb, who's in her early thirties and an editor at a women's-interest website. Because of this she's sometimes skeptical when female colleagues are overly inquisitive about her job. "I think, *What are you trying to do here?*" she says. "*Why are you trying to ask me about my relationship to the boss?* I worry, *Is this a mean girl?*"

But like with mean girls in high school, mean girls in the office is a stereotype. There are individual women in work-places who try to take down other women, who have insecu-rities and male-dominated thoughts and a sometimes poor way of doing things, but being wary of every seemingly am-bitious woman at work isn't helping more women get power.

It's making it so the women who do get ahead don't trust other women enough to lift them up too.

Devin knows this and is making a point of being less suspicious of other women at work. "It takes a lot of energy to go down the path of wondering what another woman's every move means," she says. "Instead I try to just take the coffee date, see what's there, and think maybe we'll turn out to be friends."

This doesn't mean that women have to stop competing at work or cheer each other's office accolades because we share the same sex. Alison Blough, an executive at a music company, has bonded with women throughout her career but knows not every woman is going to be over the moon each time she has a workplace win. "I hate the term 'catty,'" she says, "but you have to realize that everyone doesn't celebrate your success. That's the way it is in all of life. There's an ebb and flow to it. Sometimes other women will be happy for you. Other times they won't. You have to realize that we're in a work environment and they're looking out for number one. It's not 'Kumbaya' and we're going to braid each other's hair and all advance together. I expect that you have the honor not to mess with my career during your ascension, but I reject the groupthink that says we all have to love each other all of the time. I don't like being boxed in and that feels boxed in."

At work and in life, I didn't want to sabotage or scrap with other women; I just wanted to get away from them. I believed that in order to be successful, and to not be penalized because of the fact that I was female, I had to stand on my own. Leaning on other women would only reinforce that I was one of them.

Part of the allure of being one of the guys—whether it's at work or in your social life—is that it makes you special. You are not one of the mass of faceless, interchangeable girls. You are in the unique position of having been accepted by the other sex, but it's always understood that this designation applies only to you—all women are not welcome. You are the exception, not the rule.

For a long time, Jaya Saxena, who's in her late twenties, loved being one of the guys. "Being the girl who was friends with the guys felt like a superpower," she says. Growing up in Manhattan, she thought she had more in common with the boys around her than with the girls. She didn't like ballet or pop music; she liked sports, video games, sci-fi movies, and alternative rock. "I felt that binary 'boys are for romance and girls are for friendship' was bullshit," she says. So when she was thirteen, she met a group of guys at an arts camp, and they quickly became her core group of friends. "Everyone was a bit of a weirdo," she says. "It felt very refreshing to be around these people who didn't care how I looked, or if I'd hooked up with anyone. It was just, let's talk about this band or this book we like." She and her guy friends were playing the board game Risk or listening to bands like Incubus and Blink-182 while she imagined the other girls her age were listening to pop music and trying on perfume. One night, when one of her guy friends made a joke about her being a girl, another one said, "Jaya isn't a girl, she's just a guy with long hair." "At the time, I took it as the highest compliment," she says.

The fact that these guys had been such good friends to her in her teens—she'd call them in the middle of the night with a crisis and have deep conversations with them about her fears and anxieties—meant that when she went to college, she rushed to be friends with only guys again and ignored all the women around her. But these guys were different from her childhood pals. "One of the biggest things I hear girls say about having guy friends is, 'There's some things you can't talk about with them,'" she says. "For a long time, I was like, 'What are you talking about? I talk to my guy friends about my period all of the time. That's what friends are for.' And then I got to college and there were certain times where I'd try to re-create that and these guys would be grossed out, like if I was complaining about my period or something about body hair. They were like, 'I don't need to hear that.' Meanwhile, they'd be talking about their dicks all of the time. They had no problem talking about their experiences, but didn't want to listen to mine."

She started to realize that now she was the one letting gender get in the way of whom she could be friends with. She was buying into all of the ideas about what your sex meant about you that she was trying to reject—girls were prissy; guys were not—and limiting herself to only being friends with guys, even as she was noticing that all men weren't as supportive as she wanted them to be and some girls did like the same hobbies she was into.

In a theater class, she met a girl who, for the first time, seemed to be on her wavelength. She surprised her by asking her on a friend date to see an apocalyptic film starring dragons. "I was excited about it because it was more the type of movie I'd want to see," Jaya says. "I had the stereotype that all other girls want to watch chick flicks, but not me. I'm super cool. Later it made me realize that it doesn't have to be this division. I'm allowed to like chick flicks and wear makeup if I want."

Eventually she stopped feeling like being one of the guys was an essential part of her identity. Her guy friends saying "you're not like other girls" was no longer a compliment. "For a long time it made me feel cool and like I wasn't a weirdo for liking things boys are supposed to like," she says. "But that was me buying into the idea that girls are inherently not into that stuff. Once I realized they were, that line of reasoning couldn't be used on me. I was like, 'What are you talking about? I know a ton of girls who like that stuff. Have you not talked to a woman before?' We have a ton of varied interests. It's not that I'm like other girls or not like other girls. I'm like me."

At *Details*, my obsession with watching boys do stuff paid off. For someone who had never been "our guy," or any guy at all, I was great at coming up with stories that he—or at least the editors at the magazine—liked. "From my point of view as a boss, you were an editor that really understood and were able to produce content that was right in our sweet spot," Dan says.

Notably, men often aren't able to know women this same way. The writer Junot Díaz says the women he teaches can usually credibly write from a male point of view, but the guys can never write from a woman's. "If you're a boy writer, it's a simple rule: you've gotta get used to the fact that you suck at writing women and that the worst woman writer can write a better man than the best male writer can write a good woman," he said in 2012 at Word Up, a community book shop in New York. "And it's just the minimum. Because the thing about the sort of heteronormative masculine privilege, whether it's in Santo Domingo, or the United States, is you grow up your entire life being told that women aren't human beings, and that women have no independent subjectivity."

The first item I ever published in the magazine was two hundred words on the last X-rated drive-in movie theater in America. I read about porn drive-ins existing from the late sixties to the early eighties and wondered, *What if one is still around?* No matter how evolved the *Details* guy was, he was still interested in pretty much anything involving porn. The features editor I sat next to had been working for months on a story about straight guys who did gay porn. (The headline was "Gay for Pay" when it ran in the magazine.)

So in between mailing contracts and coding invoices, I called drive-ins to see if I could find such a place. And I did! The Apache Drive-In Theatre in Tyler, Texas. After I'd written the item, the executive editor sent me a two-word e-mail: "nice job." I kept it open on my computer for a long time, elated that my work had been noticed.

I got promoted to a position where part of my job was to come up with stories. I wrote about chubby guys who thought their guts indicated how successful they were ("The New Fat Cats"), men who swore by workouts favored by women, like

Pilates ("How to Get the Body of the Moment"), and how to decode a department-store fragrance counter ("The Ultimate Guide to Buying Cologne").

At the time it didn't occur to me that I was writing about the same topics—sex, body image, fashion, and grooming habits—I'd sneered at in women's magazines. All I saw was that I had impressed the men around me, even if that was by figuring out where they could see some fifty-foot-tall penises and Volkswagen-size breasts.

Succeeding in this men's world, though, also meant learning how to act around them. At the poker table at home or in the conference room at the office, I was always looking for cues. I absorbed what they thought was cool and what annoyed them and reflected it back. I learned when to talk, what to say, and when to shut up. I learned, in their eyes, what was the right balance of woman to be.

Traditionally what men want, to use the writer Gillian Flynn's brilliant label from her novel *Gone Girl,* is a Cool Girl. "Men always say that as the defining compliment, don't they?" Flynn writes. "She's a cool girl. Being the Cool Girl means I am a hot, brilliant, funny woman who adores football, poker, dirty jokes, and burping, who plays video games, drinks cheap beer, loves threesomes and anal sex, and jams hot dogs and hamburgers into her mouth like she's hosting the world's biggest culinary gang bang while somehow maintaining a size 2."

In my personal life and at work, I was trying to be a Cool Girl. I don't know if any of my poker bros would have recoiled if I'd done something a little too ladylike in front of them, like if I'd decided to paint my nails during a slow hand, because I never would have let myself do that. I was always mindful of being the kind of girl they'd want to have there, which meant never being offended when the conversation inevitably turned to outrageous sex acts or never being bored when one of them talked about another idea for an art project that was absolutely going to be amazing. I didn't want anything from them except to be around them, and they loved me for it.

In work meetings, too, I was focused only on how I was presenting myself. I was conscious of the way I was sitting, of how much I was talking, of nodding a lot when someone said something Dan was into, and of laughing only when the rest of the room did. I did not flinch when we talked about getting an actress to "go there," which was code for her being willing to strip off at least some of her clothes at the photo shoot.

"You never struck me as a girl's girl," Dan says, "and it's true frankly of a number of the women who worked at the magazine over the years, they were incredibly comfortable sitting in a room of male editors who were talking about a wide range of subjects, most of which would have made a lot of women blush. While our content was wide-ranging, we would talk about things related to sex, hone in on the male point of view of something, and I was always mindful of that sitting in a room with mostly men and only a few women. I always thought you were somewhat fluent in these subjects. I did notice that you were comfortable sitting in a roomful of men talking about these subjects."

I might have seemed comfortable, and sometimes I was, but as I got older, there were moments when I knew I was ill at ease underneath my Cool Girl costume. I wasn't sure what to do about this. Once I had established myself as this chill person who happily soaked up anything men say, I had no idea how to express opinions or emotions that didn't sync up with theirs.

Because of this my professional relationships and friendships started to seem less secure. There was always the threat, in my head at least, that if I started acting like a Not Cool Girl, they wouldn't want me around anymore. I'd no longer fit in.

Eventually, obscuring any objectionable parts of my femininity started to feel wrong, in part because I realized that no matter how much I pretended to be the woman guys wanted around, I still wouldn't ever fully belong. I wasn't invited to one of the poker guys' bachelor parties, and I was bummed about it. (There is an episode like this on *My Boys,* where P.J. has to go to the bridal shower instead of the bachelor party and is horrified.) There'd been a billion nights where I'd been out with them and been the only girl, but now I couldn't come because it was symbolic? Or, another time, I wrote "we" in an article for *Details* and was stung to see an editor's comment: "Can't use 'we' here because it's a woman's byline."

I'd believed that being too girly would hold me back, but that wasn't true: I was holding myself back by pretending to be a one-dimensional woman. Plus, I was undermining and dismissing my sex by not seeing us as complex people who shouldn't have to conform to anyone's standard of what's cool or not.

met Ruthie at *Details*. She was hired as the new assistant to the managing editor after I got promoted. I was so accustomed to ignoring women at this point that I do not remember our first lunch together. How important Ruthie is to me now makes me hate that blank spot in my brain. I wish I had that memory. She says she asked me to lunch to have one of those how-did-you-make-your-job-happen advice sessions, and that I was very nice, which is a relief.

We went to the diner one street over from the office. I've learned since that Ruthie's standard diner order is chicken fingers, but she says, "I probably didn't have chicken fingers because I was being professional." At the end of the lunch there was a tell that we'd go on to become friends—one that I'm relying on Ruthie's memory for, and again, I am disappointed it's not in mine. We both pulled out identical USAA credit cards to pay. (USAA is the military bank—I have the card because my dad was in the Air Force; Ruthie has hers because her dad was in the National Health Service Corps.) This has gone on to be one of those friendship signifiers that we both think is really funny but no one else is ever amused by. But at that first lunch, it didn't mean anything to me because I wasn't looking to have anything in common with her.

A few months later, *Details* moved offices and Ruthie and I wound up sitting side by side. I began noticing what she said and did, and how much it amused me, like when she talked about her favorite Halloween costume. She'd worn a pink sweat suit and pig's nose and asked people what they thought she was. "You're a pig," they'd say.

"No," she'd answer. "I'm a sexy pig."

At the same time, she was observing and appreciating me, in a way that I was super-pleased by, even though she was calling out girly things I'd never wanted anyone in the office to identify before, like when she noticed I got my eyebrows shaped or had a new tiny earring in my cartilage. For the first time at work I was attuned to another woman. I wanted Ruthie to like me.

Toward the end of my time working for *Details,* we worked on a story together. It was about guys going to Lilith Fair, the all-female musical festival headlined by Sarah McLachlan. I wrote it and Ruthie edited it. I talked with a lot of sensitive men who were spending their weekend listening to ladies strum acoustic guitars, and when the piece was ready, one of the pictures that we wanted to run with it was of two topless women posing happily on the lawn. They knew their picture was being taken to be published in a magazine and were fine with that. Still, one of the male editors stepped in and said we should cover their eyes with black bars so they couldn't be identified. This seemed wrong to me, but I couldn't articulate exactly what was bothering me about it.

I was explaining, badly, why I didn't think we needed the black bars when Ruthie spoke to back me up. Unlike me, she knew exactly what was wrong with putting black bars over these topless women's eyes. "It's not a sexual picture," she said. "Putting a black bar over their faces sexualizes it."

She had said exactly what I was thinking but couldn't

articulate, and I was grateful to her—a feeling that was unfamiliar to me, yet welcome at the same time. She'd been there and hadn't held back her opinion. She didn't pretend to be fine with the situation even though that would have been the Cool Girl thing to do. (We didn't get what we wanted, though; the pictures ran with the black bars.)

For the first time in years, I felt a real kinship with my own sex, and the more I looked around, the more I started to realize that there were plenty of smart, funny, warm girls around me to be friends with. Why wasn't I reaching out to them?

CHAPTER 4

A New Focus on Friendships

I don't know what I would have done so many times in
my life if I hadn't had my girlfriends. They have literally
gotten me up out of bed, taken my clothes off, put me in
the shower, dressed me, said, "Hey, you can do this,"
put my high heels on and pushed me out the door!

—Reese Witherspoon, actress and producer

"Not yet," I said to my boyfriend as he knelt in front of me. He'd just asked me to marry him, and I shocked both of us with my answer. We'd been dating for a decade, ever since meeting in college, and I had been assuming for at least the last five of the years we'd been together that we would eventually marry, even though we didn't live in the same city.

It was late afternoon; we were visiting his parents in Austin and hanging out by the pool for the last hour of our trip. It was hot. I was sweating even though my bathing suit was still damp from being in the water a few moments before. The whole proposal felt rushed, like a formality we were checking off. One minute we'd been sitting side by side in lounge chairs dozing and drying off, gearing up to go inside and pack for our separate flights to our separate homes, and the next he was kneeling next to me asking if I wanted to get married.

I was terrified as soon as I realized what was happening.

I didn't see waking up next to him every morning. I saw leaving the city I loved and had built a life in. I didn't see the family we'd have together as a married couple. I saw all of the stereotypical duties designated by my sex (dirty dishes, diapers). I didn't see growing old together. I saw having to stall the career I felt was only just starting to be a substantial one.

I saw all of the independence I'd worked so hard for being stifled; I couldn't say yes.

I'd been ready for marriage, I thought. My parents have been married for almost fifty years, as have most of my aunts and uncles. Growing up, I never thought of marriage or children as optional. As life steps, they seemed nonnegotiable, to be done somewhere in between getting my driver's license and watching my hair go gray. Looking back, I don't think I knew even one single woman when I was younger. In my memory, every adult lady in the suburban Texas town I was raised in had a husband. If there was a single woman she'd been widowed or maybe divorced; she certainly wasn't single because she'd never wanted to get married in the first place.

Marriage was something to look forward to, I was taught. Without a husband, you were supposed to feel incomplete. Even in elementary school, some of my friends were already actively planning their wedding days. One day in fifth grade, I was riding home from school with a friend I'll call Casey.

Her mom was driving, and we were in the back of the van. Casey pulled out a photo album from under the seat and opened it. Inside, sealed under clear protective covers, were dozens of pages ripped from wedding magazines of three-tier cakes, white tulle gowns, diamond rings and tiaras ("I can really see myself in a tiara," Casey said), and even flower-girl dresses (at only ten ourselves, we were probably still young enough to *be* flower girls).

At that point, my biggest fantasies included becoming a backup dancer for Janet Jackson and being allowed to drink Dr Pepper regularly. It never even occurred to me to dream about my wedding, but almost immediately after I saw what Casey called her "wedding inspiration album," I felt pressure. Before she'd pulled that book out, I'd felt like the future was open for anything I wanted, and as we flipped through the pages, it seemed to narrow in front of me. Marriage was looming—to someone, someday—and part of what I was supposed to do was put my focus and energy into preparing for it.

About a decade later, the guy who I assumed would be that someone I married arrived, the same guy I quit my sorority for. I was crazy about him. He was the president of the university's rugby team, and so handsome and charming that I wanted to be everywhere he was immediately. Sometimes I wondered how I got lucky enough that he seemed to like me that much too. As I got to know him better, I liked him even more. He was warm, generous, intelligent, and opinionated. He made me laugh and was up for any adventure. He challenged me to think about the world in bigger ways than I had before. He encouraged my writing and listened to me. He gave me a cat. I threw myself into the relationship with the kind of intensity I reserve only for people I want to be in my life for a long time. Together, we tested each other in all kinds of ways, trying to determine if we really could be partners in life.

But after college, neither of us was ready to get married. I wanted to go to New York to be a writer, and he got accepted to study aerospace engineering in a graduate program at the University of Colorado in Boulder. We built separate lives in both places but made sure to visit each other enough that it felt like we were still growing together. I didn't feel lonely or like I needed to spend every day with him. I was ambitious and naïve, confident that if I just kept working hard I'd get to some patch of success that I could be happy with. I thought that when I did, I'd finally be ready to get married. We kept dating even as he finished school and found a job in Denver, and I chose to stay in New York.

We'd get the usual pressure, disguised as well-meaning concern about wanting to see us settled. "When are you two going to make it official?" my aunt would ask. Once my dad insinuated that I was waiting for a proposal that was never going to come. "If I wanted to be married, I would be," I said angrily.

By this point, most of my friends from childhood had gotten married. My fifth-grade friend Casey's wedding was, unsurprisingly, one of the first I was invited to. At the reception I heard another friend's mom whisper, "I'm honestly surprised she waited this long." I'd gone happily to many of these ceremonies, usually with my boyfriend. We would always have a really fun night, dancing, drinking, and occasionally sneaking away from our assigned table to have a whispered conversation in the corner about how wild we were about each other. We assumed our own wedding would be happening soon enough that we'd sometimes comment to each other about a detail we'd want to copy, or a tradition we'd absolutely be skipping.

Before the day he proposed, I was equal parts excited and scared about getting engaged, but it was not something I'd ever thought I'd actually decline.

And yet, when he asked, I blurted, "Not yet."

In the movie version of this part of my life, after I said "not yet" to my boyfriend's marriage proposal, my friends step in to support my decision and me. They scoop me from my fetal position on the floor while Carly Rae Jepsen's "Boy Problems" starts to play over a montage of us dancing in leather pants, waving champagne bottles in the air, and finishing off the night with slices of pizza and smeared eyeliner.

In reality, what happened was that my boyfriend and I had a lot of thoughtful conversations and plenty of fights about the proposal and our hesitations about marriage. The straight line we thought we had to walk as a couple was gone, and neither of us was sure what to do next. We tried to work through the upheaval together over the next few months, but I also started to really believe, for the first time, that my life was more than just groundwork for couplehood and marriage. No matter if I figured out my future with this boyfriend, or another down the road, I saw my options expanding and part of what I wanted to do was latch on to the bunch of super-smart, accomplished, brave, kind, silly, and generous women I am lucky to have as friends.

In the years since I'd evolved from being one of the guys and snapped out of the dumb idea that girls had nothing to offer me, I made friends with all kinds of women. I met them everywhere, through work, through other friends, through hobbies. Some were writers and editors; others were fashion stylists or nonprofit executives or start-up founders. They were all inspiring to be around—the kind of women who are enthusiastic, opinionated, and caring at all times. They never seemed like they were too tired or had better things to do than listen to me or be geniunely concerned about my life. All of them let me know they were there for whatever I might need and told me over and over that everything would be okay. Really, better than okay, they insisted. They trusted me, even as I was doubting myself, and reinforced that although it might not feel like it, I knew what I was doing. It was comforting to know that they saw me as a completely capable person on my own—no one second-guessed my decision or even hinted they thought I was making a mistake.

I started making dates with my friends, with an intensity I hadn't bothered with before. Previously, I saw them often-ish. It wasn't uncommon that a friend and I scheduled something, and one or both of us wanted to cancel the day of our date. The reason didn't really matter. Sometimes it was because one of us had to work, or preferred to hang with a guy instead, or even just wanted to be alone that night. But now I was up for anything: dinners, cocktails, trips to the terrible movies I might have once been too embarrassed to invite another person along to, or appointments to get leopard-print nail art.

For the first time in my life, I treated pursuing and tending to friendships seriously. It could have gone other ways: I could have sequestered myself in my apartment and numbed myself with television or forced myself to go on fifty first dates in fifty days. Instead, what I wanted to do in the hours when I wasn't working or sleeping was spend time with other women.

I didn't see this as a stopgap. I wasn't after low-stakes friendships or people who felt safe to hang out with while I regrouped and tried to figure out the marriage thing. I wanted my friends to consider me as necessary as they had become to me. I wanted them to know that these were long-term relationships and that I'd be there for them, too, in any way they might want. The e-mails, texts, weeknight dates and weekend outings, secrets, jokes, and tears all rolled up into a big ball, giving my female friendships weight and importance that they'd never had before in my life.

Prioritizing friendship is sometimes tricky; society often indicates to women that it's not on the same level as the other relationships in our lives, such as the ones with our romantic partners, our children, or even our jobs. Devoting ourselves to finding spouses, caring for children, or snagging a promotion is acceptable, productive behavior. Spending time strengthening our friendships, on the other hand, is seen more like a diversion.

For unmarried women, in particular, it can feel like choosing to focus on friends instead of dating means your preferences are misplaced. "We live in a world that prioritizes romance so much," says Shasta Nelson, the author of *Frientimacy: How to Deepen Friendships for Lifelong Health and Happiness.* "Women feel like we're nothing if we're not chosen, and we are conditioned to think friendships are less important. If something has to slide, it's friendships."

Elizabeth, who is in her mid-thirties and works in marketing in New York, wants to meet a man she wants to marry, but also often chooses to go to dinner with her friends after work instead of going on dates. Her mom tells her that she's never going to find a husband that way. "If I call her and tell her I'm meeting friends for dinner," Elizabeth says, "my mom's like, 'Elizabeth, there's no point to that!'"

Even other friends can make you feel like dating is all you should care about. Julia Chang, who is in her early forties, works for a financial planning company, and is one of the few single women in her group of friends, says that sometimes her girlfriends assume that she won't be happy until she gets what they have: a spouse and, in most of their cases, children.

"I never bring it up," Julia says. "I never talk about guys. It only comes up if they ask me about it first. They want it for me. They think I'm such a great person that I deserve to be with someone who's also a good person and that being alone is not the eternity that I should maintain."

For a long time, she wasn't sure what she wanted for

herself, possibly to be married and have children, possibly not. "The thought of having to see someone every day, it stresses me out," she says. "So I want it, but I don't. All of these other things in my life would have to change, and I don't know if I want that." Her uncertainty never gave her panic attacks in the middle of the night, but it did infect her with constant low-level dread. "It was always this underlying threat of 'your biological clock is ticking,'" she says. "You're getting old. If you want to do something about it, you're going to have to do it right now." So, she made a pact with herself that if she wasn't seeing someone by the time she turned forty, she'd stop assuming she was supposed to get married and have children. This opened up her life for a new-found passion writing and directing short films, one of which won the audience award in a film competition. "People can't just accept that you can be happy and be a single person," Julia says. "They're just like, 'No. That doesn't even calculate in my head why you want to be single or enjoy being single.' It's possible; you can enjoy it."

Kathryn, a journalist in New York in her twenties who asked that her name be changed, feels the same way. She recently hooked up with a groomsman at her friend Jennifer's wedding. "So cliché," she says. "I knew it wasn't going to go anywhere because we don't live in the same city." The bride, though, texted her a few weeks later to ask if she'd heard from the groomsman. Kathryn told her no, and Jennifer replied, "Oh, are you dating anyone else?" When Kathryn said no, Jennifer suggested a dating app she could try.

"I was a little mad, like, 'You texted me to ask me if I was dating? You haven't asked me what I've written lately.' I have a lot of other stuff going on," Kathryn says. "Friendships aren't valued the same way. Jennifer wouldn't text me and ask how my best friend was. She doesn't care about the most important person in my life. She only cares if he's male and is going to propose to me."

Briallen Hopper, a lecturer in English at Yale University in New Haven, in her late thirties, writes a lot about wanting to change the perception that friendships are ancillary relationships. She's single and, as she wrote in an essay for *New York* magazine's website, "not ashamed to admit that my friends are my world. They are responsible for most of my everyday joy, fun, and will to live." She goes on to explain that, despite this, it can be terrifying to make friendship your main support system. The relationship is "chronically underrated and legally nonexistent," she writes. It's scary to rely on people who, when it comes down to it, may not value you as much as people they're tied to by blood or paperwork. "There are times where people who are in nuclear family situations or couples feel like they're maxed out with what they have going on in their own space, and they don't necessarily feel like they can open themselves up for being present for friends the same way," Briallen says.

A close friend once told her that her priorities were her kid, her partner, her work, her friends, in that order. "Like suits in a deck of cards," Briallen wrote in the essay. "In her life, a kid thing would always trump a partner thing; a work thing would always trump a friend thing. This was the best way she knew of trying to impose some order on life's complexity, but to me it seemed like a terribly reductive way to think about human relationships—plus it was no fun to know that I would always be the lowest priority in her life. Our friendship didn't last."

Briallen's doing what she can to solidify and sustain what could be ephemeral relationships, in part by creating rituals to protect them and signify how special they are to her. She tells her friends she loves them on a regular basis and lights a *The Golden Girls* votive candle at night when she's counting her blessings. "There are a lot of kind of built-in rituals with other relationships," she says. "Yes, with romantic relationships, but even with things like Mother's Day, or naming ceremonies with your kids. I like thinking about friendship as something that has rituals too. It's about taking friendship as seriously as any other relationship and not thinking about friendship as a plan B to tide you over until you get married or meet a romantic partner."

"Why wasn't friendship as good as a relationship?" the writer Hanya Yanagihara wrote in her 2015 bestselling novel *A Little Life*, about a group of male friends. "Why wasn't it even better? It was two people who remained together, day after day, bound not by sex or physical attraction or money or children or property, but only by the shared agreement to keep going."

She makes friendship sound romantic, a notion I like. I think the most solid, supportive friend alliances are as hard to come by and as heady as any fairy-tale love. During my early thirties, I started to tell my friends I loved them, and I did it a lot. On the way home after a night with a friend, I felt almost the same way I would after a good date with a guy, intoxicated by how understood I felt and hopeful for how the relationship might develop even more. It was an unexpected emotional rush, one extremely different from how I'd once felt about my female friends when they'd been orbiting my life as odds and ends that I'd reach out to occasionally.

Now I was fully committed in my pursuit. In one instance, I spent a few months trying to get a fellow writer I admired to go out to dinner with me. We had met once, at drinks with her boyfriend, and I'd left that evening wanting to get to know her better. When we finally did hang out, it was like we'd been on parallel life tracks and felt exactly the same way about what we wanted to do next. I related to every single thing she said (the bottles of wine we drank in the new French restaurant we were trying may have helped with this). Still, we had a ton in common. We had moved to New York around the same time, were both writers, and lived in the same neighborhood (and were thinking it was time to move out of this neighborhood). She'd just broken up with the boyfriend who introduced us and was trying to figure out what she wanted next, and so of course we talked about men and dating, but we also discussed much more, things I don't typically share with someone I'm just sitting down with for the first time. Before I went to sleep, I sent her the kind of "amazing night" text I would send to a first date I was sure I wanted to see again. The next day I texted my mom: "I have a new best friend," I wrote. "I love her."

Other women court friendships too. Sara Eckel, the author of *It's Not You: 27 (Wrong) Reasons You're Single,* was single throughout her twenties and thirties. During this time, she was dating in hopes of finding a romantic partner, but she was also always on the lookout for friendships. "It was really important to me to have female friends," she says. "I'd pursue them the way I would a relationship." As she was leaving one party, she saw a woman who seemed familiar, but Sara didn't think they'd met. She looked glamorous and tough, like a 1940s movie star. Sara thought, *Who are you? I must know you.* She introduced herself, and the two of them talked for half an hour by the coat check as other guests squeezed around them to get their jackets. It turned out they lived in the same neighborhood. They exchanged e-mail addresses and started hanging out most days.

"We'd talk about the same stuff as you do on dates," Sara says. "She was really smart, and we had a lot of the same kind of feelings about politics."

Soon they were RSVPing for two on invitations without consulting the other, going to what Sara calls "slit-your-wrist documentaries, like about Wall Street corruption," and taking an impulsive bus trip to Ohio to campaign for John Kerry before the 2004 election, where they shared a tiny room at the Days Inn and saw Bruce Springsteen play at Kerry's final rally. "It was a big adventure," Sara says.

Another time she approached a woman at her book club. "It was like, Wow, there's a new girl," she says. "She's great." Sometimes women asked her to get together too, and "I was always so happy about that," Sara says. "There's that feeling when you meet a new friend."

Often she'd be at events hoping to meet guys, but end up vibing with women instead, like at one speed-dating event where the men were decades older than the women. "It was dire," she says. She remembers the women being in the bathroom laughing and empathizing with each other. "They were like, 'How are you doing?'" she says. "We were all on the same bad date together." Instead of going out with a single guy she met there, she asked one of the women to dinner.

Sara was as picky about whom she tried to befriend as she was about whom she dated. "I didn't want to go out with a guy just to go," she says, "and I didn't want to have a friend just to have a friend." She wasn't looking for someone who was only a physical presence in either relationship. "I have a friend who'd talk about a 'warm body' friend," she says, "as in, you're a warm body I can go out to dinner with. Even as lonely as I'd get sometimes, I didn't want that. I remember making a decision that it would be better to be at home and be lonely than to be using someone like that."

But just because she wanted to develop a friendship with someone didn't automatically mean they were interested too—sometimes figuring out if someone is into you as a friend is as awkward as discerning if a crush reciprocates your feelings. "It can still be a little bit of a dance where you have to make the initial, 'Hey, we should get lunch or coffee sometime,'" Sara says. "A lot of times, people are super-receptive, but sometimes you realize I asked this person to coffee and she went, but at this point it's on her. It's a dance in that way. You want to make sure people actually want to hang out."

I got lucky. When I started to make friendships my main

focus, I rarely felt alone; what I gave out in friend love, I almost always got back times two. It was sort of like we were all starved for this kind of friendship, for straight-up, openly, and honestly being thrilled we were in each other's lives. One day, I e-mailed Ruthie to invite her to something she'd been planning to go to by herself. She wrote back:

> KAYLEEN I AM SORRY I AM GOING TO WRITE
> THIS EMAIL ALL IN CAPS BECAUSE I CANNOT
> THINK OF ANOTHER WAY TO EXPRESS MY
> STRONG FEELINGS OF HAPPINESS AND LOVE
> FOR YOU.

Okay, maybe writing that sentence in caps was enough. Actually, no.

> YES, I WANT TO GO WITH YOU TONIGHT.

We didn't work together anymore, but I'd moved to Ruthie's neighborhood, and she'd been showing me around. She took me on her favorite walks and to the local sushi restaurant and the best bagel shop. We also went to trash movies, trendy nail salons, and one barre class that neither of us expected to be as intense as it was.

"Even the locker room situation was more intense than I wanted it to be," Ruthie remembers.

We had some bigger adventures, like one night of parties that we needed weeks afterward to dissect. And when I lost a bracelet on an early road trip we took with a group of people, no one was more concerned than she was. Ruthie called it "the Miracle in Baltimore" when I found it a few hours later in the hood of my coat.

As we got closer, we began to share more, both secrets from our pasts and fears about our futures. We freely admired different aspects of each other, like how I think Ruthie has perfect taste in books, music, and theme outfits, like the retro Philadelphia Eagles T-shirts she wears for big games. I started to trust her. I gave her a set of my keys in case I locked myself out, which I've since done at least six times, and Ruthie's always been there to let me back in.

It turns out that women are biologically predisposed to reach out to each other, although it took decades for scientists to uncover this impulse. In the 1990s, researchers didn't think about—or test—the ways men and women might be different. Medical psychologist and Penn State associate professor of behavioral health Laura Cousino Klein, Ph.D., was in her early twenties at the time, starting graduate school. "The idea of talking about sex differences was really frowned upon," Klein says. "We were trying to talk about how men and women were similar." Consequently, most of the studies were done on men only. Data gatherers assumed men and women with the same disease would show the same symptoms (whether the illness was physical or mental). This is not true. Women's and men's symptoms for everything from HIV to depression aren't identical, and today the National Institutes of Health has a rule that when a disease affects both genders, both men and women have to be included in the clinical trial.

Klein was passionate about including women in her studies before this rule. For her study, as a student, on the "fight or flight" response to stress—the impulse to face danger or flee from it—she observed both male and female rats. She was looking for the rats to hold still when they were put under stress. "This is part of 'fight or flight,'" she says. "The way rodents respond is this 'freezing' response, like if a rabbit stops in the middle of the road so their prey doesn't see them." The males froze, but she couldn't get the female rats to do the same thing. "My females revealed more stress, in cortisol [the hormone that spikes when the body is under stress] or other biomarkers, but behaviorally the males seemed more reactive," she says. Instead of freezing, the female rats climbed into the same cage, where they groomed and licked each other. "We called it the 'sorority study,'" Klein says. "I thought they were just having a party."

No one would publish her research because of the inconsistent results, and it wasn't until she met Shelley E. Taylor, Ph.D., a psychology professor at the University of California, Los Angeles, that she got a clue about why the females had been reacting the way they had. Taylor told her that a notable gender difference in psychology was that in times of stress women turn to their friends more than men, which made Klein wonder if her female rats were showing her something important, not just having a party. "We thought, *Maybe it's possible women have a different biological response to stress,*" she says.

In 2000, Klein and Taylor, along with Brian P. Lewis, Tara L.

Gruenewald, Regan A. R. Gurung, and John A. Updegraff, published a landmark paper in *Psychological Review,* a journal of the American Psychological Association, that showed that women often have a "tend-and-befriend" response to stress, instead of a "fight-or-flight" one. They based their finding on analyzing biological and behavioral studies of thousands of stressed humans and animals, and theirs was the first new model to describe people's response to stress in more than sixty years.

What they concluded was that when women feel tense or agitated, they often instinctively calm themselves by reaching out to and nurturing others. Stressed women get a surge of oxytocin, a hormone that propels women to seek out their friends. "When you think about it from an evolutionary perspective, for women to only have a 'fight or flight' response doesn't always work," Klein says. "If you're a mother with a child facing a predator, and you have to decide whether to leave your child and fight the predator or scoop them up and run away, in either case it might not work. When you go through the animal reports, there are many instances of females gathering in groups to create a safety net. They'll have a call and get together in a circle and fight off a predator."

This "tend and befriend" response makes sense to me and reflects what I was doing when I turned to my friends with an urgency that hadn't been there before, but I don't think I was moved by hormones alone. What I was also going through was a mind shift where I started to see that my friendships could be valued and celebrated as seriously as any other relationships in my life. They didn't have to be consolation prizes until I found someone to marry. They could be as fundamental as any other designated pairing society okayed, even though they're not secured by anything beyond feeling.

When I saw these friendships clearly, I realized how extraordinary it was that the women I knew were caring for me and for other friends for no other reason than that they wanted to. "Friendship is really unconditional love," the pop singer Sophie B. Hawkins says. "We know that all marriages are not binding. Even our children can leave us, and they might. Friendship is stripped of all of that illusion."

As I piled up the triumphs and failures of being young in a big city, I kept pushing the idea of marriage off. And as I moved farther away from my childhood and my hometown, the road maps for how I could live my life broadened far beyond the one that said I wasn't officially an adult until I had a husband.

I'm not sure exactly when I'd say my adult life began. It might have been when I finished school, feeling smart and very sure that my career would fall into place exactly as I wanted it to. Or maybe it was a few months later, when I got my first job at a trade magazine that covered the shoe industry, beating out what felt like hundreds of other candidates for it. Perhaps it was even a couple of weeks after that, when I realized that this coveted job was actually pretty terrible, and I needed to find a new one as quickly as I could. It could have even been when I threw my first dinner party, or took a vacation by myself, or invested in the stock market with money I'd earned. No matter which moment it was, it was clear that as I was going about my days purposefully, this was my real grown-up existence—I wasn't waiting for marriage to kick it off.

It's not that I didn't occasionally dream of the comforts and security a husband could provide. Sometimes I was tired of having to always call the landlord myself, or wished someone else would fill the fridge with groceries, or that it wasn't only up to me to build up an emergency savings fund. I understood the appeal of having a life partner and legal commitment that validated the relationship.

For the most part, though, I was fine without those things and wasn't waiting until I got them for my life to begin. I'd moved beyond viewing marriage as a platform to take flight from—and I was getting further from seeing it that way each day. I was up in the air already, dreaming of buying my own apartment, of being a boss, and of writing a book.

In another time and place, I could have easily been like my mom, who never had this experience. She got married when she was twenty-six, which she says "was considered very late." She went to work as a teacher immediately after college, but "it was always in the background that I would meet someone and get married," she says. "Most of my friends were married right out of high school, while they were in college, or right after."

After watching her sorority sisters and post-college roommates get married, she says, "It felt like it was my turn. I should get married because everyone else was married and I was one of the last ones." She started dating my dad, and even though she was about to start graduate school, she still got engaged and planned the wedding while getting her degree. "Back then, your life truly didn't begin until you got married," she said. "What you did prior to that wasn't all that important."

From 1890 to 1980, the median age of first marriage for women hovered between twenty and twenty-two, but today it's around twenty-seven—and is higher than that in many cities. In 2009, possibly for the first time in American history, there were more single women than married women (meaning those who'd never married or were widowed, divorced, or separated).

Today, for women in their mid-twenties to their mid-thirties, being single is more likely to be the norm. From 2000 to 2009, the number of women between twenty-five and thirty-four who'd never been married rose from thirty-five percent to forty-six percent.

"Young women today no longer have to wonder, as I did, what unmarried adult life for women might look like, surrounded as we are by examples of exactly this kind of existence," Rebecca Traister writes in *All the Single Ladies: Unmarried Women and the Rise of an Independent Nation*. "Today, the failure to comply with the marriage plot, while a source of frustration and economic hardship for many, does not lead directly to life as a social outcast or to a chloral hydrate prescription."

In the 1950s, when women entered the paid labor market, they started to move to cities by themselves, according to Eric Klinenberg, Ph.D., a professor of sociology at New York University, the author of *Going Solo: The Extraordinary Rise and Surprising Appeal of Living Alone,* and the coauthor of *Modern Romance* with comedian Aziz Ansari.

"It became more common for women to spend much of their adult life single and living alone," Klinenberg says. Since then, this way of life has only intensified. There are more single people living alone in cities—often far away from their relatives—for longer periods of time. "The key to living alone is to build relationships," he says. "You can live alone and be tightly connected to work or friends who are like a substitute family for you."

These friends who intertwine themselves as if they were legally or biologically related are often called "chosen families" or "urban families." Today the terms are sometimes used interchangeably, but they have different etymologies. "Chosen families" comes from the queer community in the 1980s, as used in anthropologist Kath Weston's *Families We Choose: Lesbians, Gays, Kinship.* It refers to how gays and lesbians formed their own support systems either because they'd been turned away from their birth families (or turned away themselves) or because they were not legally allowed to marry or adopt children.

"Urban families," on the other hand, were comprised of young, never-married city dwellers, both gay and straight, who relied on each other as if they were blood relatives. In *Bridget Jones's Diary,* which was published in 1996, author Helen Fielding gives her singleton heroine, Bridget Jones, an urban family but the label isn't used until the movie, which was released in 2001. In the book, Bridget's friend Tom says, of his friends' support, "I know we're all psychotic, single and completely dysfunctional and it's all done over the phone, but it's a bit like a family, isn't it?"

In the movie, after Bridget (Renée Zellweger) tells a lie at work, she says: "Jan 4—emergency meeting with urban family. Great joy of single life is replacement of frightful real family with specially chosen group of friends."

"It's great if people realize that there isn't just one way to live," Fielding has said. "That's an old-fashioned concept, and I think it's losing its grip on us. Life in cities is very similar all over the world, and people do tend to live in urban families as much as in nuclear ones. They're not worse off or better off; the point is that it's no longer abnormal to be single."

Alternate families first began to be prevalent in pop culture in the 1990s. They were meant to resonate with Generation Xers, who no longer looked to work for fulfillment or respected authority figures the way their parents had. Instead what they had was each other.

They were in movies, like *Singles* (1992) and *Reality Bites* (1994), and on television, the most popular sitcoms were about groups of codependent pals—an evolution from shows centered on families or workplaces that started in 1989 when *Seinfeld* debuted on NBC with a plot about nothing more than the whims of four friends who lived near each other in New York City. Cocreator Larry David's credo was "no hugging, no learning."

It was followed in 1993 by *Living Single* on Fox, a show about six black twentysomethings (four women, two men), who spent a lot of time in the Brooklyn brownstone where most of them lived, sharing their professional and romantic struggles.

In 1994, *Friends* on NBC did the same thing with six white twentysomethings (three women, three men) in a Manhattan apartment building. "The well-hidden secret of this show was that it called itself *Friends,* and was really about family," former *Time* magazine television critic James Poniewozik wrote in 2007 when he included *Friends* on his list of the top one hundred shows of all time.

Brit Bennett, who's in her twenties, was influenced by her surrogate friend family when she wrote the 2016 bestselling novel *The Mothers.* The book is about Nadia Turner, her closest friend, Aubrey Evans, and the man they both fell in love with, Luke Sheppard, but instead of focusing on the romantic relationships, Brit chose to make the friendship between Nadia and Aubrey the emotional center of the story. She did this because her own friends are so vital to her. "I've got a couple of friends who are married, but not many people are married or have children yet, so really my friendships are so important to me and particularly my friendships with women," she says.

These women don't live in Los Angeles with her. They're scattered around the country but have been a constant in Brit's life, unlike boyfriends, who "come and go," she says. Her friends visited her when she was in graduate school at the University of Michigan in Ann Arbor, she's been to see them in San Diego, and they've flown to Las Vegas together for fun. "My friends have been there for me in such an emotionally supportive way across distance," she says. "It's kind of a dumb metric but I'm always aware of how many states have I hung out with this friend or that friend in. They're there for me through whatever stress I have about trying to figure out my career and my life. I've always been really grateful for them being that sort of foundation for me."

Briallen Hopper, the Yale lecturer, didn't think it was possible for friends to give each other the kind of care family would until a friend with incurable stage IV cancer needed her. Briallen witnessed her friend's will, helped her compare insurance plans, and learned the spellings and side effects of various chemo drugs. She also gossiped about cute doctors with her and, after her friend insisted, read *The Fault in Our Stars,* a young adult book by John Green about a girl also living with incurable stage IV cancer. "It really showed me that friendship can do anything that any of these other relationships can do," Briallen says. "There's the same level of commitment, the same level of care, the same level of loyalty and trust."

Briallen also learned that her friends could help her, too, like when she was struggling financially and a friend offered to let her move in with her. "It made me realize that in material and huge ways you can count on your friends," she says. "It helped me think of friendship as not just a relationship for fun, but a primary life relationship."

Being single, for Briallen, doesn't mean being alone. She'd rather be reading a book with someone else sprawled on the couch with her instead of curled up by herself, and prefers to write with other people around too. She and a friend have synced their teaching schedules so they both have Mondays free to write together. Sometimes they'll exchange work halfway through the day. She tells her friends to call her anytime and means it. Recently, when a friend was trying to finish a big project, she called Briallen at five forty-five A.M. "I was glad to be able to be there for her," Briallen says. "If people are marrying less or later, all of the nitty-gritty of life like picking someone up from the train station, all of the basics where it's helpful to have someone there, people just make that happen with other people. Back when almost everyone paired off and married young, their romantic partner did it, and now that's not true anymore. Now all of these functions are being fulfilled by friendship."

I worried that I'd failed my mom when I decided I wasn't ready to get married. I wasn't following the same model she had and wouldn't be having a wedding or children anytime soon. I felt like it was part of my duty as a daughter to do these things, even though my mom has never said—or even hinted—anything like this. I remember apologizing to her, one day when I was visiting my hometown, telling her that I was sorry that I'd messed up on marriage.

She didn't even consider accepting. "You don't have anything to be sorry for," she said.

I protested and leaned into the apology, calling myself a failure.

"You're not," she said. "Just look at all you've done."

Even now, years later, I still occasionally fall down on the supposition that I should have a husband and children, and it can be hard to expel the fear that I'm doing it wrong. The idea that women are supposed to be wives and mothers is so deeply implanted in me that I'm still working to loosen its thrall.

Other women feel this too. When she was a child, the essayist Emily Rapp Black saw how much her mom cherished her friends, but she also observed her parents' long marriage and, in her early twenties, did all she could to find a husband.

She'd moved to Geneva, Switzerland, to work at a relief organization. There she met a trio of women who were thirty years older than her. They immediately opened their group to her, jokingly calling themselves "the Wrinklies," inviting her to their weekly dinner, and passing her chocolate and affectionate notes at the office. Like Emily, they were single, living alone, and working to assist people in need in countries around the world, but as much as Emily loved being with them, she also felt sorry for them, as if they'd failed because they hadn't married and had children. She was busy dating, consumed by the superficial worries she was convinced would thwart her finding the love of her life, like if she was a few pounds too heavy. The Wrinklies questioned why she was spending all of her time in bars when she said she wanted to have a big career, but she didn't listen. Emily felt like her real life would start only when she was married and a mother. "I did feel like, Oh, these old women who were like fifty or something," she says. "They're missing out because they never did this other thing."

While she was in Geneva, she watched them support each other every day as they worked at helping others survive. One afternoon, she witnessed them attempting to get a mother an antibiotic for her child. A corrupt doctor was withholding it for an enormous amount of money; they were trying to force him to release it, sprinting between their offices, shouting into their phones, and rushing again and again to the fax machine. But eventually it was too late; the baby died. In the aftermath, the Wrinklies grouped together, crying and passing around a bottle of whiskey.

Fifteen years later, Emily was married and had a nine-month-old son who had just been diagnosed with Tay-Sachs disease, a fatal illness that put him in a vegetative state and caused his death before his third birthday. After her own friends, who she knew from various stages of her life, cared for her during her son's illness and death, she realized what the Wrinklies had possessed (and that she had dismissed). "I thought back to the way those women interacted with one another," she says, "and I really misunderstood that and was too wrapped up in my own stupid shit at twenty-one to understand that those were choices that they made and that those relationships were just as important as any romantic relationship would likely ever be."

Emily's friends visited from other states and other countries. They sent food. They started a fund to pay for her son's needs that medical insurance wouldn't cover. They got her horribly drunk. They cleaned her house. They took her dancing. They cooked her dinner. They went on walks with her. They got to know her son and reminded her that he was loved, and that she was loved. "They entered this space of sadness with me in a full way," she says, "and I was not fun, and there was no reciprocity with me. I was just a fucking ball of grief and need, and I never felt judged for that, and I never felt like people were getting annoyed with me even though they likely were. I just felt really supported in a time in my life when I had no patience to be anything other than how I felt, and I'd never experienced that before. I'd never been so undone by an experience and so that's when I was like, 'Oh, right. I allowed myself to allow help.'"

When Emily wrote about the experience in an essay for *The Rumpus,* she describes, based on her own deep relationships and the bond she'd seen with the Wrinklies, the validity of female friendship. Instead of not being important, she writes, it actually shows us connection, kindness, generosity, and humanity—in a way other sanctioned relationships may not. In other words, our friendships make us bigger than ourselves. "It's possible to transcend the limits of your skin in a friendship," Emily writes. "A friend can take you out of the boxes you've made for yourself and burn them up. This kind of friendship is not a frivolous connection, a supplementary relationship to the ones we're taught and told are primary—spouses, children, parents. It is love."

In the years after Emily's son died, she became a better support for her own friends, guided by how they acted while he was alive. "One thing I learned a lot from that period was you show up and you just listen," she says. "You allow the person to experience the extremity of whatever it is they're going through and try not to have judgment and also to offer help and advice if it's asked for. I think that's the role of a friend, and it's one I take pretty seriously."

After *Details,* I went to work at a start-up digital newspaper. By this point, I had a lot of solid friendships, a network of pals I was happily entrenched in. Carmel, the woman who sat next to me in the office, however, knew almost no one in the city. She had moved from Sydney, Australia, leaving her parents, siblings, and long-term boyfriend behind.

Our desks, in the back corner of the office, had so little space between them that if I stretched out my arms, I might smack her in the face. "I liked your boots," she says years later about a pair of flat knee-high boots that I wore all the time. "I saw them and thought, *I might like this girl.*" She started asking me about my life, my career, and for advice about how to get along in the city. During the workday, we took walks, had lunch in the park, and foraged for midday snacks. ("I'm going to get a brownie/muesli/slice/cookie. Want to come?" Carmel would instant message me.) She soon became someone I saw outside of work too, hangouts that weren't restricted by time or place. After work, we'd go for drinks or to the gym. On the weekends, we'd have pizza in the park or take the train to the beach. She'd come to my apartment or I'd go to hers. We'd meet up with my other friends or hers.

Carmel talks a lot; I'm quieter, but I never felt like she didn't hear or appreciate me. Our workplace was, we often commiserated, a difficult one for women. All of the top editors were male, and the leadership often made us feel as though our jobs were contingent on their whims, not our skills. One night after an office party during which an editor had insinuated he could have me fired, I cried in Carmel's arms about how crushing the encounter was. I backed her at work too, often reassuring her that it was okay to refuse to write stories she thought were sexist. "You were a champion for me," she says. "I would not have felt comfortable confiding in my male friends at work about how I felt treated by the male editors. I don't think the level of bro culture that we felt—I don't think they would have realized it. Even enlightened, sensitive men don't perceive that as acutely as women do. But I found that in you. I knew how you felt there, and you knew exactly how I felt."

We took care of each other. I brought soup to Carmel when she had tonsillitis for what seemed like two months straight; she helped me move apartments on New Year's Eve. When Carmel broke up with her boyfriend back in Australia, she says, "You never judged me for making the decision to break up a long-term loving relationship with a really nice dude," she says. "You never once said, 'Just get back together with him.' Other friends said that, and I'm not as close to them as you."

We accepted each other and let each other exist, like I do with my family, but this felt different because it was a choice. "You were never trying to impose your moral code on me," Carmel says. "You were only ever thinking about what's best for me." In a way that was natural and unforced, we meshed our lives together.

When Carmel decided to go back to Australia to take care of her mother, who had been diagnosed with breast cancer, we had a last lunch in the park before she left. Neither of us knew if she'd be back, which made me feel helpless. There was a real chance we might never see each other again. I remember walking her to the train knowing that this was one of the pitfalls of chosen families. Affection would always keep us together in one way, but it'd never be as easy again to make sure she'd be there for Thanksgiving. Still, because she's Carmel, she remains optimistic about the idea that we can form whatever bonds we want to in this life. "I moved to the other side of the world, but I still feel as emotionally connected to you as I ever did," she says. "That's an adult friendship."

About a year after she returned to Australia, her mom died. When she did, I sent flowers and, later, talked to her on the phone about how she was doing. She told me about an old friend, Claudia, and a new one, Milka, who'd been her anchors since she'd returned. While her mom was sick, they'd ask her to go on walks, or the grocery store so they could pick up dinner together. They were there every day, being supportive and warm, just so she could have someone to talk to about what was going on with her mom if she needed to. At the funeral, while her sister sat with her husband and sons, and her brother was next to his partner, Claudia and Milka sat behind Carmel. "They both had a hand on my shoulder and were massaging my back," she says. "I had these two friends that were there for me. I was sitting by myself. I didn't have a partner in the romantic sense, and they were there for me. They were my friends who function as family."

There is a holiday for celebrating your girlfriends, although it didn't come from Hallmark or Congress. "Galentine's Day" was introduced to the world by Leslie Knope, a fictional midlevel bureaucrat in an Indiana parks and recreation department on the NBC sitcom *Parks and Recreation*.

The series starred Amy Poehler and was created by Greg Daniels and Michael Schur. Schur wrote the first "Galentine's Day" episode, which aired during the second season, but doesn't want to take credit for creating the holiday. "There are a lot of writers on the staff so it's possible that one of them came up with it," he says, "but I remember that when the idea was pitched, whether it was me or someone else, it was immediately like, 'Oh yeah, this is great.' It was an immediate sort of no-brainer, and I imagined it being a regular thing as long as the show was on the air." He recalls the holiday being called Galentine's Day in the initial pitch too. "We never spent one second thinking about a different name," he says.

"What's Galentine's Day?" Knope asks on the episode that aired on February 11, 2010. "Oh, it's only the best day of the year. Every February thirteenth, my lady friends and I leave our husbands and our boyfriends at home and we just come and kick it, breakfast style. Ladies celebrating ladies. It's like Lilith Fair, minus the angst. Plus, frittatas!"

Parks and Rec did continue to celebrate Galentine's Day, and before long women who weren't Knope's friends were observing it too. As BuzzFeed's Maggy van Eijk writes, in a piece called "23 Reasons You Need to Celebrate Galentine's Day This Year," "It's the perfect chance to get your best gals together: your friends, your mum, your coworkers, that lady who works in your favorite coffee shop with the amazing hair, get all those women together and CELEBRATE. Cherish your fond memories, make plans for the future and talk about how much you ADORE each other (preferably in song). Why? Because romantic relationships are fleeting, and messy and Valentine's Day makes a lot of people feel miserable. But friendships are EVERYTHING."

Every year, Briallen Hopper hosts an elaborate Galentine's party at her home in New Haven. She bakes all sizes of heart-shaped red and pink cakes and sets up Galentine-making stations stocked with construction paper, markers, and glitter. Her guests write each other love letters while drinking pink champagne and eating cake. One year, for a friend getting a joint Ph.D.-M.D. in studying the brain, Hopper drew her a picture of a brain and wrote, "I hope your year is full of dopamine." "I sometimes even forget there is a Valentine's Day," she says. "It's just not the main event."

Galentine's Day is sometimes mistaken as a replacement for Valentine's Day, as something women do *instead* of commemorating the romantic holiday, either because they're against it on principle or because they don't have a date, but that isn't the way it was presented on *Parks and Rec*. On the show, Knope has her festivities on February 13, the day *before* Valentine's Day. "Leslie's feminism was something she wore on her sleeve and was proud of and excited about," Schur says, "but that deep and abiding interest that she had in her female friends didn't replace other things in her life. So she didn't invent Galentine's Day because she hated Valentine's Day. She loved Valentine's Day. She thought Valentine's Day was great. When she fell in love, she was extremely public about her sexual attraction to her boyfriend and then fiancé and then husband."

The holidays were distinct on purpose so the show wasn't playing into the usual dichotomy Schur saw on television, and in the media in general, about feminism. "It was always that you have to choose," Schur says. "You can be a girl who likes smooching boys and looking pretty or you can be a feminist. The idea was that she invented a holiday that didn't replace a different holiday. It was in addition to another holiday. There was one day that she celebrated her female friends for all of the wonderful things that they did for her and that she did for them, and the next day you celebrate your boyfriend or girlfriend or whoever."

On the surface, *Parks and Rec* was about the role of government in people's lives, but the core of the show, especially as it went on, was the friendship between Knope and Ann Perkins, a registered nurse who was played by Rashida Jones. "The main relationship we wanted to have was a female friendship between a striver in government and politics and a very pragmatic, straightforward thinker, and the ways in which those two women would complement each other and the ways they would learn from each other," Schur says.

Having a sitcom revolve around female friendship was unusual at the time. Most shows were about whether a guy and girl would get together, "a 'will they / won't they' thing," Schur says. "That playbook has been run so many times on so many TV shows. A huge part of telling stories and a huge part of TV comedy specifically is just trying to surprise people. When you tell a different story, people are interested for a reason, so when Amy was at the center of this show because I loved Amy and I thought Amy was a unique talent, then it was a very simple sort of decision that we should do a show about her and another woman instead. We just tried to do something that was different, and doing a show about two women who were friends was different at that time."

Knope's love for Perkins—and how she often phrased it—was over the top yet also seemed exactly right. A few of her best bizarre compliments include: "Ann, you cunning, pliable, chestnut-haired sunfish"; "You're Ann Perkins! Sperm that is worthy of your perfect eggs does not grow on trees"; and "Ann, you beautiful tropical fish. You're smart as a whip and you're cool under pressure."

While other women on television at the time were often annoyed, floundering, stressed, or bitter, Knope was always cheerful and hopeful. "This was something I talked about with Amy all of the time," Schur says. "Leslie's fundamental belief was that optimism beats pessimism. That was the essence of who she was. She thought that it was better to be positive, to try and to hope and to believe, than to give up and say, 'There's nothing we can do. We're screwed.' She was a person who's going to keep fighting as long as she had a breath in her body." This optimism influenced how Knope and her pals celebrated Galentine's Day. "They don't talk about their boyfriends or their husbands," Schur says. "They don't talk about bad things or strife or pain or misery. They set aside one day a year to just tell each other that they're important and that they're great and they're wonderful people and just celebrate and drink champagne at ten in the morning."

Their Galentine's Day party was always a brunch during a workday. Knope loved breakfast food, especially waffles. On one episode, she says, "We need to remember what's important in life: friends, waffles, work. Or waffles, friends, work. Doesn't matter, but work is third." And Schur wanted the event to be cheery and happy. "It was like Valentine's Day is for romance and so you go to a candlelit dinner at night, but Galentine's Day is very bright and fun and festive," he says. "And part of the celebration with this was they play hooky a little bit because it's like nothing is more important than your friends so everybody just says, 'I got to take two hours and leave.'"

Each year, Knope gives her girlfriends (and her mom) homemade gifts. On the 2010 episode, she gives them all a bag with a bouquet of hand-crocheted flower pens, a mosaic portrait of each of them made from the crushed bottles of their favorite diet soda, and a personalized five-thousand-word essay on why they're all so awesome. Schur came up with a backstory that Knope sleeps only four hours a night. This is never mentioned on the show, but he thought that it was the only way to explain how she had time to construct these intricate gifts. "If you really look at the things she makes for her friends," he says, "she makes tile mosaics of their faces using their birthstones, and she makes personalized coffee cups and mugs and whatever. The only way this could happen is if the person sleeps four hours a night. There was no way she could do all of this stuff unless she was a crazy robot who was awake all of the time."

Today, there's mass-produced merchandise that would make good Galentine's Day gifts, like "Uteruses Before Duderuses" mugs (that's another Knope quote). On Galentine's this year, I got a present from my friend Erica. "Happiest Galentine's Day!" she wrote on the card, "I ♥ you like crazy. All the Xs & all the Os!" The gift was six adorable handmade ceramic bowls she knew I'd been wanting. I was overjoyed with my new kitchen gear, but more with how great it felt that Erica had been thinking about me.

Each year on February 13, Schur tweets "Happy Galentine's Day." "I'm very proud that the show introduced Galentine's Day," he says. "I think that's great, and I love it when people tweet gifs of Leslie Knope in any context. When Wendy Davis was doing her filibuster in the Texas legislature [to block an antiabortion bill] there were tons of Leslie Knope gifs flying around. I love that she stands for something or multiple things and I love that people connected with her. I love that February thirteenth will be Galentine's Day for some people forever. All of that stuff warms my heart."

CHAPTER 5

Our BFFs, People, and Soulmates

You are my best friend! Don't you ever call anybody
else that!

—Ilana in *Broad City*

Ruthie and I call each other soulmates. The kind of lifeline I have in her—"I feel exactly the same way" or "Same, exact same" is something we say a lot to each other—isn't one I ever expected I'd find in my adult life. Other women have soulmates (or "queens" or "ride or dies") too, and these heightened friendships, these connections, make us feel less alone, no matter who else is in our worlds.

We now have big stakes in each other's lives, trust established through things like me going to Ruthie's childhood home for Thanksgiving and being enamored with her immediate and extended family, or her walking through the apartment I'd bought without anyone else seeing it and being confident that, even though it was filled with rubble, it was going to be a perfect place for me to live.

The time we spend together these days is less restricted by formal plans. She walks by my apartment hoping to see me, and I do the same to her. She's invited me over for dinner after we've run into each other on the train. I've answered her text in the middle of a post-work run to say that I could meet her for an impromptu drink in an hour. We text each other from our separate couches about what we're watching on television.

I always try to be kind to her, in a way I have a more difficult time being in romantic relationships. She's that way too.

We're purposeful about protecting and caring for each other. A few months ago, I called her in tears and asked if she could meet me at a bar near our apartments. When she did, she gave me flowers she'd bought from the bodega and hugged me while I bawled. "It'll be okay," she said. "I love you so much." Strangers stared.

Little girls are encouraged to have best friends. They're often asked by nosy adults, "Do you have a best friend?" I had one, named Sarah. We played Barbies, built backyard forts, and were average at gymnastics together. I passed her notes in school and saved the ones she slipped me. If we weren't at each other's houses, we were probably riding our bikes, which had matching streamers on the handlebars, around our neighborhood.

We're supposed to seek out best friends when we're young. The relationship, our parents hope, will teach us how to play nicely with others. And kids have all kinds of ways to show

how proud they are to be in a best friendship: Sarah and I wore matching woven bracelets and parted our hair the same way.

As we get older that prominence that a best friend holds can fall away—adult women are more likely to be asked if they have a boyfriend than a best friend and to wear an engagement ring instead of a BFF charm.

Because of this, it can be frustrating for some women to get across how fundamental their attachment to their best friend is. Stephie Grob Plante, an essayist who lives in Austin, found this out about a year ago when her best friend, Julia, died in a car accident. The car she was riding in was struck by a drunk driver. Julia's sister called Stephie to tell her, and Stephie started sobbing before she finished explaining what had happened. She immediately booked a flight to Irvine, California, where she and Julia grew up (and Julia had still been living).

They met when they were three. "I don't have any memories before she was my best friend," Stephie says. When they were younger, Julia was outgoing while Stephie was shy. Later, at parties during high school, if Stephie felt like she should bail, Julia would say, "No, you're not going anywhere." "She was one of those people you could be around and be like getting a contact high," Stephie says. "She had a really generous laugh. She'd make you feel like you were funnier than you were."

The two never fought, which Stephie knows might sound like whitewashing now that Julia is gone, but "she was the only person I never got mad at and vice versa," she says. "We were in this little bubble together in an 'us against the world,' sort of way." Even after Stephie moved away from their hometown, Julia was a constant presence in her life. They saw each other whenever Stephie came back, even if it was a last-minute trip. "She'd drop everything she was doing just to be with me," Stephie says. "She'd pick me up at the airport."

When Julia died, Stephie was bothered by some people not understanding how important Julia was to her, as if you weren't supposed to mourn best friends with the intensity you do family members. "I have gotten the sense with different people that they didn't really get it," she says. When she asked for time off from work to help her deal with her grief, she didn't feel like the company was particularly supportive. She ended up leaving the job a few months later.

"It's easier for people to say, 'Oh my gosh, you lost your mother, you lost your sister,'" she says. "It's hard to communicate to people who don't know or understand, 'This was my best friend for my entire life.' I think there is a need to justify why this is taking the toll it is on me. Because I want to make sure people don't misunderstand. It doesn't matter if they do or not, but it feels invalidating when they don't."

Even before Julia died, the two of them wanted to make it clear that their friendship was special, stronger and stretchier than that of childhood pals who scrawl "BFF" in each other's high school yearbooks but are distant by their five-year reunion. "'Best friend' gets thrown around a lot," she says. "It isn't strong enough. It doesn't carry the same weight as 'brother' or 'sister.'" So they became each other's BFF!F—they added an exclamation point for emphasis and another F for an extra "forever." If Stephie could, she'd invent a completely new word. "'Best friend' doesn't convey the closeness and the necessity and the intensity of that bond," she says.

At Julia's memorial service, Stephie spoke to the six hundred people there. She told a story about five years before then, when she and her husband were talking about her tie with Julia. Stephie said to him, "Look, you know I really, really love you, but Julia is my soulmate."

"Duh," her husband said. "I know."

She told the story because she knew people would laugh, but "it's the most serious joke," she says. "'Soulmate' gets applied to romantic relationships, and it's somewhat cheesy, but 'soulmate' applies to these really close friendships. It was so steadfast. There was no stress in our relationship. We didn't actively try to be friends with each other. I don't know what this was other than like our souls are connected. It sounds so silly, but we are forever soulmates."

The night after Julia died, Stephie and Julia's mom went into Julia's bedroom. They found a card Stephie had sent her that said, "Thank you for being my best friend in the world for the past 22 years. I can't wait to celebrate another 40, 60, 80 years of best friendship with you." Her mom started crying and said, "I'm sorry you're not going to have that."

Stephie says it's true that she won't have the relationship she expected to when she wrote that card, but she still feels Julia's presence every day. At night, when she can't sleep, she has conversations with her in her head. "I'll just tell Jules about my day, tell her something funny," Stephie says. "I can hear her voice. I can hear her laugh. I can hear her say, 'Oh my gosh, you're such a dork,' or 'Oh, that's so gnarly.' I do still feel her. I feel like she's my little shoulder angel. I'm going to have lots of different relationships, but she'll always be my BFF!F."

For a long time, the only two adult women I ever saw en-
thusing about each other were Oprah Winfrey and Gayle
King.

Gayle made her national debut as Oprah's best friend in
1986, during the first season of *The Oprah Winfrey Show*. Both
of them wore cardigans and long double strands of pearls.
"We've been friends for over ten years," Gayle said on the
episode. "We worked together in Baltimore at WJZ-TV, and
that's how we became so close. That's when it all started."

In total, by the time the show ended in 2011, Gayle was on
it 139 times, more than anyone except Oprah, who always
introduced her with some variation of "Gayle King is my best
friend in the whole world."

Oprah talked about Gayle when she wasn't on the show
too. In 1995, Oprah told the audience about putting on a
Wonderbra before filming a live episode. "It was not the time
to try it live, let me tell you," Oprah said. "Cleavage for days!"
Afterward, she was in a meeting and got an emergency call
from Gayle.

"Gayle, what's the matter?" Oprah said.

"Well," Gayle said. "I've got a black eye."

"Oh my God, what happened?" Oprah said.

"I passed the monitor in the newsroom and one of your
breasts hit me in the eye," Gayle said.

Today, the two of them are still raving about—and
roasting—each other in public. In 2016, Gayle, who's now the
cohost of *CBS This Morning*, Instagrammed a picture of

herself on air wearing a necklace the size of a salad plate made out of turquoise, green, red, and pink rhinestones in the shape of a flower. Her caption said:

> Note @oprah sent to my asst this am "plz tell Gayle I'm on treadmill & it's hard to focus w/the circus around your neck" I think she's WRONG

> thoughts?

In response one woman wrote, "This friendship gives me so much goddamn hope."

There's nothing reserved about their friendship. In 1994, for the episode celebrating Oprah's fortieth birthday, singers Patti LaBelle and Aretha Franklin, as well as her fiancé Stedman Graham, came out to surprise her, but she didn't start crying until Gayle appeared. "This is so touching to me because when Patti was here and then Aretha came and then everybody was coming, I thought, 'Gee, I wish Gayle could be here to see this,'" Oprah said.

Oprah and Gayle could have been more circumspect, presenting themselves as friends because of all they had in common when they met as young, single, working African American women. They do make this point, but their proclamations about each other have gone way beyond being friends because of a shared experience. In an interview with Barbara Walters, Oprah said about Gayle, "She is the mother I never had. She is the sister everybody would want. She is the friend that everybody deserves. I don't know a better person."

In *The New York Times*, Gayle said about Oprah, "Who doesn't want to be her best friend? . . . I never feel I'm in her shadow. I feel I'm in her light, that's how I look at it."

Oprah and Gayle's real friendship played out on Oprah's talk show, but fictional best friends were on television for decades before it debuted, starting in the 1950s and lasting through the 1980s, starring in shows like *I Love Lucy*, *Laverne & Shirley*, and *Kate & Allie*. The characters on them were always getting into scrapes, sometimes immensely silly ones if their names were Lucy and Ethel, but they never left each other. They were committed to the adventure and to the friendship.

But by the nineties, the best friend got downgraded to one note, or didn't exist at all, with the rise of shows about single professional women like *Murphy Brown* or *Ally McBeal*. Instead of being given a whole personality, the best friend got a single characteristic, and usually not one that the star of the show would ever want, like being wacky, bitchy, or slutty.

Best friends started to creep back into television in the 2000s but not as a show's main subject. In 2005, Shonda Rhimes, the creator of *Grey's Anatomy*, gave us a great modern portrayal of female best friends in the middle of hospital drama about a fraught romance between surgical intern Meredith Grey and neurosurgeon Derek "McDreamy" Shepherd. The friendship between Meredith and her fellow intern Cristina Yang was "the secret core of Grey's," *Boston Herald* critic Mark Perigard wrote.

"I know a lot of people like to think that Derek is [Meredith's] soulmate," Rhimes told *Entertainment Weekly*, "but I think that Cristina is her soulmate and Derek is the man she loves, and that's lovely. I have these friendships, you know? And I've had really close friends, who were [and] still are my closest friends in the world, move away, and it's devastating. And I was surprised by how devastating it was—being a grown woman and having my own life and my own family and everything. But it's devastating in a way . . . You are somebody special when you're with that best friend."

The fact that *Parks and Recreation* was about Leslie Knope and Ann Perkins's friendship was also concealed, at least initially. "There was a lot going on in the show at the beginning," cocreator Michael Schur says. "We were able to tell this story of a female friendship in part I think, because we built a little bit of a Trojan horse. The show was originally announced as being a spinoff of *The Office*, which it wasn't ever, but that's how it was announced. So there was that. And then just Amy Poehler doing a show was a thing. Then there was the fact it was about government and it being done at a time when Obama was running for office, when the economy was collapsing, when the sort of role of government in people's lives was coming under much more scrutiny. There were a lot of aspects to the show that took precedence over the concept of it being a female friendship. I don't want to say that people weren't receptive to it. I just don't know that they were even aware that they were being asked whether they were receptive of it. I think that the first seven things they thought about the show was probably not that it was a show about a female friendship."

On *Grey's,* Rhimes also gave best friends a boost when she had Cristina tell Meredith she was her "person." A person is not just someone you drink too much wine with. A person is essential.

"The clinic has a policy," Cristina (Sandra Oh) says to Meredith (Ellen Pompeo) after she tells her she's pregnant and made an appointment for an abortion. "They wouldn't let me confirm my appointment unless I designated an emergency contact person, someone to be there just in case and to help me home, you know, after. Anyway I put your name down. That's why I told you I'm pregnant. You're my person."

"I am?" Meredith says.

"Yeah, you are. Whatever," Cristina says.

"Whatever," Meredith says and puts her arm around her.

"You realize this constitutes hugging?" Cristina says.

"Shut up," Meredith says. "I'm your person."

When Oh left the show in 2014, she told *Entertainment Weekly* that when they were filming the scene she didn't know that the moment was going to be so significant, but eight seasons later, she realized what it meant. "It's the beginning of this friendship," she said. "It was so great to see, because you can see Cristina's reluctance to depend on Meredith. And then Meredith turns around, and Meredith is filled with this need and warmth that—oh, this person is letting me in. And then the way it just happened that Ellen as Meredith puts her head on Cristina's shoulder—it's just, like, oh this is the beginning of the *big* relationship of the show."

Aminatou Sow, who's in her early thirties and hosts the podcast *Call Your Girlfriend* with her long-distance bestie Ann Friedman, uses "person" because she wants to be clear that her best friends aren't extraneous. She isn't very close to her family, and her mom passed away a couple of years ago. She's also committed to being single for a long time. "So for me, friendship holds such a central place of importance," she says. "It's always been a really big deal."

She wants to see it become more commonplace to use friends for purposes (or spots on forms) that traditionally have been filled by spouses, parents, children, or siblings. For the past two years, she's been sick and, consequently, in and out of hospitals. "My emergency contact is a friend," she says. "It's not my dad. It's not my siblings." The people who've come to stay overnight with her in the hospital have also been friends, which is confusing to the staff. "It's always such a burden to have to explain," she says. "The hospital is always like, 'Oh, are you two married? Are you two dating?' It's like, 'No, but this is my person.' Because it's family only usually in super-emergency things."

Aminatou also puts friends down as the beneficiaries for her 401(k), her life insurance, and other insurance benefits. It's all legal; you can write in anyone you want as a recipient. "But it's the kind of thing where it's like 'relationship' and there's not a box for friend. Like 'husband,' 'brother,' 'sister,'" she says.

Whenever she starts at a new company, she says, "I'm always like who do I love at this new job, and you call your friend and say, 'Hey, what's your social?'"

She's tired of feeling like her most important relationships aren't recognized and wants them to be. "Friendship is paramount to me and tied into even a lot of my political activism," she says. "I think that we're seeing some different depictions of friendship. Do I think that it's going far enough? Or that we're seeing too much of it or even enough of it? No, absolutely not. There's always room for more and on this particular topic there's room for a lot more. The fact that there's not really a model of family that's not very heteronormative is really insane."

In fact, engaged couples have actually co-opted the best friend title. A lot of people are thrilled to be marrying their best friend (Kim Kardashian was).

"More and more people want their romantic partner to be their best friend," says Stephanie Coontz, a historian specializing in marriage and family studies who's the author of *Marriage, a History: How Love Conquered Marriage.*

The jeweler Zales even used the idea to sell an engagement ring with two diamonds: "One diamond for your best friend, one diamond for your true love, for the one woman who's both."

But the concept of marrying your best friend is getting some pushback, both from experts and from men and women who want a best friend and a mate in different people. "There is this tendency to look at the couple as the only source of gratification," Coontz says. "A counter is the rediscovery of female friendship and the rediscovery of male friendships."

Historically, marriage wasn't supposed to provide you with a best friend, according to Esther Perel, a couples therapist and the author of *Mating in Captivity: Unlocking Erotic*

Intelligence, who gives speeches around the world about how to keep desire high in long-term relationships. "Marriage was an economic institution in which you were given a partnership for life in terms of children and social status and succession and companionship," Perel said in her 2013 TED Talk. "But now we want our partner to still give us all these things, but in addition I want you to be my best friend and my trusted confidant and my passionate lover to boot, and we live twice as long. So we come to one person, and we basically are asking them to give us what once an entire village used to provide."

My mom, who was married in 1967, says she would have never called my dad her best friend. "He was my husband," she says. "That's what he was. Men his age didn't want to communicate or commiserate or have the kind of empathy guys are expected to today. Your dad would say, 'I don't want to talk about this,' and that was accepted."

None of her sisters or girlfriends at the time were looking to marry a man they could call their friend either. "They were looking for physical attraction," she says, "and that he could support you. That's what you were looking for."

Perel also says it's uniquely American to want your spouse to be your best friend. In other parts of the world, "they have best friends, and that's not their partner," she said in an interview with NPR. "Their partner is their partner. That's a different thing. And frankly, many people [in the United States] treat their partners in ways that they would never treat their best friends and allow themselves to say and do things that no best friend would ever accept. Friendship does not operate along the same lines."

Marianne Kirby, who's in her late thirties and lives in Al-exandria, Virginia, doesn't call her husband her best friend. She has a best friend, whose name is Lesley and whom she met a year before she met her spouse. If something good or bad happens to her, her instinct is to tell Lesley first. When she got laid off from her job at a design company, she texted her before she told her husband. "Her reaction was the one that made me feel better, versus his, which was, 'Okay, we have to freak out,'" she says.

This isn't to say that she doesn't think her husband is incredible—"I wouldn't have married him otherwise," she says—but she doesn't want to roll multiple relationships into one person. "They're all so important," she says. "I don't think we need to narrow them down. When we perpetuate this idea that you should marry your best friend, we're saying you should only have one relationship in your life, and that ends up eroding any support network you have outside the marriage. It's this sort of isolating tactic and maybe it's fine but maybe you wind up cut off from literally everything else and you don't have anyone to turn to if you need someone."

Her husband is supportive of how close she and Lesley are, even if he sometimes doesn't totally get it. Sometimes, on a Saturday when he sees her grab her phone and head to the bedroom, he'll say, "Are you going to spend four hours on the phone with Lesley right now?"

"Yes, that's what's going to happen," Marianne says.

"He respects that it's something I need to be happy and functional," she says, "and he doesn't have to fill the role of my best friend so it takes some of the pressure off him. And I think that's something important too. He's only going to go to yoga with me so many times. I don't think that love is finite and I think that the more people that we care about and care about passionately, the more we have to put in all of our relationships. It makes me a better romantic partner to have really strong friendships."

Best friends are also cofounding businesses, proving that this relationship can be part of our work lives too.

"We're really aware that people want to hear us say we're best friends," says Keeley Tillotson, who cofounded nut butter brand Wild Friends with Erika Welsh. "People don't want to know how the sausage is made. It's way better talking about the fact that we're best friends versus 'all I did today was analyze charge-backs from our distributor.'"

Erika jokes, "We'll milk it for all it's worth."

They met in high school but became friends when they lived together as freshmen at the University of Oregon in Eugene. As roommates, they made their own peanut butter for the first time when their shared store-bought jar was empty. (It was raining and neither wanted to bike to the store to replace it.) They used the food processor Erika had gotten for Christmas and a recipe they found online. Eight months later, in 2011, they dropped out of school to make peanut butter full-time. They tell this story on the label of any Wild Friends product, from cinnamon raisin peanut butter to chocolate almond butter. "We tried to write it so it seems real," Keeley says. "We didn't want to be cheesy, like 'Erika and I delight in our friendship.'"

They had to decide to quit school together and never considered another option. "It wouldn't have worked for us," Erika says. "You have to feel confident that when you're doing something the other person is doing it too. If you're working late at night you want the other person to be too."

For the first two and a half years of running the company, they were always in the same space: They went to the same six A.M. yoga class, worked next to each other all day, and then went home to make dinner together. "It was bordering on unhealthy," Keeley says.

When Keeley met her boyfriend, Peter, she was torn about whom to spend her time with. At night, she'd think, *Do I make dinner with Erika or Peter?*

"We had no other friends," Erika says, laughing, "and I was like, 'What is happening? Who is this person?'"

The cofounders of news digest *theSkimm*, Carly Zakin and Danielle Weisberg, were also roommates before and during the launch of their business. They came up with the concept, a skimmable first-thing-in-the-morning e-mail that rounded up world events, from their shared couch while they were both working as NBC news producers. Together they had four thousand dollars in savings and talked on the same couch about how much money they wanted to spend beyond that. "We agreed to go into credit-card debt together," Carly told Business Insider, a website that covers finance, tech, and media. They quit their jobs on the same day to start *theSkimm*. "It was the scariest day of our life," Danielle said. "That was not easy."

For the first six months, they devoted every second they were awake to the start-up. During the day they approached possible advertisers and, around dinnertime, started writing the newsletter and kept working until past midnight. At night, they'd take turns waking up every hour to check their news sources until they sent out the e-mail at six A.M. "Those first months, we only got through it because we didn't have a backup plan," Danielle said. "We didn't have a safety net financially or emotionally. This was everything."

"We were feeding off the other's enthusiasm and belief," Carly told *Fast Company,* a business magazine.

Their friendship, both the Wild Friends and *theSkimm* founders say, makes them better business partners, not worse, and they do all they can to protect it while running their companies. "No one thing is going to break us up," Keeley says. "It's a work in progress. As long as both of us are trying to do our best, our relationship's not going to burst in flames on a random Tuesday."

Jessica Morgan and Heather Cocks, best friends who founded the celebrity-fashion-criticism website Go Fug Yourself in 2004 and write novels together, agree. "You have to be careful about what hills you need to die on," Heather says. "The friendship comes first. I don't want to do without this friendship, so how badly do I want my way? How badly do I want to be right? We've always approached every discussion with, 'You're more important to me as a human than as a writing partner. This fight isn't worth blowing that up to me.'"

They work from separate homes in Los Angeles, but chat online from the moment they sit down at their laptops to the moment they shut them. Sometimes Jessica will go over to Heather's after work too. "I'll be like, *I haven't seen Jessica in forever,*" Heather says. "*I need to see her face.* She's my work wife. She's my life partner. She was my mate before I chose a romantic mate. I love hanging out with this person."

In 2012, a pair of best friends put a show about best friends back on television, but for only one season. Jessica St. Clair and Lennon Parham created and starred in *Best Friends Forever* on NBC, about a divorcée (Jessica, using her real name) trying to get over her breakup by moving in with her childhood best friend (Lennon, also going by her real name), but not getting along with Lennon's boyfriend, who also lives there.

Jessica is a boisterous blonde. Lennon is a more subdued redhead. They met when they were both studying sketch comedy at the Upright Citizens Brigade in New York, but didn't interact beyond passing each other in the hall and noting that they were dressed alike, in cardigans from Express and "like a real weird cropped pant," Jessica says. "We looked like girls who should not have found their way down into this basement."

A few years later, they both moved to Los Angeles, where Jessica went to see Lennon's one-woman show, *She Tried to Be Normal.* Jessica found it so outrageous that she kept punching the arm of the male comedian sitting next to her. "No one had ever made me laugh that hard," she says. "So then I started a slow and secret courtship of her. I knew she was vulnerable. She was out in LA separated from her friends and family. And I thought, *This is when you can strike.*"

Jessica asked Lennon to yoga, which she'd never done

before. Lennon accepted, even though she'd never done yoga either. Neither one admitted their inexperience, and midway through what turned out to be an advanced class, while in modified headstands with their legs spread wide and their heads resting on blocks, they made eye contact. Both realized the other one had also lied.

"We were like, *This is forever*," Lennon says.

They decided to try writing a script together, and during their first session, "we laughed so hard that we were like having seizures," Jessica reminisces. "It felt like when you're in elementary school and you meet your first best friend. You just think everything they say is so fucking funny and the world sort of melts away. I never thought in my thirties I would meet somebody like that."

She went home and told her husband, Dan, "This is it. I want to write with this woman for the rest of my life."

"That is so creepy," Dan said. "Do not ever say that to her. That sounds like you're going to kill her and wear her face as your own."

Jessica answered, "I will have her, and I won't stop until I have her."

A few years later, they wrote *Best Friends Forever* because they wanted to tell a story no one else was telling about a deep, real female friendship like theirs. "That's who we are in real life; our friendships are the most important thing to us," Jessica says. Critics praised it, but the show was canceled after a single season. In a piece that's partly a eulogy for the show, *The Atlantic*'s Julie Beck wrote that it was "the best portrayal of female friendship I've ever seen, the one that rang the truest."

Lennon says it would have been a "crazy fluke" if the show had gotten a second season. Beyond the fact that NBC didn't promote it, the first four episodes were shown in April and the final two aired in July. "It was sort of bananas," Jessica says. "That we even went from script to pilot to series was insane."

A few years later, in 2014, another series about best friends debuted, but *Broad City* on Comedy Central was well promoted and watched—the show averaged 1.2 million viewers an episode during its first season. (Comedy Central promoted the second season with T-shirts that said "Broad Fucking City." A guy wearing one got kicked off a Southwest Airlines flight, news that was reported everywhere from BuzzFeed to *The Daily Show* and only helped to stoke interest in the series.)

Abbi Jacobson and Ilana Glazer, the real-life best friends who created and star in *Broad City*, conceived of it as a web series first. Each episode never had more than hundreds of thousands of views, but "we just started to get a response from our community—the comedy community in New York—and that was enough to make us feel like it was something good and relatable and that we should keep making them," Ilana told *Fast Company*.

Initially when they tried to pitch it as a television show, after sixteen web episodes, no one was interested. Abbi and Ilana's talent manager, Samantha Saifer, recalled, "I had one agent, a woman, tell me, 'I don't get why we'd watch this. Are they going to get married?'"

Amy Poehler was a fan of the web series. She agreed to film a guest role in its thirty-third and final episode, and later to be an executive producer as Abbi and Ilana continued to pitch it as a television show. With her help, Comedy Central ordered ten episodes.

Broad City doesn't have a high-concept plot. Nothing obfuscates the fact that most of what the main characters, who are also named Abbi and Ilana, want to do is hang out together. They go to menial jobs, have tenuous romantic relationships, and smoke a lot of pot, but all of that whirls around what's really important in their lives: each other. Their friendship isn't the secret core of the series; it is the series.

When *The New Yorker* writer Nick Paumgarten profiled Abbi and Ilana in 2014, he wrote that *Broad City* owed a debt to *Laverne & Shirley* as well as Cheech and Chong, "but it also offers something that, oddly, seems to be new, and that, to its legions of fans, is deemed long overdue: an unpretentious portrait of a friendship between women in which they don't undermine each other or fret over how they look or define themselves by whom they're sleeping with. The love affair at the heart of the show is between Abbi and Ilana."

In the first season, Ilana does have a steadyish guy she has sex with, played by comedian Hannibal Buress, but he's the one who wants more commitment. Poehler said it was important to sideline him. "We really wanted to make sure that everybody knew that at the end of the day, this show was a love story between Abbi and Ilana," she said at a panel at the New York Comedy Festival. "They're the couple, they're the two that you have to care about."

They're comedically codependent; they Skype each other from the bathroom (or in Ilana's case, while having sex), skip work when the other one asks, and help each other scrape together money for anything she might desire (weed, Lil Wayne tickets). In the second episode of season two, they're snuggled in bed together talking about how Abbi's worried she might poop one day while she gives birth. Ilana calms her, saying, "If it happens to me, you have my permission to look away."

Abbi answers, "I'm going to see you give birth, then?"

"Bitch, durr, durr, duh durr durr," Ilana says. "Who else would be my focal point?"

In the meantime, as soon as *Best Friends Forever* was canceled, Lennon was secretly planning to get pregnant. "I was like, 'Oh, I've gotta get this show on the road,'" she says. Jessica, not knowing this, came over to her house to pitch ideas for a new show. An executive at USA Network had told them he'd work with them on anything they wanted to do. They were brainstorming, and Jessica said, "This is the dumbest thing I've ever said, but what about like 'Two Ladies and a Baby'?"

"Done and done," Lennon said.

They were now in their late thirties, and in a different stage of their friendship. "We wanted to write about what we were actually going through," Jessica says, "the beginning of making our families, having a baby."

Eventually their daughters were born within five months

of each other, and now, as three-year-olds, they play together. "Our daughters are best friends in real life," Lennon says. "They didn't really have a choice. But they also like each other."

"I'm just so excited for them to grow up in a world in which like, yeah, you've got your best friend next to you and that means you can fucking do anything," Jessica says. "Any-thing."

On the new show they created, *Playing House,* which premiered on the USA Network in 2014, Emma (Jessica) and Maggie (Lennon) are childhood friends who became less close as adults. Maggie married and stayed in their Connecticut hometown, while Emma followed an all-consuming career to Shanghai. In the first episode, after a pregnant Maggie splits from her husband, Emma quits her job and moves in with her, setting up a series about best friends supporting each other the way romantic partners have traditionally done. The final scene of the pilot episode is a twist on the classic "rush to the airport to tell her how you feel" scene; it's Maggie asking Emma to stay with her. "It is a fantasy, right?" Lennon says. "That your best friend can move into your house and you can decorate it like your perfect Pinterest board and no one would think there were too many doilies."

Behind the improbable setup and the pair's ongoing hi-jinks, like accidentally soaking themselves in a neighbor's shower, is an ordinary, wonderful best friendship. Maggie and Emma have a secret language ("totes kewl" means *not* cool) and an ironclad love for each other. "Most of the conflict comes out of them caring too much for each other, which I think in our real lives probably is where a lot of the comedy comes from," Lennon says.

In September 2015, while they were promoting the second season of *Playing House*, Jessica was diagnosed with breast cancer. Lennon was with her at the doctor's office when she was diagnosed, and for the double mastectomy, year of chemotherapy, and breast reconstruction that followed. During chemotherapy, Lennon, Jessica's husband, and other close friends would distract Jessica by reading old *Oprah* or *In Touch* magazines out loud and feeding her Cheez-Its and Teddy Grahams. For her infusions, Lennon packed Jessica in ice "like a choice piece of holiday meat so that I didn't get like any nerve damage," Jessica says. "When you are faced with a life-or-death situation, your best friend is the one you need next to you. Women instinctually know how to take care of each other."

At all of Jessica's doctor's appointments, "Lennon would take all of the notes and ask all of the hard questions," Jessica says, "because my husband and I were in shock." At one appointment, Jessica was supposed to choose her breast implants. The surgeon showed them the options and asked, "Which one feels most like your real breast?" Jessica wasn't sure and asked her husband and Lennon for help.

Her husband poked Jessica's boob from the side and said, "I don't know."

Lennon stepped in, grabbed Jessica's breast, then felt each implant carefully and said, "It's number two."

"It was like, 'Let's not fuck around here,'" Lennon says.

Today, Jessica is healthy, and she and Lennon wrote about

and reenacted the experience for the third season of *Playing House*. Initially they weren't sure it would work on the show. Could they make the audience laugh about Emma having cancer and Maggie caring for her? "We really hemmed and hawed about it," Jessica says. "But the truth is a lot of funny shit happened to Lennon and me during this. Her choosing my boobs. The craziness that went down in chemo, so we decided, 'Yeah, we're going to do it.' We're going to tell the story because the truth of the matter is I wouldn't have literally survived physically or emotionally if I hadn't had Lennon with me."

This isn't to say that best friends don't annoy or anger each other. I like to stress-pick at my nails or what I see as flaws in my clothing, and sometimes when I'm intently absorbed in this Ruthie will say, "I can't handle you doing that right now." Or, this winter, while it was snowing, Ruthie texted to ask me if I could help her carry a mattress up her stairs. I didn't want to leave my apartment and wrote back, "That sounds terrible." But I also wasn't going to let Ruthie struggle with it herself, so I met her outside her building and we shimmied it up to her apartment together.

A boyfriend once said to me, when we were fighting, "I wish you looked at me the way you look at Ruthie." I knew what he meant. I'm sure when I see her, my face is all love.

I talk about her all the time, to the point where I wonder if I'm bringing her up too much, but that doesn't stop me from doing it. "Did you know that Ruthie made a resolution that she has to eat a slice of pizza every week?" I'll say.

"It's the exact same way with you," Ruthie says. "I feel like I talk about you all of the time."

This understanding and acceptance we have with our best friends, I think, is only becoming more remarkable—and something more people are attuned to and appreciative of, whether they see it on television or with their own soulmates.

When the creator and star of *Insecure*, Issa Rae, was developing the show for HBO, based on her web series *Awkward Black Girl*, she made it mostly about the Issa character. HBO executives saw the pilot and suggested that, instead, she focus on Issa and her best friend, Molly, who is modeled after Issa's real-life BFF, a corporate lawyer who grew up in South Central Los Angeles. "People will watch if Molly and Issa have chemistry," Prentice Penny, the showrunner, told her.

Issa liked the idea. She wanted to show ordinary, supportive black female friendship, not the melodramatic, manipulative relationships she saw on reality shows like Bravo's *The Real Housewives* franchise or VH1's *Love & Hip Hop* and *Flavor of Love*. She wanted Issa and Molly to act like she and her real-life friends did: mocking each other and bringing over chips and dip to apologize after they've been insensitive. When the pilot aired in 2016, it ended with Issa showing up at Molly's with Cheetos and Frito-Lay dip after embarrassing her by performing a rap Molly knows is about her called *"Broken Pussy"* ("Maybe it's really rough / Maybe it's had enough / Broken pussy"). In the season finale, Issa says to Molly, "I can't imagine my life without you. You're my best friend."

Of her real best friend, who inspired Molly, Issa told *Cosmopolitan*, "I always look up to her because I feel like I constantly have to get it together. She always calls me to the carpet when I'm fucking up, but even when I'm fucking up, she has my back. I can say that for a lot of my friends, and to not see that [on-screen]—to constantly see black women fighting and plotting against each other, really gets to me because that's not what I see to be true of my friends."

With Ruthie and me, it feels like we're both trying to accomplish the same things at this point in our lives: work hard, be there for our parents, siblings, and other friends, and figure out whether, or how and when, to start our own families. "I feel like I can consult with you," Ruthie says. "We have such similar circumstances that I do feel, not necessarily what's right for you is right for me, but I never feel like your perspective is one where I'm just like 'you don't know my life.'"

What we give each other is the assurance that we're doing what we need to and want to as best we can. Mostly, though, I watch my friend and am so impressed with her. I feel lucky that she's so rooted in my everyday and wants me just as much in hers.

Or like she said when we met the other night, when I hugged her and apologized for still being damp from a post-run shower, "If I could wring you out and drink you up, I would."

CHAPTER 6

Strength in Numbers

You don't climb the mountain alone because you get to
the top and it's no fun. I'd rather climb the mountain
with my girlfriends and get to the top and have a party.

—Erin Wasson, model

A couple of years ago, I did something I hadn't done since second grade: I had a birthday party and invited only girls. I'd just moved into the apartment I'd bought on my own, and it hit me, in a way it hadn't when I was busy applying for the mortgage and selecting a stove I wasn't planning to use, that the space was totally mine. I'd never expected to live alone. I thought my track would be to go from splitting a home with roommates to sharing one with my husband. But now I was in a place that I'd picked out every single item for, down to the white plate that went over the intercom. It was like living in my fingerprint. The first day, as soon as the moving crew left me alone in my apartment, I remember running around the L-shape, from the bedroom to the kitchen, overjoyed to be by myself there.

This turn of my life felt special, and the more I thought about it, the more I wanted my female friends to commemorate it with me. I wrote in the invite:

> *To my favorite ladies,*
>
> *I finally got a couch, so please help me celebrate my birthday by coming to sit on it. I'll have booze, cheese, and other delicious snacks that do not require cooking.*

A dozen women, not all of whom knew each other beforehand, came over. I remember peeking in on them in the living room while I was in the kitchen. They looked so relaxed around my coffee table—sitting on the couch or the floor, nestled in the windowsill, or standing to get more snacks— talking to each other as easily as if they did this every Wednesday. They seemed as at home in my new home as I was. *I love this,* I thought, watching them. At the end of the evening, the few of us left were all sitting on the floor, drinking a final glass of wine, and having the quieter conversations that tend to wait until most of the party has gone. It got later and darker; my playlist ended, but my apartment still felt warm, like there was no pressure to leave. The women who'd been there and the ones who were still had imbued it with something good. That night is still one of the best I've ever had in my apartment.

I feel this sense of greatness a lot now when I'm with all girls. Recently, I went to Palm Springs with a group of six women. We rented a house to hang out in for the weekend, and at the time, I was dazed from a romantic breakup that had happened a few weeks before. I couldn't sleep, barely ate, and was trapped in my head thinking about almost nothing but what had gone wrong with the guy. I was a zombie, but when I could see through the fog of my own misery, I noticed and felt grateful for the same sense of comfort I'd had in my apartment the night of my birthday, as if being encircled by my girlfriends would keep me safe. They just let me be, only gently shifting aside my layer of sadness occasionally to hug me or check in if I'd been alone for too long.

I haven't been surrounded by groups of women since college, and now that I am again, it feels like a relief. Part of that is the security that comes from being buffered by people of the same sex—there is a way in which the women I love relate similarly. When we're together, the energy and adoration are striking. But underneath that, there's a subtler sense that we're intertwined, knit together. This combination makes me feel like I could go from their company and straight to the moon. My friends inspire me to pull myself together, to shake off whatever might be trying to rattle me that day, or to own what I've done well. Just being around them is often all the propping that I need.

We don't have a lot of in-your-face examples of women being together happily. We have more today than we ever have before, but for many people, the default thinking is still that a bunch of girls can't be cool with each other.

Karen McCullah, who cowrote *Legally Blonde,* a 2001 movie about sorority member turned law student Elle Woods (Reese Witherspoon) triumphing over dismissive male lawyers while wearing hot pink, says people often tell her they didn't expect Elle to have positive friendships. "One of the things always mentioned about *Legally Blonde* is the female friendships in the movie and how the women all support each other—her sorority, her friendship with the manicurist—and that really surprised me that it was considered noteworthy because all the girls in my sorority were very supportive and kind to each other," she says.

Paul Feig, the director of 2016's all-female *Ghostbusters,* recalled how he was warned by his male colleagues to expect on-set turmoil. "I had some male producer say, 'Oh boy, get ready. It's going to be tough, you're going to have catfights,'" Feig told an audience at a producers' conference in Los Angeles. "And I said, 'Who the fuck are you?' It was the most wonderful experience I've had."

Before starting to shoot *Ocean's Eight,* a spin-off of the *Ocean's* trilogy that stars eight women, Sarah Paulson was asked by Hollywood news site *The Wrap* if she thought there would be "actress in-fighting" during the shoot.

"Not in the slightest," Paulson said. "I've never had anything like that happen on that set. I don't come from a world where I expect that. I just think it's sort of sad, really, that that would be the expectation."

Groups of men don't get these questions. In the sixties, no one wondered about infighting in the Rat Pack of singers Frank Sinatra, Sammy Davis Jr., Dean Martin, and more, who were so tight they often made surprise appearances at each other's gigs. In the 1990s, no one doubted that the group of actors known in Hollywood as the "Pussy Posse"—with members like Leonardo DiCaprio, Tobey Maguire, Lukas Haas, and Kevin Connolly—were real friends when they were out at nightclubs together. In 2004, the only talk about the filming of *Ocean's Twelve,* one of the *Ocean's* trilogy with all-male stars, was about the good time the guys were having playing pranks on each other, like when George Clooney put a bumper sticker on Brad Pitt's car that read, "Small Penis on Board."

But the knee-jerk reaction to women together is that we can't possibly get along, that we're only pretending to like each other. Sarah Berkes, who's in her mid-twenties and works at a sportswear company, gets this a lot because she lives with 374 other women. She has a room in the Webster Apartments in New York, a stately rooming house that was opened in 1923 as a residence for single working women. It was founded by brothers Charles and Josiah Webster, who earned a fortune working with Macy's department store. When Charles died in 1916, he had his estate set aside to create the Webster to help care for the Macy's shopgirls, who often moved to the city with no money or social network. He wanted them to be able to live somewhere affordable, comfortable, and close to their jobs. "I direct that the said apartments shall not be conducted for profit but solely for the purpose of providing unmarried working women with homes and wholesome food at a small cost to them," he wrote in his will. The Webster has 375 single rooms, all occupied by women (in the 1920s, between thirty and forty Macy's shop-girls lived there). "When I tell people where I live," Sarah says, "the first question I get is, *'Is it really catty?'*" She tells them it's not. "We're all adults," she says. "You don't know everyone in the building. We don't have pillow fights in our underwear. That's not real life."

The Webster is one of the few remaining all-female resi-dences in New York, although the city used to have many. The most famous, the Barbizon Hotel for Women, once housed Grace Kelly, Joan Crawford, Ali MacGraw, Liza Min-nelli, and Sylvia Plath. Plath used it in her 1963 novel *The Bell Jar,* disguising it as the Amazon, a building she wrote that was for well-to-do girls whose parents "wanted to make sure their daughters were living in a place where men couldn't get at them and deceive them," she wrote.

Sarah lived in her sorority house during college and was thrilled to find a similar setup in the city at the Webster. "I was used to living with all girls and not having boys upstairs," she says, "and in a way I prefer it." She likes that home feels low-key. She can run down the hall to the bathroom in her bra or show up hungover to brunch on Sundays. "In the com-munal space, I can just wear pj's or no makeup or booty shorts and I don't have to worry that there's a guy who's going to see me," she says.

Men are allowed only on the first floor, where women can sit with them in one of the six "beau parlors," small alcoves with armchairs, a love seat, and a coffee table, but no door that they can close for privacy. The staff at the Webster is serious about enforcing the "no men upstairs" policy. Recent suspicion that a resident had a guy in her room resulted in a supervisor hunting him down. She knocked on the resident's door, calling out, "Can I come in your room? We think you have a man in there."

When the young woman opened the door, there was no one else in the small room, furnished with a single bed, desk, and dresser. Then the supervisor asked her to open the closet, where she found a terrified male crouching inside. He sprinted out of the room as soon as she saw him.

Sarah says living in the Webster is different than living in the sorority house because she doesn't know everyone there—residents call their rooms "apartments"—but the girls aren't shy about making friends in the shared areas, like the roof deck with the view of the Empire State Building or the cafeteria. "They'll come up and say, 'Yo, I'm new. Can I sit with you at dinner?'" Sarah says.

She met her best friend in the second-floor television room, while they were both waiting for ABC's *The Bachelorette* to begin. (Whenever they go out to bars together, they don't tell any guys they meet where they live. "We figure out, *'What's our story tonight? Are we roommates? Did we meet living in the city?'"* she says.)

She and another girl started a Facebook page for the Webster girls, so anyone could gather a group for going to the Brooklyn Botanical Garden or on a Hudson River boat cruise. The Webster also has events for the residents, like watercolor classes—Sarah has a painting of high heels she made at one hanging in her room—movie nights with popcorn, and workout classes. When her mom came to visit, she slept on a cot in

Sarah's room, ate in the cafeteria, and met all of her friends. At the end of the trip, she didn't want to leave.

Sarah and her best friend are planning to move out of the Webster and into an apartment together, but they're not ready yet. "Everyone thinks we're cloistered nuns and we're not allowed to drink, but I've had the most positive experience," Sarah says.

The term "frenemies" is almost exclusively applied to women's friendships. No matter how effusive women are about each other, outsiders—and sometimes the women themselves—often perceive a rivalry, especially if they have reason to clash over anything, like professional success. This makes frenemies, women who are nice to each other but don't necessarily like each other.

This way of being, or of people thinking women are, comes from two incompatible things we're taught: First, we're socialized to always be good girls. Anne Helen Petersen wrote about good girls on BuzzFeed: "There's still an expectation that any sort of activity that is not traditionally feminine should be countered with niceness. It's okay to be an aggressive soccer player, in other words, so long as you're not a bitch off the field."

At the 2016 Olympics in Rio, gymnast Gabby Douglas was shown looking serious on television while watching her teammates compete in the individual all-around competition, which she'd missed qualifying for (a loss that meant she couldn't defend her gold from the previous Olympics).

Twitter users criticized her for not smiling (they used #crab-bygabby). This led to Douglas actually *apologizing* for her expression.

"Everything I've gone through has been a lot this time around," she said, "and I apologize if [I seemed] really mad in the stands. I wasn't. I was supporting Aly [Raisman]. And I always will support them and respect them in everything they do. I never want anyone to take it as I was jealous or I wanted attention. Never. I support them, and I'm sorry that I wasn't showing it."

Women aren't allowed to be jealous, angry, or vengeful, at least if we want to go on being seen as good girls.

But we're also led to believe that if another woman gets something—a medal, a promotion, or even a committed relationship—then another one of us won't. There's a sense, among women at least, that achievement is a zero-sum game, and we're supposed to be cutthroat at all times.

It's the incongruity between stopping ourselves from seeming anything but pleasant while ambitious, on one hand, and the belief that all women can't have good things, on the other, that creates frenemies.

Girls, a series creator Lena Dunham based on her own friends that premiered on HBO in 2012 and ended in 2017, was largely about dysfunctional friendships. It made a point of being grittier than most of what was on television, which included showing awkward sex, fleshier bodies, and the characters screaming at each other that they were bad friends.

In the first season, the main character, Hannah (Dunham), has a frenemy named Tally (Jenny Slate). Tally has written a memoir while Hannah is still struggling to become a writer. At Tally's book party, Hannah says, "All she used to write about were her sexual escapades, and then she got into a monogamous relationship, you know, and so I thought she'd reveal her true, boring nature and start writing travelogues or something, but no, her boyfriend up and killed himself."

But by the fifth season, Tally returns and runs into Hannah, and they spend the day, in between eating hot dogs, stealing a bike, and smoking weed, being honest with each other. Tally admits that all of her success in writing hasn't made her as happy as she hoped, that her opinion of herself is based solely on what she finds when she Googles her own name. She's envious that Hannah hasn't been stuck being known for one thing. "Look at you, you've had all of these, like, boyfriends and jobs and moments," she says, "and you've lived all this truth."

"It didn't feel like very much while it was happening," Hannah says.

"But it is so much, and you have so much to say," Tally says.

When women stop seeing each other as rivals, whom they nonetheless have to be nice to, we'll be free from this clumsy middle ground of being frenemies. We can compete against each other. We can face off and admit what we really want and that it hurts when we don't get it. But we can also understand each other—and with that kind of empathy, instead of disingenuous smiles, we might be able to lift each other up too.

F emale athletes, especially at the highest levels where so few others can relate to what they're doing, have been examples of how women can battle each other while also treating their competitors as people they actually like and depend on—without being fake about it. "It's hard and lonely at the top," Serena Williams has said about her friendship with her tennis rival Caroline Wozniacki. "That's why it's so fun to have Caroline." During the 2016 Olympic Games in Rio, New Zealand runner Nikki Hamblin tripped during the first round of the five-thousand-meter race, two thousand meters from the end. When she fell on the track, she took American Abbey D'Agostino with her. D'Agostino had twisted her knee and didn't think she could keep going, but helped up Hamblin and told her to go on. Then she collapsed on the track again. Hamblin didn't move and instead stayed there until D'Agostino got up and kept running too. Eventually they both crossed the finish line and made it to the finals. "When someone asks me what happened in Rio in twenty years' time, that is my story," Hamblin said of her moment on the track with D'Agostino. "She is my story."

Kim Vandenberg, an Olympic swimmer who won a bronze medal in Beijing in 2008 in the four-by-two-hundred-meter freestyle race, has been relying on the women she competes against since she first got in the pool at age eight.

"I grew up racing my best friend," Kim says of a friend she calls Alice, whom she met when they both started swimming at a country club in Moraga, California. As kids, they spent hours together, both in and out of the water. Kim plucked Alice's eyebrows for the first time. At first, they weren't sure how to balance their friendship with trying to beat each other in the pool. At one meet, they decided to tie, pacing themselves so they finished at the same moment, but "we got in trouble," Kim says.

As she got older she learned that she could still be friends with the other swimmers and race against them. Some girls would freak out when she'd beat them, but she didn't let that stop her from trying to swim her fastest. "I'm not going to not beat someone even though we're friends," she says.

When they were sixteen, she and Alice both made the Olympic trials, a first for each of them. Even as they were both trying to earn a spot on the US team, they backed each other. "If one of us had a bad swim, we'd cry about it in the warm-down pool," Kim says. "We were sisters. You're away from your family, training for four to five hours a day. Even if we fought, we'd get over it. Our friendship was more important. We'd swim and then in the locker room, we'd be talking about our latest crush, where we were going shopping, or what movie we were going to see." Their high school coach told them, "You need to cut the cord."

Kim and Alice's friendship faltered only when Alice wanted to stop swimming. They were both on the team at UCLA at that point, and Alice wasn't performing as well as she had been in high school. To tell her she was quitting the team, Alice sent her a long handwritten letter, making sure to say that her leaving the sport had nothing to do with Kim. "It was still hard," Kim says. "Every memory I had in the pool was with her."

Before the Olympic trials in 2008, though, Alice was there again. Kim was stressed and sore and had a horrible migraine. Alice came to her house, made tea, and sat in Kim's room with her in the dark because any light would make her head hurt more. "She was just there taking care of me," Kim says.

In her early twenties, when Kim started competing internationally, she met a friend she calls Chloe, a swimmer just as driven as she was. They bonded when they were stuck in an airport in Germany, trying to get to a competition in Turkey, so they killed time eating chocolate, "like these giant bars of Toblerone," Kim says. "We were so tired and had eaten so much sugar. We couldn't stop laughing." They had the same goals, "to be the best in the world," Kim says. Sometimes they'd do three workouts a day. "All we wanted to do was get our asses kicked," Kim says.

Before competitions they'd encourage each other to be calm. "We'd be sitting in the room putting on the swim caps," Kim says, "having so much fun getting ready for our races, and just being there to ease each other's nerves." After competitions, they'd celebrate together. At the World Championships in Australia, in 2007, they both won medals and were hyped up, running around their shared hotel room topless with their medals covering their breasts. "We had one silver and one bronze on each breast," Kim says.

They were focused on winning themselves, but also wanted the other to do well. "We were always suggesting the other person get more sleep, or saying, 'Use this product, or take this vitamin,'" Kim says.

The friends she swam with, Kim says, matter more to her

than her medal count or her race times. "Our connection is genuine," she says. "Our care for each other isn't superficial. My friends are my soulmates, and I love them all. I want the best for them in their lives."

Social media moves fast, and #squadgoals is now a dusty hashtag, to be dumped in the same pile as #yolo before it. But that it feels dated today makes it easy to forget how revelatory the pictures of women showing off their friendships were when #squadgoals was at its most popular in the back half of 2015, especially on Instagram. (To put the time period in perspective, pictures of pool floats shaped like flamingos or doughnuts were also all over Instagram.)

The hashtag applied to many groups, like a bunch of cute puppies or the Teletubbies. Companies also used it for marketing: Burger King attached it to a tray of cheeseburgers. But mostly #squadgoals meant female friends, who also called themselves #girlsquads. They used the hashtag when they were flashing peace signs at the beach, flanking a bride, or stretching out their hands to show off fresh manicures.

On *The Mindy Project*, Mindy Kaling's sitcom about Mindy Lahiri, a young ob-gyn, Mindy tells her colleague Danny that her best friend from college Maggie is coming to a party with her.

Danny: "How many best friends from college do you have?"
Mindy: "Best friend isn't a person, Danny, it's a tier."

Model Gigi Hadid talked about why she and her famous friends, including pop singer Taylor Swift and models Kendall Jenner and Karlie Kloss, used the hashtag. "'Squad Goals' is a big social-media thing right now," she said, "and that's what we want to inspire in other groups of friends—to be proud of the power you all have when you're together, which can be amplified so much by each person. That's what has been cool about everyone's willingness to be there for each other, and we don't want to be like other generations who are infamous for their cattiness. We want to be the new generation."

These squad goals pictures, then, were women chipping away at the judgment that when we get together we're awful to one another. While we were documenting our lives on social media, we were also presenting visual evidence that groups of women are supportive. Before female friends co-opted the word "squad," it was used by military units, sports teams, cheerleading groups, and hip-hop collaborators, all to make the same point: We're tight-knit, whether we're executing a strategy or a play, propping up a verse or a human pyramid.

In 2015, the Hadid-Swift-Jenner-Kloss-and-more squad was the most famous one around, and Swift was seen as the center of the group. Katy Waldman wrote in a piece in *Slate* about the history of squads that no article about the topic can go more than a few sentences without mentioning her. On tour, Swift showed clips of her friends—including Hadid, Kloss, pop singer Selena Gomez, the sisters of the band Haim, and more—rhapsodizing about hanging out with her. ("We pretend like our life is a karaoke bar," one said. "We're an epic squad," another said.) "It was a public service announcement for the healing powers of female friendship," Jon Caramanica wrote in a review of a show in Louisiana in *The New York Times*. "Ms. Swift has been actively cultivating these friendships as part of her retreat from the tabloids in recent years. Rather than be known as a serial dater, she'd prefer to be thought of as a serial befriender."

Swift herself said of the shift, in *Rolling Stone,* "When you're not boyfriend-shopping, you're able to step back and see other girls who are killing it and think, 'God, I want to be around her.'"

At some shows, her friends joined her onstage. They made a music video together for the song "Bad Blood," about Swift's rivalry with another female performer that showed them training for revenge in sleek outfits with swords and machine guns. And they spent the Fourth of July at Swift's beach house in Rhode Island, where they Instagrammed themselves jumping on the beach, wearing American flag onesies, or clutching sparklers.

The flip side of girl squads, especially as an Instagram trend, is that they can seem more like possessions worth bragging about than genuine friendships, especially if the women in them all look and dress alike. They could be modern cliques, with #squadgoals having the same effect as the *Mean Girls* line "You can't sit with us." Critics of Swift's squad have said that it seems too uniformly cast to be inspiring—most of the members are white and many are supermodels.

Teen Vogue's Elaine Welteroth worries about this. She

doesn't want all girls to feel pressure to belong to a group of friends that's Insta-friendly. "If it's authentic, there's nothing more beneficial or helpful, as a woman, than to have a band of strong women who support you behind you," she says. "That being said, not every girl is going to fit into this construct of a squad, and I think it can become exclusionary in a way that isn't healthy or beneficial to all girls."

I understand this, but I also think these pictures were an important start in seeing groups of women in a different way. The users of #squadgoals in 2015 were starting an image shift. They were capturing and highlighting friendships they were proud of as they were going through life together. Anything on Instagram is a little bit perfected, but the emotion behind the photos didn't feel airbrushed.

Showing women's friendships, on-screen and off, is so important because it changes the narrative in society that says women must be adversaries, on some level, no matter what. The more we see women together, the more these relationships become real and nuanced. Women together can be strong and crack each other up with filthy jokes, but they can also be petty and have arguments that aren't about the real reasons they're mad at each other. The recent movies and television programs that show these kinds of friendships have been written by women who lived them. Annie Mumolo and Kristen Wiig cowrote *Bridesmaids,* which came out in 2011 and showed women unafraid to test and fight about their friendships. (It also showed them being unafraid to shit and vomit in and around a bridal shop, in the movie's infamous food-poisoning scene.)

"We wanted to show women being funny in a way we know them to be, to capture their behaviors, both the good and the bad," Mumolo said. "We also wanted it to resonate emotionally, 'cause that's where it came from for us—the way it feels when it seems like everyone else's life is going along swimmingly and your own is just snowballing from bad to worse."

The story centers on Annie (Kristen Wiig) feeling like she's losing her best friend Lillian (Maya Rudolph) to Lillian's perfect new friend Helen (Rose Byrne), at a time when she feels more imperfect than ever. At one point, at Lillian's Helen-thrown bridal shower, after Helen gives Lillian a trip to Paris as a gift, a feeling-totally-left-out Annie ransacks the party, destroying an enormous heart-shaped cookie and splashing out the chocolate in the chocolate fountain. "Why can't you just be happy for me and then go home and talk behind my back later like normal person?" Lillian screams.

"I think it's a slightly pandering idea that all women just want to see romance and they'll always respond and show up," the director Paul Feig said. "Even though *Bridesmaids* had that component, it was a story of female friendship. For me, that's just a much more fun area and one that is less explored. I've seen my female friends with their girlfriends, and how strong and important those relationships are. I've also seen my wife over the years struggle to find the right female friends, and it's, in a way, more complicated than trying to find guy friends. I think they're deeper friendships too.

If you show these kinds of stories that are important to women and that they don't normally see, it really means a lot to a lot of people." *Bridesmaids* earned 169 million dollars and became the highest-grossing R-rated female-led comedy of all time.

In the same way, *Pitch Perfect*, a 2012 movie about a female a cappella group that made 65 million dollars and has two sequels, was partly inspired by writer Kay Cannon's experience with her college track teammates. At first, Kay was only interested in writing about a cappella groups, which she thought sounded preposterous. When she was a writer on *30 Rock*, Tina Fey's sitcom about a live sketch-comedy show, there was a joke about one of the writers having been in one at Harvard.

"Who made that up?" Cannon asked. Her boss said no one did; a cappella groups were real, and they competed against each other. "Someone needs to write a movie about that," Cannon said, thinking it could be her.

Kay read Mickey Rapkin's nonfiction book *Pitch Perfect: The Quest for Collegiate A Cappella Glory*, in which he follows three different competitive groups for a year, and learned that all-women groups are usually the underdogs, so she decided to make "a very strong female-centric girl-power kind of movie," she says.

The notes Cannon got from the studio executives on her first drafts of the script were that they wanted to see more romance. *"How about a love triangle between one of the Bellas, a Treblemaker, and another guy?"* they suggested. "There were many times I had to be like, 'Guys, this is about an a cappella group who wins the championship,'" Cannon says. "This is about an all-girl group. It is not a romance."

Pitch Perfect is set at the fictional Barden University, with the Barden Bellas going up against the guys, the Treblemakers, to try to win the national title. Part of the Bellas' initiation oath is: "I solemnly promise to never have sexual relations with a Treblemaker or may my vocal cords be ripped out by wolves."

"The Trebles don't respect us," explains coleader Aubrey (Anna Camp), "and if we let them penetrate us, we are giving them our power."

"I treated it like a sports movie, where they're Rocky and they're up against the big, bad all-male group," Cannon says.

Cannon wanted the Bellas to mimic the way she and her track teammates leaned on each other. "That bond that I have with them, it's forever," she says, "so I really understood that and I really lived that. It was exciting to write *Pitch Perfect* knowing that the girls are Bellas for life. I understood how you will do anything for your best friends. You just have this shared common experience and you trust each other, and I think that's a really beautiful thing."

A real-life friendship between Nicole Kidman and Reese Witherspoon got the HBO series *Big Little Lies* made. The two were introduced by Bruna Papandrea, Kidman's childhood friend and Witherspoon's former partner in her Pacific Standard production company. They both wanted to work together on a project focused on women and found the right one in Liane Moriarty's novel *Big Little Lies*, a mystery about a murder in a beach town where figuring out who did it becomes less interesting than seeing the complex women at the story's core empower each other.

"Reese called me up with Bruno and said, 'There's this book, read it,' and that was the beginning of it," Kidman said to *Entertainment Tonight*.

The two of them, who wanted to co-executive produce and star in the series, then pitched *Big Little Lies* to television studios like HBO, Netflix, and Showtime, sparking a bidding war.

"It was kind of amazing to feel the interest—that's what happens when women combine their powers," Kidman told *Vogue*. "If I'd gone by myself to try and do it, it wouldn't have worked."

While Kidman and Witherspoon were promoting the show, they told lots of cute stories about how much the stars, who also included Laura Dern, Zoë Kravitz, and Shailene Woodley, liked each other. During filming they'd go out to dinner every night and share their lives. Dern introduced Witherspoon to Red Vines candy and brown lipstick. "We couldn't get enough of each other," Witherspoon told *Vogue*. They keep in touch through a WhatsApp group.

But they made it clear that what they really wanted to point out about their friendship was that it had been crucial for getting this story on television and would hopefully lead to other narratives centered on women.

At the 2017 Emmy Awards, the show won Best Limited Series, along with many other awards. While accepting the award, Kidman and Witherspoon held hands, their affection for each other as evident as their elation over the series' acclaim.

"This is a friendship that then created opportunities," Kidman said in her acceptance speech. "It created opportunities out of a frustration because we weren't getting offered great roles. So now, more great roles for women, please."

I used to think women in groups were scary. When I stood outside of them in the middle school yard or sat apart from them at the dining tables in the sorority house, I felt excluded and intimidated. I couldn't see how I could be part of these circles, and I didn't know if I really wanted to.

That's changed. Now when I see groups of women, I'm drawn to them. It's not because I had a "Kumbaya" moment where I think all women need to be friends—they don't. But I realized that I had in women what I always thought I got from men: strength and reliability.

My friends started this. The respect I have for them opened up a wider scope in my heart, where I saw clusters of women as places I also wanted to be. I started to look for gaps in their circles, openings for me.

This search—and standing with other women—felt more urgent after the election of Donald Trump as the forty-fifth president of the United States.

The night of the third debate between Trump and Hillary Clinton, I interviewed Linda Bloodworth Thomason, the creator of *Designing Women*. We were primarily talking about *Designing Women*, but Bloodworth Thomason has also been a good friend of Clinton's for almost four decades. She rang the doorbell of the governor's mansion when Clinton was the first lady of Arkansas and introduced herself. As we were talking, I kept thinking about how incredible it was that not only were we going to have the first female president, but that person was her friend. I couldn't resist asking, "How does it feel watching your friend possibly become the first female president?"

I said "possibly," but at that point I was sure she was going to see her friend win, so I was dismayed by her hesitation.

"Well, it's exciting," she answered, but quickly changed the subject to telling me about Clinton's mom, Dorothy Rodham, whom Bloodworth Thomason had been close with before she died and whose ring she was wearing that night as she prepared to watch the debate. Dorothy Rodham had been born to teenage parents in Chicago who put her on a train at age eight to go live with her grandparents in Los Angeles. Then, when she was fourteen, she moved out and supported herself as a nanny and maid.

"Now Hillary is where she is," Bloodworth Thomason told me that night. "Now she's almost there. But all of it began with this little girl who had no prospects, who did not know what love was. It's such a testament to towering female strength that you can not only survive this, but you can figure it out. You can give everything you didn't get to your little girl and then she can go out and give it to millions of women. That's sort of emblematic of what women can do for each other, even if you're not related. Throughout the oppression of women, this is how we advance and prosper emotionally and every other way, because we stand on each other's shoulders. How Dorothy did this, how the hell she did it, I'll never know. She had so much to overcome, but look at the steel rod she placed in her daughter's spine."

Truthfully, when Bloodworth Thomason told me this, I was not all that moved. I put what she was saying in the past. In my head we were right where we should be. Respect, parity, and belief women could lead the country would fall in line when one of us was president. I thought it was all easy from here.

Before Trump was elected president, being a feminist wasn't something that connected me to other women. If anyone asked, I would have said I was a feminist, but it wasn't something I ever mentioned or planned any political activism around. I thought of it as a sensible position to have, a personal evolution that I'd reached after realizing that it was no knock on men to consider myself equal to them, but I didn't consider what it meant to be a feminist outside the bounds of my own body and brain.

I would read about the fuss when a female celebrity—Shailene Woodley, Lady Gaga—declined to call herself a feminist, then go back to thinking about something I wanted to purchase online or what I was going to eat for lunch.

"I think our generation thought we had to just, like, work hard," *Teen Vogue*'s Elaine Welteroth says. "Grind it out. But don't talk about feminism. Don't talk about it. That was unattractive. There was a stigma."

Jessica Testa wrote on BuzzFeed about how mainstream feminism before 2017 was mostly about personal and professional advancement. Feminists leaned in; they did not march. "By President Obama's second term, there simply wasn't a women's movement, at least in the raucous political sense," she wrote. "Feminist activists were still out there—fighting for reproductive rights and against sexual violence, joining Black Lives Matter—but the movement that attracted the most attention was the up-the-corporate-ladder kind. Empowerment was catchier than equality. Powerful women in business became the faces of modern (white) feminism, even if they expressed little interest in feminism itself."

Feminism wasn't, for me, a reason to stretch to other women or care about what issues were important to them. But on election night, the first thing I did was, as Bloodworth Thomason had portended, reach toward other women. Some friends had come to my apartment to watch the returns, and before Ruthie and Erica left, around two A.M., the three of us hugged. I'm a hugger and will pull my friends close for whatever reason, but this was more instinctual. Even as we didn't really believe the result of the election yet, we were already creeping toward each other, on impulse.

Hours later, in a Facebook post, Teresa Shook, a retired lawyer in Hawaii, suggested a march on Washington, as did a few women on the East Coast. Tens of thousands of women pledged to join them and, by mid-January, the Women's March was shaping up to be the anti-Trump demonstration, despite a few proclamations that the name was too narrow.

"The opposite turned out to be true," Amanda Hess wrote in *The New York Times Magazine*. "Women led the resistance, and everyone followed."

Women are stepping up together, loudly and publicly, like we've had to do before and will again, like Dorothy Rodham did for her daughter and like her daughter did for me. A country so clearly governed and controlled by men isn't going to be realigned overnight, but we turned out in massive numbers for the Women's March on Washington, DC, and its worldwide satellite protests. The total attendance at various events around the country was estimated to be between 3.2 million and 5.2 million, making the Women's March what's thought to be the largest single-day demonstration in recorded US history, according to *The Washington Post*. The sight of women in pink pussyhats, carrying signs that said KEEP YOUR LAWS OUT OF MY VAGINA or GRAB 'EM BY THE PATRIARCHY, with their daughters, sons, mothers, friends, and partners, dominated my headspace for days afterward.

This isn't to say that female friendship is equivalent to political organizing. Liking other women isn't going to guarantee us equal rights. How anyone votes and what they believe is, in the end, personal. But for me right now, being with other women is crucial, for feeling comfortable and seen. For the first time, I'm not thinking of feminism as about slogans or intellectual arguments. It's about standing and yelling and looking around and learning how other women want to transform our culture.

I am aware that within the women's movement and the feminist space there is division, for example, between women who are abortion-rights advocates and those who are anti-abortion, or between those who believe feminism is too strict and those who believe it's become too inclusive and is now meaningless. There has also been too little acknowledgment of the experiences of women of color. What contributes to our individual selves beyond our sex—our race, class, ethnicity, and religion—informs our experiences. Intersectional feminism asks white women to recognize that they have had it easier, that other, nonwhite women have been oppressed and discriminated against differently.

"For me, there's a double whammy with being a woman of color and a young one," Welteroth says. "There's ageism, sexism, and racism. The trifecta. How do I parse these out? Which one do I deal with first? Which one is contributing to this particular interaction that I'm having that's uncomfortable? But 'intersectional feminism' is a term now! It's one that people are talking about and little white girls are talking about!"

In the past, the experiences of women of color were not acknowledged by mainstream feminism, and in the same way, there have been very few representations of nonwhite friend groups in pop culture. Only a smattering of movies and television shows have captured both the universal theme of female friendship and the cultural specificity of women of color. On network television, there have been some shows featuring casts made up of minorities, but for the most part, these have been sitcoms about families and mostly black ones. More often, when there's a female character of color on television, she doesn't have friends who are of the same race. These women, like Olivia Pope (Kerry Washington) on *Scandal,* Mindy Lahiri (Kaling) on *The Mindy Project,* or Gloria Delgado-Pritchett (Sofía Vergara) on *Modern Family,* are presented in white, mostly male worlds. "They have mostly white friendships," says Nancy Wang Yuen, a sociologist and author of *Reel Inequality: Hollywood Actors and Racism.* "There's an orientation toward a white culture. It would be so great to see women of color talk amongst women of color, but you don't see many relationships like that." Cable television and streaming services are starting to show more of them, like the friendship on *Insecure,* but network television largely does not.

The UPN show *Girlfriends,* which ran from 2000 to 2008, was an exception. It was created by Mara Brock Akil and was about four black friends—Toni (Jill Marie Jones), Maya (Golden Brooks), Lynn (Persia White), and Joan (Tracee Ellis Ross)—dealing with, and laughing about, career setbacks and disastrous romantic relationships. The show was sincerely interested in showing real-seeming black women. "*Girlfriends* doesn't get the credit it deserves for how uniquely it approaches the particular professional and personal issues black women have to deal with," wrote Angelica Jade Bastién in *The New York Times.*

That the show existed at all was because of UPN's commitment at the time to series that featured casts of black characters—there were at least ten—but a merger with the WB changed the direction of the programing so eventually there were no more black shows on the new network, The CW.

Brock Akil has wanted to make a movie version of *Girlfriends* since the series ended but hasn't gotten the studio that owns the rights to it to want to go ahead with it, which has been frustrating for her. "I was like, 'Guys, don't you understand the money you're missing? Do you not know how black women shop? Like, what are you doing? You have the analytics for it, why don't you want this money?'" she told *The Fader,* a music magazine. "Sometimes you can't help but think, 'Is there some conspiracy? You just don't want black women to feel good about themselves?' I don't understand. A lot of times, there's oversight. They don't think about us. There are blinders on and, whether they're deliberate or not, it doesn't make any sense."

Movies starring groups of women of color have been few and far between. In 1993, *The Joy Luck Club* had a cast of mostly Asian American women. It is based on Amy Tan's book of the same name about four Chinese women who immigrated to the United States—they get together to play mahjong—and their relationships with their American-born daughters. Critics liked it. "Handsomely brought to the screen with a cast of dozens of actresses and no men of any consequence, *The Joy Luck Club* is anything but a traditional women's picture," Janet Maslin wrote in a review in *The New York Times*.

And it was a financial success. It was shown in only about six hundred theaters and made 33 million dollars. But in the decades since then, no other movies have been released around a group of Asian American women. When the writer Jenny Han announced in an Instagram post that her young-adult romance book *To All the Boys I've Loved Before* was going to be adapted into a movie, she wrote "Guys, I'm over the moon. The most important thing for me as the author is seeing an Asian American girl in the starring role, and with this movie, we get to see not one but THREE! That is truly groundbreaking. I haven't seen Asian American women centered on the screen since *Joy Luck Club*, which was nearly 25 years ago."

In 1995, *Waiting to Exhale*, starring four black women, was an even bigger hit. The movie was adapted from Terry McMillan's book of the same name (she also cowrote the screenplay), and the tagline was "Friends are the people who let you be yourself—and never let you forget it." The four friends, Savannah (Whitney Houston), Bernadine (Angela Bassett), Robin (Lela Rochon), and Gloria (Loretta Devine), are all in various stages of being screwed over by men while leaning on—and whooping with—each other. I saw the movie at least fifteen years ago on cable but I can still recall them clinking champagne flutes and having a spontaneous dance party to TLC's *Creep*.

When the movie, which cost 15 million dollars to make, earned 45 million dollars in seventeen days, Elaine Dutka wrote in the *Los Angeles Times* that the movie was "part entertainment, part social phenomenon . . . Industry observers point out that the picture continues to build in suburban theaters catering predominantly to whites," she wrote. "And African American women are still turning out in droves." It would go on to make 67 million dollars total. "It showed women that in spite of fractured relationships, joy, peace, love and kinship are always a possibility," Bassett has said. "It broke perception, preconception and history."

Even so, it took decades for another movie starring black women who weren't historical figures to be made. In 2017, *Girls Trip* opened, about four college friends getting together to behave badly in New Orleans. Screenwriter Tracy Oliver told *The Hollywood Reporter* that she wanted to portray "black women being carefree and having fun just like everybody else.

I think we need to show all aspects of black lives. I love *Moonlight*, I love *Hidden Figures*, but I also want to see some people who are having fun and just showing female friends hanging out."

The women, Ryan (Regina Hall), Sasha (Queen Latifah), Lisa (Jada Pinkett Smith), and Dina (Tiffany Haddish), who call themselves the "Flossy Posse," drink, dance, and tell plenty of dick jokes ("All this NBA dick and she sucking a baseball player?!" Dina says about the woman having an affair with Ryan's husband), but they also show each other tons of loyalty and hard-earned love. To date, the movie has made 114 million dollars (it cost just 19 million dollars to make).

"I wanted some real relationships," the director Malcolm D. Lee told *The Hollywood Reporter*. "And my wife's book club watched the movie as one of my first audiences, and they laughed and loved it and said, 'I love how soft they are with each other.' If that's part of the takeaway of this bold, outrageous comedy, that's great."

I'm in a club of women. What we had in common at first was that we all watched *Scandal*, Shonda Rhimes's ABC show about Washington, DC, crisis fixer Olivia Pope, which is why it's called Scandal Club. It was Ruthie's idea to watch the premiere of the second season with four of our other friends, Amanda, Claire, Erica, and Marisa. She asked me if I'd host it at my apartment, and I e-mailed everyone, promising red wine and popcorn (Pope's only sustenance) and permanent adoration if anyone wore a white pantsuit (her uniform).

They all came—no one in a pantsuit—and we drank wine, double-fisted popcorn, and swooned over the outfits and Scott Foley. "I think I looked at it as a onetime thing," Ruthie says, "but I'm always trying to make groups happen, to be like 'now we're in Scandal Club, we're getting matching tattoos at nine P.M. sharp, you're welcome.'"

I'm not sure when we officially started calling it Scandal Club, but we met again and again and, even though we'd all known each other individually before, as a group everything about how we interacted became more intense. We shared more personal opinions, on superficial topics, like how to justify buying Isabel Marant boots, to more emotional ones, like what birth control we preferred. We talked through the nuances of big life changes—when Amanda got engaged, Claire and Erica sold their business, or Ruthie bought an apartment. We always hang out in each other's homes, never at restaurants or bars, which I think adds to the intimacy of the group. Getting together now feels necessary, and Scandal Club, which is really just being in a room with these women, helps me feel more grounded in who I am.

I don't remember the last time we watched the show. "For a while I would try to be like, 'my Scandal Club, but also sometimes we meet and don't watch *Scandal*,'" Amanda says. We now have text and e-mail chains so that we can volley our thoughts in between seeing each other in person. And we get together when we want to. It never feels like an obligation. We keep showing up because we like being together as a group. The comfort is compelling. "My number one pet peeve of groups of women is they're like, 'We all hate each other and we dread this and don't want to do it all, but we have to,'" Amanda says. "This is a choice, which makes it really nice. I'm like, 'No, I want to do this. I didn't get suckered into this.'"

What we have in common beyond similar tastes in pop culture is that we are all independent, married or not, and all in on listening to, advising, and cheering on each other's minor and major decisions. It's not like we always have a love-fest. We amuse ourselves plenty with petty gossip about celebrities and acquaintances. But I know whenever I'm with them, I can figure stuff out, out loud.

Lately, one thing I've been turning to my group of friends to talk about is the subject of kids. Of my friends who aren't yet parents, some of them know they want children, others know they don't, and some are unsure. We talk about our careers, our worries about the future our kids could grow up in, growing old, and how to make this choice deliberately. I never thought about having to figure out whether to become a mom. I haven't felt much societal pressure—my mom has literally never brought it up, which I understand is rare, at least from some of my friends who've had the opposite experience. For a long time, I assumed that, like marriage, having kids was something I'd do, that my life would lay out the moment I decided to get pregnant as part of a neat sequence, without me having to set the course. That didn't happen—and continues not to happen. There's a happy chaos in this. Life hasn't gone in the order I assumed it would, but what's happened instead has given me so many astonishing experiences and friendships I never could have scripted and am grateful for. It's freeing but it also forces me to think more consciously.

Until recently I wasn't absolutely sure that I did want to try to have a child. But talking to my friends about how this now has to become my choice, and the fears that come with that choice, made me realize that I do want to try to become a parent. All the angst that goes along with this decision—*Is this guy right? Am I too old? Should I do this by myself? Do I have enough money?*—is quieted when I turn to my friends, who root for me and calm me.

The friendships that are those safe spaces, the ones that feel more like tribes than anything else, are important. No matter what makes you feel like you belong with people—whatever specific set of characteristics you have in common, whether they're as broad as race or as frivolous as your love of *Gilmore Girls*—there's a sense that they can empathize with your experience in a way someone outside it can't. You can confide in each other without much worry that you might be misunderstood or come off as a jerk.

"With most groups, I'm desperate to be part of them," Ruthie says about Scandal Club. "And then when I am, I feel so isolated because I realize I'm my own person. But this group is based on genuine affection and mutual interest, not my fear of being unpopular. Our friendship is stable and real and rewarding. Also you're the coolest people I know."

These days, our tribes often come together electronically, through whom we interact with on social media, what newsletters we subscribe to, or which group chats we're in. Online, it's possible to corral people with common interests or experiences without any preamble or need to be in the same physical location.

When Elizabeth Spiridakis Olson, a creative director who was living in San Francisco, California, was pregnant with her first child, she noticed that a woman she'd met once and followed on Instagram was pregnant too. Their babies were born a week apart, and in the first month afterward, they'd both be up in the middle of the night nursing them, scrolling through Instagram, and liking each other's posts. They started texting. "I'm up for the one A.M. feeding," Elizabeth would write. "I'm doing the four A.M. feeding," the other woman, who lived on the East Coast, would respond.

"She became one of my most important touchstones," Elizabeth says. "I've only met her once but I feel close to her because I've talked to her about all of this stuff in my darkest hours. It all came out of having this shared experience of this newborn. I think with her I'm very honest about things, in a way that I'm not with friends I've known for years."

Another friend added her to a private Facebook group for moms, "a funny environment of mom real talk," Elizabeth says. "When I was up late at night, still sleep deprived, that was such an amazing community of women being like, 'Dude, I've fucking been there. I'm in it, or I'm still fucking there.' I'm on it every day still checking and it's been so important."

She never thought she'd be into mom groups online, but she found herself enjoying the freedom of being able to admit anything and knowing the women in the Facebook group would understand. "You need a safe space," she says. "There was a lot of shit going on. I surprised myself. Becoming a mom can be super-isolating, especially at these moments when it's the middle of the night and you're the one who's up. Even if you have the greatest partner, you're the one who's got to be the one in the shit with the baby and you feel super-alone. It's hard to tell yourself millions or billions of women have gone through this. You're in the dark. You're nursing the baby and you have your phone in your hand, and so I'd write the Facebook group: *'I'm ready to cry. My nipples are killing me. I wish I could drink some wine.'* And you have a ton of people who are like, *'Girl, I feel you.'"*

I feel the same way as I think about my choice to try to become a parent and the challenges if it happens. My friends will be there, even if they can't erase the anxiety—and there's a lot that's buoying about that. My life isn't organized like I thought it would be, but I can always tell my friends about my uncertainties and keep repeating them, and they will hear me every time. No matter how scared or vulnerable or far away from myself I might feel, they remind me that it's going to be okay. They make me feel safe.

How Our Friendships
End, Change, and Endure

Louise, no matter what happens,
I'm glad I came with you.

—Thelma in *Thelma & Louise*

I realize all of the time how much the women I love mean
to me: when I run into Ruthie on the street, when I have
coffee out of the mug Valerie sent me, when I instant message with Andrea in a panic about work or my personal life,
when I have one last glass of wine with Stephanie, or when I
close my door after the Scandal Club leaves.

And inevitably sometimes I'm struck by how much I don't
want to lose them. I want to preserve this moment where I
know I'm as important to them as they are to me. These relationships are as a crucial as any I have with men or blood
relatives or bosses, and I want these women in my life forever.

For so long I think, there's been a tacit, depressing assumption that our friendships, unlike our other relationships, should be temporary. We're made to believe that at some point we will have to distance ourselves from each other, whether that's to find romantic mates, raise children, assist elderly parents, or go after promotions. These ties of friendship, we're told, are not the ones that contribute to our being busy improving ourselves at all times.

But we're pressing back on this notion. We're caring for each other—loudly and continuously—for no reason besides wanting to. We're saying and showing: Our friends matter as much as our other attachments.

No matter how old we are, or what our lives look like, the women around us are essential. They're our travel buddies, spare key holders, preferred dates, secret keepers, cheerleaders, inspirations, and emergency contacts.

They have our trust. Amy Poehler wrote of Tina Fey in her memoir *Yes Please*, "Sometimes Tina is like a very talented bungee-jumping expert. All it takes is for Tina to softly say, *We can do this, right?* and I suddenly feel like I can jump off a bridge."

They have our hearts. At a movie screening, Michelle Williams said of Busy Philipps, "I'm here with my best friend. I'm so in love with her. She's proof that the love of your life does not have to be a man! That's the love of my life right there."

And we're not letting go. Recently, when Ruthie and I were at country singer Jason Isbell's concert, he played a song, "Cover Me Up"; part of the lyrics are "know you're enough / to use me for good." He said he wrote the song for his wife, but after Ruthie and I swayed to it, she joked, "I guess it's our song now."

Hundreds of years ago, there was a period when women's friends were supposed to be as valued as the other people in their worlds. In England in the nineteenth century, women were expected to keep their friends close, both before and after they married. "If a woman didn't have any friends, she wasn't a proper young lady," says Sharon Marcus, the author of *Between Women: Friendship, Desire, and Marriage in Victorian England.*

Unlike men and women, who weren't allowed to spend much time together unless they were husband and wife, women could see each other as much as they wanted. "No one restricted the freedom of female friends," Marcus says. "They were allowed to go on walks together. They were allowed to sleep together in the same bed."

Because of this, women were often closer to each other than their husbands by the time they married, between the ages of eighteen and twenty-five. Men weren't suspicious of, or threatened by, women's intimacy during this time. They didn't worry that it would jeopardize their marriages, make their wives less available to them, or impede their dominance in any way. "I think they mostly didn't care," Marcus says. "The safe generalization is that men didn't think much about women's relationships with women."

It was a time when people used passionate language even if they weren't talking about a lover, and women gushed about each other, as shown in journal entries Marcus includes in her book. In 1854, a young woman named Anne Thackeray (later Ritchie) writes about how she "fell in love with Miss Geraldine Mildmay" at one party and Lady Georgina Fullerton "won [her] heart" at another. In 1881, another woman writes about a deep childhood love for an older cousin while recounting her life for her daughter: "From my earliest recollections I adored her, following her and content to sit at her feet like a dog."

Friends wrote each other letters and visited each other's homes, trips that could last for weeks if they lived far apart because it was difficult to travel long distances. Women often kept a diary throughout, writing about how great it was to be there with their friend.

They maintained these strong bonds after they had children as well. In the mid-1800s, a woman named Mary Lundie Duncan wrote to her friend six weeks after the birth of her first child: "My beloved friend, do not think that I have been so long silent because all my love is centered in my new and most interesting charge. It is not so. My heart turns to you as it was ever wont to do, with deep and fond affection, and my love for my sweet babe makes me feel even more the value of your friendship."

Some female friends lived together during the nineteenth century as well, an arrangement chosen either as a way to maintain their independence and freedom or because they preferred their friend's companionship to anyone else's. Louisa May Alcott's 1869 novel *An Old-Fashioned Girl* introduced two artists, Becky and Lizzie, who "live together, and take care of one another in true Damon and Pythias style. This studio is their home—they work, eat, sleep, and live here, going halves in everything. They are all alone in the world, but as happy and independent as birds; real friends, whom nothing will part."

These partnerships came to be called "Boston marriages," a name most likely inspired by Henry James's 1886 novel *The Bostonians*, about two cohabiting women who were devoted to each other. James describes the main character, Olive Chancellor, as "unmarried by every implication of her being." He wrote that "she was a spinster as Shelley was a lyric poet, or as the month of August is sultry." Olive suggests to her protégée, Verena Tarrant, that they live together, imagining them enjoying "still winter evenings under the lamp, with falling snow outside, and tea on a little table."

Our friendships today aren't being shaped by society saying they're important for our propriety, but by women changing the rules themselves. We're reappropriating our friends as our people and soulmates. We're writing movies and television shows that take the way we are together seriously. We're tilting our culture by insisting on a solid spot for ourselves and our friendships in it, and a wider audience is responding.

The web series *Brown Girls* is about two best friends in their twenties in Chicago, Leila, a Muslim South Asian American writer, and Patricia, a black musician, who are trying to harmonize their cultural backgrounds with their career aspirations and romantic interests. The story is inspired by the writer Fatimah Asghar's own ten-year friendship with the singer Jamila Woods. "The people of *Brown Girls* are not caricatures," she told *Elle*.

The realness resonated. In 2017, HBO bought the rights to *Brown Girls* to turn it into a cable series, but it was nominated for an Emmy well ahead of its possible television debut, for Outstanding Short Form Comedy or Drama Series. "When I made it, I kinda thought it was just gonna be me and my friends watching it in our rooms," Fatimah has said. "To see the way that people have been responding to it has just [made me think,] no, people want shows like this."

Women talking about valuing and loving each other—and other people listening—is rounding out the way we see ourselves and the way others see us. We're pushing past the stereotypes of mean girls, one-note best friends, and single ladies. We're opening up more space for who women really are when we're together.

This doesn't mean that we won't ever step away from each other for something else. Sometimes we will.

About a year ago, two friends who I'll call Melissa and Alexandra were at their favorite beachfront bar in Naples, Florida, when Melissa told Alexandra she was moving. They both lived in New York and had been best friends since meeting in law school a decade before. They had established routines, like taking these wintertime trips to Naples or texting each other at the end of long workdays to see if the other had eaten dinner. On Saturdays, they'd be on the couch in one of their apartments watching TV and scrolling through their phones, barely talking. To work events and parties, they'd bring each other as their plus ones. "If I was invited to something, I could say, 'Oh yeah, we'll be there,' and that meant me and Melissa," Alexandra says. They dated guys, sometimes had boyfriends, but "there were so many periods where we were both single," she says, "and even when we weren't, but especially when we were, she was my person."

Now Melissa was telling Alexandra she was moving to Austin. Partly she wanted to live closer to her mom in Dallas, who would be a three-hour drive away. She also thought she was working too much. In Austin, she hoped to find a law-firm job that wouldn't dominate her life. But she was also trying to get some space from Alexandra so she could force herself to date. She wanted to marry and have children. "It's not going to happen for us if we stay in the same place," she told Alexandra. "You and I are kind of holding each other down because it's so easy to be together that we don't force ourselves to go out and look for real partners."

Alexandra was upset. She wanted to have children too, but she'd been thinking about reshaping her previous mind-set that she needed to have a husband to do so. "I was very content and I was sort of at a place in my life where I thought maybe if I could have a child and have a significant relationship, it didn't need to be a sexual, romantic relationship," she says.

Alexandra thought that she and Melissa could have moved in together, been artificially inseminated by the same sperm donor, and raised their kids as siblings—a present-day version of the nineteenth-century Boston marriage. "I don't think I would do it with anyone else," she says, "but I would have done it with her. I'm kind of never not in awe of her. She's so smart. She just really educates herself in so many ways but is still fun and likes all of the right pop culture. We're always saying to each other, 'You like all the right things.'"

Even as she was considering this altered future, Alexandra knew that it wouldn't work for Melissa. She was more traditional than Alexandra and wanted a romantic relationship with the person she chose to start a family with, "and that's totally fair," Alexandra says.

Melissa kept trying to reassure Alexandra that their friendship wouldn't change. At dinner the night before she left, she kept saying, "It'll be the same. We'll see each other all of the time."

Alexandra wasn't as optimistic. "It felt like such a loss, such a profound loss," she says, "and I think that what's the weirdest thing is that she went and had this whole new life and I was going to our same places. She had this escape plan."

About six months after moving to Austin, Melissa met the man who'd become her fiancé. Alexandra likes him and knows he wants her to be his friend too (when they met, he emphasized how much he'd heard about her). "He totally appreciates how smart and great Melissa is," Alexandra says, "and he's that way himself and it's sort of amazing to me that she found someone who complements her so well, that is worthy of her."

The two friends are less entwined now. For example, if Alexandra has a work trip, she won't automatically suggest Melissa join her anymore. Melissa's busy planning her wedding and traveling with her fiancé. But Alexandra still calls

Melissa her best friend. "I have people that I probably wasn't as close to when she was here that I've become closer to," she says, "but not that one person, which I wouldn't want. I would be super-upset if she had one person in Austin. But I have people. I have a really busy life. I don't go home and cry every night. But I think that when she was here, I felt like I had a person to be my person, and I don't have that anymore. And again I don't want to replace her, but it's hard not to have that."

It is impossible to keep our friendships static. I wish it wasn't, but it is. I know that I had different priorities and goals a decade ago and I may change just as much in the next ten years. My friends might too. The people who are part of my everyday right now—who invite me to dinners and plays and movies and yoga, who amuse me, and who understand me—may be less present someday. Or I may not be there for them anymore. I accept that everything evolves. I can't will my friendships to stay exactly as they are today.

We move, get new jobs, fall in love, or give birth, and sometimes there isn't going to be a way to equalize everyone in our lives, whether the imbalance comes from logistical or emotional upheaval, or some combination of both.

Susanna Fogel and Joni Lefkowitz, who are both screenwriters in Los Angeles, tried to work through the shift in their friendship when Joni met her now wife.

They'd been best friends and writing partners for six years and had just reached a professional high point: being in

Baltimore for six weeks overseeing the filming of a script they'd written that, if all went well, could lead to an HBO series.

"Had we both been single, it would have been an adventure that was just about us," Susanna says. They would have had martinis in the hotel lobby and watched movies in each other's rooms. But Joni had brought along her new wife, whom Susanna barely knew. "I was quickly getting to know her while having this professionally overwhelming experience that I wanted to share with only Joni," she says. "I felt like I'd lost my person and the celebration we'd been working for had to be shared with someone I didn't know."

The two of them met in 2002 when they were both twenty-two, in a comedy writing class. During one lecture, another student said something that irritated Susanna. Joni was rolling her eyes too. They looked at each other and became instant friends. "The shared experience of bonding over someone else's lameness is the glue of female friendship," Susanna says.

They realized they had similar senses of humor, whether that meant enjoying mocking the reality show *America's Next Top Model* or the customers at the American Girl store where Joni worked. They started writing together, often at the mall, because they thought that was a funny place to work, and after spending the day together would go out to a bar or dance club. They rarely saw anyone but each other. "We formed these rituals that were our whole lives together, a way to deal with the anxiety of being adults," Susanna says.

They had a secret language, which Susanna describes as

"very bizarre" and so many inside jokes that she pitied anyone else hanging out with them. "We felt like we were each
other's appendages," she says. Having success as writers
made them even tighter. "We felt like our problems were different than our friends' problems," she says. "We thought we
were the only people who could understand what we were
going through."

Joni coming out as a lesbian, two years into the friendship,
only made them better friends. Susanna was straight and
liked their new best-friend identity. "It was a fun twist on
how we defined ourselves," she says. "We were these hipster
girls with bangs and one was a lesbian and one was not." She
and Joni started going to lesbian bars together, where Susanna liked being the only straight girl.

But then Joni met the woman who would become her
wife and Susanna started to feel shut out, especially because
the other person vying for her best friend was also a woman.
A lot of what they used to do before—girls' night out, getting
massages, watching rom-coms—now included Joni's partner,
too, and Susanna wasn't always glad to have her around.

"We're force-fed the importance of the romantic narrative," she says. "You're expected to be hurtling toward this
goal of finding a partner and you're supposed to be happy for
anyone who achieves that goal. But of course there's a feeling
of loss, but you don't talk about that because you're supposed
to be one hundred percent happy."

Joni would say to her, "Aren't you happy for me? I found
this person."

What Susanna wanted to say, but didn't, was, "I'm happy

for you, but I'm also bummed out that we can't have a girls' night without your girlfriend there. I don't want to tell your girlfriend about my personal life. I want to tell my best friend about it."

Instead, she didn't say anything, which led to her being unhappy while they were on the film set in Baltimore. That was the moment when she thought, *I have to go make some new friends.*

Often it can feel easier to make a friendship a former friendship than to talk about what's going on. "We have a culture that just lets friendships drift apart," says Shasta Nelson, the author of *Frientimacy: How to Deepen Friendships for Lifelong Health and Happiness.* It can hurt to break up with a friend just as much, if not more, than to break up with a lover, but women don't grieve these losses as publicly. When boys break our hearts we cry into pints of ice cream, burn their stuff, or turn the pain into *Lemonade.*

When we lose our friends, we barely even commiserate about it, even though it's an awful absence, too. As Lena Dunham wrote in *Lenny Letter,* a feminist newsletter she cofounded, about a friend who had stopped speaking to her, "It was a loss with no upside. It was hell."

Because Susanna and Joni were still writing together, they decided to hash out why they were both hurt, a reckoning they turned into a movie about friends breaking up, called *Life Partners.* "It was our way of processing our transition together," Susanna says.

In *Life Partners,* Paige (Gillian Jacobs), who's straight, and Sasha (Leighton Meester), who's gay, have a routine a lot like

Susanna and Joni's once was, where they hate-watch *America's Next Top Model* and have sleepovers. "I just want to meet a guy that I like as much as you, is that too much to ask for?" Paige says one night while they're falling asleep.

"Yes, yes, it is," Sasha says. "I hate everyone but you. We're screwed."

But Paige does meet a guy she starts to like as much Sasha, Tim (Adam Brody). She invites him to watch *Top Model* with them and tells him all about Sasha's life, including details Sasha didn't want her to share.

"I may have told Tim that you went out with like three girls recently who live at home," Paige says.

"Oh, wow, you told Tim a lot about me," Sasha says.

In real life, Susanna and Joni had gone through a similar clash in Baltimore, where she felt like Joni's partner knew personal things about her that she didn't want her to. "Someone else was trying to share in those in-jokes about my life," she says. "It felt like a violation." Joni, on the other hand, thought Susanna was being selfish and not accepting her wife.

After they left Baltimore, they kept disagreeing about how to keep their friendship going now that one of them was in a serious romantic relationship. Joni wanted space to focus on her new marriage, while Susanna wanted the friendship to be as intense as it used to be. She called Joni once after a fight with her boyfriend and was upset when she didn't hear back from Joni for two days.

"I was in Palm Springs with my wife," Joni said when they finally talked.

"But I needed you," Susanna said.

There's a similar moment in *Life Partners* when Sasha says to Paige, "Guess I should've known that as soon as you found someone else to couple up with that you'd be done with me."

"Sasha, that is not fair," Paige says. "Okay, yes, I am less available to you now than I was before when there was no one else in my life and we talked every night till two in the morning. But that was always gonna change when one of us met someone. I mean you don't talk to your friends till two in the morning anymore, you stop needing that."

"But you still have that," Sasha says. "You still talk to someone at two in the morning, it's just him now. Nothing changed for you. It just changed for me. Can you acknowledge that, please?"

Their friendship isn't the same at the end of the movie—they're watching *Top Model* on separate couches. Susanna and Joni, too, stopped working together after *Life Partners*. Susanna went to London to write a book, while Joni got a job as a co–executive producer on *New Girl* in Los Angeles. They're still friends, but "it's different," Susanna says. "We just don't have that much in common."

But even as our individual friendships fluctuate, we're not going to stop reaching out to each other. There is no longer an automatic endpoint for prioritizing friendships, like there was for my mom or other women her age, even if they aren't with the same women we met in kindergarten, as college, freshmen, or at our first jobs. We're continuing to stretch toward each other.

When Carla Bruce-Eddings, a publicist in New York who's in her late twenties, was five months pregnant with her first child, she felt lonely. She had a husband and lots of friends, but none of them were pregnant. With her friends, "there was always this underlying sense that they were fascinated, or shocked or freaked out, by what I told them about pregnancy," she says. "That got kind of wearying."

She wanted to commiserate with other women who were about to have their first babies too, and she wanted them to be women of color. "I'm black and I wanted to have other friends who could understand where I was coming from in multiple areas of my life, not just pregnancy," she says.

She'd never had a community like that before. "I grew up in a mostly white town," she says. "My college was mostly white. I wanted to be around people who I could relate to on a deeper level."

But when Carla tried to find a group like this on Meetup .com, she couldn't. Her husband suggested she should start the group she was looking for.

She called it "First Time Moms of Color in Brooklyn." Women found it quickly and many messaged Carla, "I'm so glad you started this group."

Eight pregnant women showed up to the first meeting, brunch at one of Carla's favorite restaurants. "It was the best morning ever," she says. "It was hours of complaining, but the best complaining ever."

Her daughter is two now and the group still exists. Some of the members see each other often, whether that's for a playdate at one of their homes, a trip to a museum, or an impromptu evening park visit to tire out the kids before bedtime.

"Knowing I have this community gives me a lot of peace of mind," Carla says. "These women more or less understand what I'm going through at every stage of parenting. There's an intimacy because we're sharing this journey."

Carly de Castro and Stephanie Danler, best friends who met as college freshmen, found that getting married and having children strengthened their relationship instead of ushering in its end.

They were sitting in Psych 101 at Kenyon College in Gambier, Ohio, when Stephanie overheard Carly say that she needed a car to visit her boyfriend in Indiana. She didn't know her but offered, "You can take mine."

"I couldn't believe it," Carly said. "It was like six hours away."

They got along well—both were studious and liked to read poetry and talk about ethics and social justice—and decided to live together while studying abroad in Rome. While their classmates were out exploring the city, the two of them felt lonely and homesick. They spent most of their time isolated in the apartment; they'd buy a wheel of Brie and eat it for dinner most nights. "Carly and I were seeing each other at our worst," Stephanie says.

After college, they lived near each other for a few years in New York, but found themselves on opposite schedules. Carly worked during the day as a publicist and Stephanie worked at night as a restaurant server. It began to take effort to see each other. At one point, Carly sent Stephanie an e-mail she blew off. She thought, *I'll see her when I see her.* Carly got mad and wrote her again, *"You can't not respond to me."*

Stephanie agreed. "She taught me how to keep this relationship going," Stephanie says. "She trained me so well. We are always available to each other." Now if Stephanie's driving on the freeway and gets a text from Carly, she'll pull over.

"She was a good escape artist with a lot of people in her life," Carly says. "I need there to be a connection. I can't have her go silent. It became part of our life to really communicate."

When Carly moved to Los Angeles to take care of her mom, who'd been diagnosed with a brain tumor, she wasn't worried about the friendship faltering. They kept talking to and visiting each other as both of their lives changed. Carly's mom died. Stephanie got married. Carly started a juice company, Pressed Juicery. Stephanie quit her job to write a novel, what eventually became the bestselling *Sweetbitter*. Carly got pregnant. Stephanie got divorced.

"Everything just shifted," Stephanie says. "We grew up. The friendship carried us into the next phase of our lives."

Carly was pregnant when their five-year college reunion was happening, but instead of flying back to Kenyon, Stephanie went to see Carly. "A lot of our other classmates didn't know what to do with me," Carly says. "We were young, and they didn't understand. Steph was like, 'We're going to do this.' I couldn't have gotten through that time without her support."

Stephanie rubbed her friend's swollen feet and read all the books she could about pregnancy and birth. "My friend was going through this crazy life change," she says. "I thought, *I'm going to learn as much as I can about it,* because I wanted to go on this journey with her. It felt like it was happening to me."

At the same time, Carly was there when Stephanie's marriage was ending. Stephanie went back to Los Angeles and spent weeks sleeping on Carly's couch. "The solace and the peace that I found there was lifesaving," she says.

Carly was also there while Stephanie was working on *Sweetbitter.* She called Stephanie before and after each publishing meeting, and Carly's publicist training came in handy once the book was released. Stephanie would also ask for her to be cc'd on important e-mails. "There's no jealousy because it feels like it's happening to you," Carly said. "There's not a lot of pettiness. We just don't have room for it. We each have a deep respect for what the other is focusing on."

Today, Stephanie lives in Los Angeles and often goes over to Carly's when Carly's son gets home from school. "Her family gives me all of this joy in my life that I don't have yet," she says. They will cook dinner; Stephanie usually does the dishes. "There is this profound understanding that comes from growing up together," she says. "Our lives look so different, but we get to live vicariously through the other person."

When we're little our friendships are encouraged, even seen as vital. The actress Molly Ringwald has talked about raising her daughter to rely on other girls. "Playdates are more important than you realize," she told *Lenny Letter.* "Connection is a skill that's taught, and girls really need to learn to trust women, to know that their women friends will have their back, and that you can talk to your female friends about things you can't talk to anyone else about. I think that's something that begins in childhood."

When we get a little older, that dependence on and celebration of our friendships is still there.

Jewelbots is a start-up company that makes bracelets for preteen girls that encourage them to learn to write computing code. Initially the cofounders thought that they could program the jewelry to light up to match the girls' outfits, but they tested the idea with some girls who hated it. "That's lame," they said.

They thought again about what the bracelets could do and came back to their trial audience with another idea.

"What if the bracelet lit up when your friends were around?"

The girls freaked out.

"Signaling affection for your friends wasn't our original idea," Jewelbots cofounder Sara Chipps says. "It was very important to them."

But sometime after we outgrow our best-friend jewelry, we can forget how much we depend on and cherish each other. It can get lost in the hurricane of hearing that we're supposed to compete with one another, find a husband already, or preempt everything else for our children.

For a long time, I shut out how much the girls around me mattered, and even though I found my way back to a tribe of women who make me light up whenever I see any one of them, sometimes it's still hard for me to believe that these kind of friendships can be sustained for the rest of my life.

Sometimes when I think about finding a romantic partner or becoming a mother, I automatically tally how that will change my behavior as a friend.

I worry, *It might be impossible to make sure everyone important to me stays that way.* If I lived with a boyfriend or husband, I think, the Scandal Club might have to stop meeting at my apartment. If I had a child, instead of going to a friend's house for dinner and talking until midnight, I assume, I'd leave hours earlier or maybe not be able to go at all.

But then I stop and see what's really happening. The women around me are adapting to these kinds of changes. I have friends whom I met when we were both single who are now partnered, raising children, or both. Even though I'm not doing the same thing, I want to stay in their lives and also get to know all of these new people they love—and they want me to as well. I see them alone, with their partners, and with their children.

It's true that some of them no longer have as much time to hang out or have interests that aren't the same as mine, but these are shifts I accept, not ones that will decimate the friendships. What I feel when we get to be in the same place— or when we talk on the phone, text, e-mail, or instant message—is the same steady appreciation of each other. I've been learning from these women in my life for years, and I don't want to stop.

When I hear my friends talk about waking up with their husbands or taking their kids to school, when I watch them balancing their families with their professional success and ambition, I think, *I love getting to see this new version of her.*

Julia Chang, who works for a financial planning company in New York, feels the same. She's single and doesn't have kids, but most of her friends are married and moms. Sometimes they meet for playdates without her. "Do I want to be at their playdates?" she says. "Not necessarily. So that doesn't create a rift in the relationship, but it's a definite pivot point. Their priorities, their goals, what their day-to-day life is like, is so different from mine."

But that doesn't mean they're not going to stay close. The history and emotional connections are still there no matter what else is happening outside the friendship.

"Some of my friends knew me when I was eighteen," Julia says. "They saw me when I had short hair and only wore baby tees, baggy jeans, and red lipstick. So they've seen me evolve. I can say the same for them, too. I've seen how they've changed. I think it's cool to watch people grow up, to watch them get married, to watch them be moms and raising kids. I'm pretty sure the friends I have now who I've known for ten years or longer will be the friends I grow old with."

Sometimes the group jokes about this. One friend texted them a photo of their future selves, a group of septuagenarian Korean women, all with short, permed hair, wearing visors and tracksuits. "This will be us," she wrote.

"I think she's right," Julia says. "I feel like I will know them until the day I die basically, and I don't think there are many people you can say that about."

We keep on figuring out ways to keep each other close. With my friends who have moved, like Carmel, social media helps. I think it's a neat trick that she can put a picture on

Instagram from Sydney, of her at the beach, at a Lana Del Ray concert, or killing it in a red gown, while I'm sleeping, and I can like it when I wake up in New York.

But I also know that with my friends who are far away, there are gaps between visits or rambling phone calls when our social media connections can become our whole relationship. I got a long e-mail from Carmel that I didn't respond to, even though it made me laugh, feel loved, and wish we still sat side by side every day. Instead, I kept feverishly liking her posts, as if these digital crumbs of affection were good enough.

Months later, I finally did write her back, a mishmash of skin-care recommendations, my confusion about deciding I wanted to have a child but not being sure how to do it, and gossip about our former coworkers. "I always feel like I can tell you anything and you'll get it and not judge," I wrote near the end.

In the morning, I had a response from Carmel, commiserating about how it sucks to be unsure about your choices, telling me her own feelings about having children, and of course offering more thoughts about skin care. She said she wished she could visit but no matter what, she was there. "I love you and think the world of you," she wrote.

There are so many ways women can be there for each other. We can be revelations. Having Renée in my life again is something I didn't expect. That evening in Los Angeles, sharing pizza, sparkling wine, and high school memories, reshaped how I thought about her. It made me realize how hard we have to try to see each other and how much I want to keep looking. Whenever she comes to New York or I go to Texas, we try to meet. She texted me after one dinner: *You are beautiful, beloved and believed in.*

We can be protectors. Ellie made me remember how we were always looking out for each other in college and how much we're still in sync even if we don't hang out often. We texted the other day about the suckiness of getting older. "At least we're in this together," she wrote.

"Forever," I responded.

And we can be rocks. What we've built and what we're sending out into the world is resilient, as strong as, or stronger than, what we have, or will have, with anyone else we might lean on in life.

The other day I asked Ruthie, "Do you think we'll stay friends?"

"I fucking hope so, Kayleen," she said.

I fucking hope so too.

In going back and thinking about my friendships and hearing about other women's, I see this: Our friends are not our second choices. They are our dates for Friday nights and for ex-boyfriends' weddings. They are the visitors to our hometowns and hospital rooms. They are the first people we tell about any news, whether it's good, terrible, or mundane. They are our plus ones at office parties. They are the people we're raising children with. They are our advocates, who, no matter what, make us feel like we won't fail. They are the people who will struggle with us and who will stay with us. They are who we text when we get home.

NOTES

INTRODUCTION:
WHY WOMEN TELL EACH OTHER,
"TEXT ME WHEN YOU GET HOME"

2   **I hear it on television, too:** *Insecure,* created by Issa Rae and Larry Wilmore, 2016, HBO, television series.

2   **"We accept this state":** Blythe Baird, "Pocket-Sized Feminism," Blythe Brooklyn, September 20, 2015, http://blythebrooklyn.tum blr.com/post/129541421701/pocket-sized-feminism-the-only-other -girl-at-the.

7   **"I just can't imagine":** Briallen Hopper, interview with the author, July 15, 2016.

7   **There just isn't only one love story in our lives:** Rebecca Traister, *All the Single Ladies: Unmarried Women and the Rise of an Independent Nation* (New York: Simon & Schuster, 2016).

7   **"The most consistent, central relationships":** Julie Beck, *"Playing House*: Finally, a TV Show Gets Female Friendships Right," *The Atlantic,* April 28, 2014, https://www.theatlantic.com/entertain ment/archive/2014/04/playing-house-finally-a-tv-show-gets-female -friendships-right/361308/.

7   **"A woman will always":** Julie Ma, "25 Famous Women on Female Friendship," *The Cut,* April 21, 2015, https://www.thecut.com /2015/04/25-famous-women-on-female-friendship.html.

8   **aggressively and sometimes nonsensically complimentary:** *Parks and Recreation,* created by Greg Daniels and Michael Schur, 2009, NBC, television series.

8   **a protective, empowering clutch:** *Big Little Lies,* directed by Jean-Marc Vallée, 2017, HBO, television series.

9   **"We don't have external structures in place":** Hopper, interview.

9   **we value them because they're beautiful:** Alexander Nehamas, interview with the author, October 17, 2016.

10   **"the world is a really hard place":** Julie Klam, interview with the author, July 26, 2016.

CHAPTER 1:
THE FRIENDSHIPS THAT SHAPED OUR OWN

13   **"As I've gotten older":** Jane Fonda and Lily Tomlin, "A Hilarious Celebration of Lifelong Female Friendship," filmed May 2015, TED video, https://www.ted.com/talks/jane_fonda_and_lily_tomlin_a _hilarious_celebration_of_lifelong_female_friendship/tran script?language=en#t-210200.

13   **My mom stayed by herself:** Judy Schaefer, interview with the author, March 10, 2017.

14   **the contemporary view of how to live:** Judith E. Smith, interview with the author, June 2, 2017.

15   **never felt lonely:** Schaefer, interview.

16   **She and her new husband lived on a cul-de-sac:** Judy Blume, interview with the author, October 19, 2016.

18   **"you don't find the word 'friend' connected to women":** Marilyn Sandidge, interview with the author, July 8, 2016.

18   **Men wrote what they thought:** Catherine Mooney, *Gendered Voices: Medieval Saints and Their Interpreters* (Philadelphia: University of Pennsylvania Press, 1999).

19   **"Only men were strong enough":** Sandidge, interview.

19   **Aristotle's breakdown of the elements:** Ibid.

20   **the pseudonym Orinda:** Ibid.

20   **"But never had Orinda found":** Katherine Philips, "To My Excellent Lucasia, on Our Friendship," Poetry Foundation, https://www .poetryfoundation.org/poems/50445/to-my-excellent-lucasia-on -our-friendship.

20 **"A Discourse of the Nature, Offices, and Measures of Friendship":** Jeremy Taylor, Reginald Heber, Eduard Koschwitz, and Charles Page Eden, *The Whole Works of the Right Rev. Jeremy Taylor . . . : Sermons* (Ulan Press, 2012).

22 **my grandmother, Christine:** Schaefer, interview.

22 **wrote more than four hundred letters to each other:** Joan Reardon, *As Always, Julia: The Letters of Julia Child and Avis DeVoto* (Rux Martin/Houghton Mifflin Harcourt, 2010).

22 **"The letters weren't emotional":** Joan Reardon, interview with the author, November 14, 2016.

25 **how important it is to have friends:** Shasta Nelson, interview with the author, July 13, 2016.

25 **my mom did exactly this:** Schaefer, interview.

26 **her mom's best friend would call:** Emily Rapp Black, interview with the author, October 27, 2016.

27 **"You never know what your kids pick up":** Mary Rapp, interview with the author, November 16, 2016.

28 **there weren't many films about women:** Mary Agnes Donoghue, interview with the author, August 11, 2016.

28 **"I knew it was a rare thing":** Walter Scott, "Barbara Hershey on Her Favorite Fairy Tale and Hanging Out with Bette Midler," *Parade,* February 17, 2013, https://parade.com/125599/walterscott/barbara-hershey-once-upon-a-time/.

29 **"all they do is fight":** Donoghue, interview.

29 **the panel's on-air disagreements:** Ryan Buxton, "Rosie Perez: Calling 'The View' a 'Catfight' Is 'Pure Sexism at Play,'" *The Huffington Post,* December 9, 2014, http://www.huffingtonpost.com/2014/12/09/rosie-perez-the-view-sexism_n_6298212.html.

29 **Mormon men practicing polygamy:** Benjamin G. Ferris, *Utah and the Mormons: The History, Government, Doctrines, Customs, and Prospects of the Latter-day Saints* (Silver Street Media, 2011).

30 **catfights were a staple of fetish films:** Irving Klaw, "Pin-Up Beauties Fight," YouTube video, posted by "Geoffe Haney," December 27, 2014, https://www.youtube.com/watch?v=PWedrtF0-IU.

30 **fought mostly over oil tycoon:** *Dynasty,* created by Richard and Esther Shapiro, 1981, ABC, television series.

31 **"*Dynasty* upped the ante":** Susan J. Douglas, *Where the Girls Are: Growing Up Female with the Mass Media* (New York: Three Rivers Press, 1995).

31 **Women could interact in ways other than:** Donoghue, interview.

32 **"I had a girlfriend who really changed my life":** "Bette Midler—Interview about *Beaches*," *Entertainment Tonight*, YouTube video, posted by "TheDivineBetteMidler," September 16, 2012, https://www.youtube.com/watch?v=hTdVRQbnJwM.

32 **"I just loved my girlfriends":** Donoghue, interview.

33 **CC racing to visit Hillary in the hospital:** *Beaches*, directed by Garry Marshall (Burbank, CA: Touchstone Pictures, 1988), film.

34 **"I'm not running Gary down":** Donoghue, interview.

35 **"It truly isn't the same":** Donoghue, interview.

36 **"the vague view that we are all life's driftwood":** Janet Maslin, "Reviews/Film; A Friendship, On and Off the Rocks," *The New York Times*, December 21, 1988, http://www.nytimes.com/movie/review?res=940DE1D6153AF932A15751C1A96E948260&mcubz=2.

36 **"Did you ever know that you're my hero?":** Bette Midler, "Wind Beneath My Wings," written by Jeff Silbar and Larry Henley, 1989, Atlantic, CD single.

36 **on a flight in business class:** Donoghue, interview.

37 **"older women in Miami":** Dustin Fitzharris, "Catching Up with the Golden Girls' Susan Harris," *Out*, October 3, 2010, https://www.out.com/entertainment/television/2010/10/03/catching-golden-girls-susan-harris.

37 **"We managed to compromise":** Stacey Wilson Hunt, "*The Golden Girls* Creators on Finding a New Generation of Fans and Giving George Clooney One of His Earliest Jobs," *Vulture*, March 3, 2017, http://www.vulture.com/2017/03/the-golden-girls-creators-on-finding-new-fans.html.

37 **"You will always be my sisters, always":** *The Golden Girls*, created by Susan Harris, 1985, NBC, television series.

38 **"wanted to elevate the concept of female friendship":** Linda Bloodworth Thomason, interview with the author, October 19, 2016.

38 **include it in the network's lineup:** Ibid.

38   **worked together at an interior design firm:** *Designing Women,* created by Linda Bloodworth Thomason, 1986, CBS, television series.

39   **"the excitement of them intellectually":** Bloodworth Thomason, interview.

39   **"hadn't been addressed on television":** Fitzharris. "Catching Up."

39   **"I wanted to have a little penisectomy":** Bloodworth Thomason, interview.

40   **personally hurtful to each other:** *The Golden Girls.*

40   **"the things that women have to overcome":** Bloodworth Thomason, interview.

40   **five friends she's been close with:** Dawn Carlson, interview with the author, March 13, 2017.

42   **"They were strapped to their babies":** Ibid.

42   **she'd moved away from the cul-de-sac:** Blume, interview.

42   **the story of Vix and Caitlin:** Judy Blume, *Summer Sisters* (New York: Delacorte Books, 1998).

43   **"It was the first thing":** Sheila Heti and Ross Simonini, eds., "Judy Blume and Lena Dunham in Conversation," *The Believer,* December 3, 2013, http://judyblume.com/reference/jweb/archived_articles/2013_12_Believer_Magazine_dunhamblume.pdf.

43   **read it six times:** Ruthie, interview with the author, August 11, 2017.

43   **"my least autobiographical book":** Blume, interview.

44   **socializing only with other couples:** Ibid.

45   **making new friends:** Schaefer, interview.

46   **a kayaking adventure in Alaska:** Ibid.

CHAPTER 2:
MEAN GIRLS AND NICE GIRLS

47   **"Gretchen, I'm sorry":** *Mean Girls,* screenplay by Tina Fey (Hollywood, CA: Paramount Pictures, 2004), film.

48   **Regina's classmates describe their obsession:** Ibid.

51   **felt the same way about *Essence*:** Elaine Welteroth, interview with the author, August 19, 2016.

51   **called Girl World:** Rosalind Wiseman, *Queen Bees & Wannabes: Helping Your Daughter Survive Cliques, Gossip, Boyfriends, and Other Realities of Adolescence* (New York: Three Rivers Press, 2002).

52   **their first response was often about how *mean* girls are:** Nancy Jo Sales, interview with the author, October 21, 2016.

53   **anecdotal examples of girls being tormented by other girls:** Rachel Simmons, *Odd Girl Out: The Hidden Culture of Aggression in Girls* (San Diego, CA: Harcourt, 2002).

53   **"relational aggression":** Kaj Björkqvist, "A Cross-Cultural Investigation of Sex Differences and Developmental Trends in Regard to Direct and Indirect Aggression: An Ongoing Research Project," Åbo Akademi University, http://www.vasa.abo.fi/svf/up/indirect.htm.

53   **working as a self-defense teacher:** Margaret Talbot, "Girls Just Want to Be Mean," *The New York Times*, February 24, 2002, http://www.nytimes.com/2002/02/24/magazine/girls-just-want-to-be-mean.html.

54   **a handbook for parents:** Rosalind Wiseman, interview with the author, June 29, 2016.

54   **how they behaved among their friend groups:** Wiseman, *Queen Bees & Wannabes.*

55   **"It's important for people to have a language":** Wiseman, interview.

55   **"The weird thing about hanging out with Regina":** *Mean Girls.*

55   **"normal, if regrettable, girl behavior":** Nancy Jo Sales, *American Girls: Social Media and the Secret Lives of Teenagers* (New York: Knopf, 2016).

56   **"You think you're really pretty?":** *Mean Girls.*

58   **a thriller about high school cheerleaders:** Megan Abbott, *Dare Me* (Reagan Arthur Books, 2012).

58   **"By and large, what's true":** Megan Abbott, interview with the author, October 18, 2016.

59   **dark comedy about high school cliques:** *Heathers*, directed by Michael Lehmann (Atlanta, GA: New World Pictures, 1988), film.

59   **"One of the things I loved":** Michael Lehmann, interview with the author, May 17, 2017.

60   **"I approach 'Heathers' as a traveler":** Roger Ebert, "Heathers," Roger Ebert's website, March 31, 1989, http://www.rogerebert .com/reviews/heathers-1989.

60   **"People saw it":** Lehmann, interview.

60   **"It's frightening and dark":** Abbott, interview.

60   **"the phrase 'mean girls'":** Lehmann, interview.

61   **"it was shocking to me":** Sales, interview.

61   **The studies that first:** Ibid.

61   **there was no proof that girls were any more vicious:** Pamela Orpinas, Caroline McNicholas, Lusine Nahapetyan, and Alana Vivolo-Kantor, "The Myth of 'Mean Girls,'" StopBullying.gov, September 10, 2015, https://www.stopbullying.gov/blog/2015/09/10 /myth-mean-girls.

62   **a backlash to the feminist movement in the 1990s:** Sales, interview.

62   **a duo who runs from the law:** *Thelma & Louise,* written by Callie Khouri (Beverly Hills, CA: Metro-Goldwyn-Mayer, 1991), film.

62   **wasn't seeing women represented:** Alex Denney, "Dissecting the Feminist Legacy of Thelma & Louise," *Dazed,* n.d., http://www .dazeddigital.com/artsandculture/article/31284/1/dissecting-the -feminist-legacy-of-thelma-louise.

63   **forcefully lifts up sisterhood:** Bikini Kill, "Rebel Girl," 1993, 7-inch single.

63   **weren't being called on in class:** American Association of University Women, "Shortchanging Girls, Shortchanging America," American Association of University Women, 1991, http://www .aauw.org/files/2013/02/shortchanging-girls-shortchanging -america-executive-summary.pdf.

63   **conversations with hundreds of girls:** Mary Pipher, *Reviving Ophelia: Saving the Selves of Adolescent Girls* (New York: Riverhead Books, 2005).

63   **"there was a momentary awakening":** Sales, interview.

64   **The dance had been built up:** *Pretty in Pink,* written by John Hughes (Los Angeles, CA: Paramount Pictures, 1986), film.

65–66   **"If you tell somebody enough":** Sales, interview.

66   **"What are little girls made of?":** "What Are Little Girls Made Of?" Land of Nursery Rhymes, http://www.landofnurseryrhymes

.co.uk/htm_pages/What%20Are%20Little%20Girls%20Made%
20Of.htm.

66 **"People are mean"**: Sales, interview.

67 **contributing to the stereotype:** Wiseman, interview.

67 **Her response surprised me:** Renée Tarwater, interview with the author, September 22, 2016.

68 **"I think 'effortlessly' is probably not":** Renée Tarwater, interview with the author, September 27, 2016.

69 **what friends did to her:** Ibid.

70 **she tried to friend an old classmate:** Ibid.

70 **"please forgive me":** Tarwater, interview, September 22, 2016.

CHAPTER 3:
ALL ABOUT THE BOYS

72 **"No man is capable":** Julie Ma, "25 Famous Women on Female Friendship," *The Cut,* April 21, 2015, https://www.thecut.com/2015/04/25-famous-women-on-female-friendship.html.

73 **Rush is not chill:** "UPC Fall Recruitment Schedule—August 2017," Sorority and Fraternity Life, Office of the Dean of Students, University of Texas at Austin, http://deanofstudents.utexas.edu/sfl/join_upc_sched.php.

74 **A video of the girls:** "Alpha Delta Pi Texas Sorority's 'Terrifying' Recruitment Video," YouTube video, posted by "Huff Levine," August 23, 2016, https://www.youtube.com/watch?v=DnyMkvb3XjE.

75 **a Delta Gamma:** Sarah Berkes, interview with the author, April 27, 2017.

77 **how distorted women on-screen were:** Alison Bechdel, *The Essential Dykes to Watch Out For* (Boston, MA: Houghton Mifflin Harcourt, 2008).

77 **her shock in reading:** Virginia Woolf, *A Room of One's Own* (Eastford, CT: *Martino Fine Books,* 2012).

79 **didn't tell her sorority friends about her engagement:** "Candlelight . . . ," *Life as We Know It,* November 14, 2011, http://kaci-justin.blogspot.com/2011/11/candlelight.html.

80 **Her real name is Ellen:** Ellie, interview with the author, September 10, 2016.

80 **"That happened maybe twice":** Ibid.

81 **before cell phones had GPS:** Ibid.

82 **force men to step back:** Ibid.

82 **"I still feel bad":** Ibid.

83 **gets good lines:** *Sleepless in Seattle,* directed by Nora Ephron. (Culver City, CA: TriStar Pictures, 1993), film.

83 **the rich guy who hired her:** *Pretty Woman,* directed by Garry Marshall (Burbank, CA: Buena Vista Pictures, 1990), film.

83 **"home with a gardening tool":** *Jerry Maguire,* directed by Cameron Crowe (Culver City, CA: TriStar Pictures, 1996), film.

83 **gets cautioned by her best friend:** *Bridget Jones's Diary,* directed by Sharon Maguire (Santa Monica, CA: Miramax Films, 2001), film.

84 **parodied the limits of the role:** "Judy Greer Is the Best Friend," Funny or Die, June 11, 2014, http://www.funnyordie.com/videos/b7b1b5799e/judy-greer-is-the-best-friend.

84 **the final scene together:** *My Best Friend's Wedding,* directed by P. J. Hogan (Culver City, CA: TriStar Pictures, 1997), film.

85 **The test audience hated it:** Patrick Goldstein, "How One Actor Changed a Movie Before It Even Came Out," *Los Angeles Times,* June 23, 1997, http://articles.latimes.com/1997-06-23/entertainment/ca-6094_1_rupert-everett.

85 **her mom had been in one:** Ellie, interview.

86 **matching anxiety-induced eye twitches:** Ibid.

86 **a common trope:** "I'm Not Here to Make Friends!" YouTube video, posted by "richfofo," July 2, 2008, https://www.youtube.com/watch?v=w536Alnon24.

87 **"For me, it's I am a woman":** J. E. Buntin, "Under the Table," *The Rumpus,* September 30, 2013, http://therumpus.net/2013/09/under-the-table/.

88 **"I was never going to be a 'chick'":** "Longform Podcast #2: Janet Reitman," Longform, August 15, 2012, https://longform.org/posts/longform-podcast-2-janet-reitman.

89 **"I gave a lot of speeches in bars":** Rachel Khong, "The Rumpus Interview with Elizabeth Gilbert," *The Rumpus,* October 29, 2012,

http://therumpus.net/2012/10/the-rumpus-interview-with -elizabeth-gilbert/.

89 **four friends on the show:** *Sex and the City,* created by Darren Star, 1998, HBO, television series.

90 **"You know what?":** Ibid.

91 **"Why can't you be happy for me?":** Ibid.

91 **"Endings count in television":** Emily Nussbaum, "Difficult Women," *The New Yorker,* July 29, 2013, http://www.newyorker .com/magazine/2013/07/29/difficult-women.

92 **identified these guys as "metrosexuals":** Warren St. John, "Metrosexuals Come Out," *The New York Times,* June 22, 2003, http://www .nytimes.com/2003/06/22/style/metrosexuals-come-out.html.

92 **The magazine's last issue:** Ravi Somaiya, "Condé Nast Closing Details Magazine," *The New York Times,* November 18, 2015, https:// www.nytimes.com/2015/11/19/business/media/conde-nast-closing -details-magazine.html?_r=0.

93 **"watching boys do stuff":** Claire Vaye Watkins, "On Pandering," *Tin House,* November 23, 2015, http://tinhouse.com/on-pandering/.

95 **it reflected her life in Los Angeles:** Betsy Thomas, interview with the author, October 14, 2016.

96 **the easy camaraderie that she felt:** *My Boys,* created by Betsy Thomas, 2006, TBS, television series.

96 **cast a woman in a significant part:** Jennifer Keishin Armstrong, *Seinfeldia: How a Show About Nothing Changed Everything* (New York: Simon & Schuster, 2016).

96 **weren't from different planets:** Thomas, interview.

97 **"Kayleen doesn't like other women":** Greg, interview with the author, August 1, 2016.

98 **recalled a female roommate:** Greg, interview.

98 **demonize other women:** Thomas, interview.

100 **women who are bullies in the office:** Cheryl Lock, "The Best Way to Deal with a Mean Girl at Work," *Forbes,* March 8, 2013, https://www.forbes.com/sites/learnvest/2013/03/08/the-best -way-to-deal-with-a-mean-girl-at-work/#30e30cc31fdd.

100 **"I've definitely worked with":** Devin Tomb, interview with the author, July 7, 2016.

101 **"It takes a lot of energy":** Ibid.

101 **we share the same sex:** Alison Blough, interview with the author, July 21, 2016.

102 **loved being one of the guys:** Jaya Saxena, interview with the author, July 16, 2016.

103 **"One of the biggest things":** Ibid.

103 **on her wavelength:** Ibid.

104 **no longer a compliment:** Ibid.

104 **"From my point of view":** Dan Peres, interview with the author, June 29, 2016.

105 **"If you're a boy writer":** Junot Díaz speaking at Word Up, 2012, posted on John Hodgman's website, October 5, 2013, http://www .johnhodgman.com/post/63169936597/if-youre-a-boy-writer-its-a -simple-rule-you've.

105 **porn drive-ins:** Steve Miller, "The Big Daddy of Drive-In Porn Theaters," *Daily Beast,* January 17, 2015, http://www.thedailybeast .com/the-big-daddy-of-drive-in-porn-theaters.

106 **a Cool Girl:** Gillian Flynn, *Gone Girl* (New York: Crown Publishing Group, 2012).

107 **"You never struck me":** Peres, interview.

108 **to go to the bridal shower:** *My Boys.*

109 **I do not remember our first lunch together:** Ruthie, interview with the author, April 5, 2017.

109 **her favorite Halloween costume:** Ruthie, interview.

CHAPTER 4:
A NEW FOCUS ON FRIENDSHIPS

112 **"I don't know what":** Julie Ma, "25 Famous Women on Female Friendship," *The Cut,* April 21, 2015, https://www.thecut.com/2015 /04/25-famous-women-on-female-friendship.html.

119 **your preferences are misplaced:** Shasta Nelson, interview with the author, July 13, 2016.

119 **meet a man she wants to marry:** Elizabeth, interview with the author, July 7, 2016.

119 **dating is all you should care about:** Julia Chang, interview with the author, July 9, 2016.

120 **"to see someone every day":** Ibid.

120 **hooked up with a groomsman:** Kathryn, interview with the author, June 12, 2016.

121 **the perception that friendships are ancillary relationships:** Bri-allen Hopper, "Relying on Friendship in a World Made for Couples," *The Cut,* February 26, 2016, https://www.thecut.com/2016/02 /single-ladies-friendship-romantic-fraught.html.

121 **"people who are in nuclear family situations or couples":** Bri-allen Hopper, interview with the author, July 15, 2016.

121 **a deck of cards:** Hopper, "Relying on Friendship."

122 **creating rituals to protect them:** Hopper, interview.

122 **"Why wasn't friendship as good as a relationship?":** Hanya Yanagihara, *A Little Life* (New York: Doubleday, 2015).

124 **was single throughout her twenties and thirties:** Sara Eckel, interview with the author, August 15, 2016.

124 **"It was a big adventure":** Ibid.

125 **picky about whom she tried to befriend:** Ibid.

125 **a little bit of a dance:** Ibid.

126 **"Even the locker room situation":** Ruthie, interview with the author, August 11, 2017.

127 **men and women might be different:** Laura Klein, interview with the author, February 8, 2017.

127 **affects both genders:** National Institutes of Health, Grants and Funding, "NIH Policy and Guidelines on the Inclusion of Women and Minorities as Subjects in Clinical Research," October 2001, https://grants.nih.gov/grants/funding/women_min/guidelines _amended_10_2001.htm.

128 **passionate about including women:** Klein, interview.

128 **"My females revealed more stress":** Ibid.

128 **a notable gender difference in psychology:** Ibid.

129 **a landmark paper:** Shelley E. Taylor, Laura Cousino Klein, Brian P. Lewis, Tara L. Gruenewald, Regan A. R. Gurung, and John A. Updegraff, "Biobehavioral Responses to Stress in Females: Tend-and

-Befriend, not Fight-or-Flight," *Psychological Review* 107, no. 3 (2000): 411–29, https://www.ncbi.nlm.nih.gov/pubmed/10941275.

129 **"from an evolutionary perspective":** Klein, interview.

130 **"Friendship is really unconditional love":** Sophie B. Hawkins, interview with the author, September 6, 2016.

131 **"was considered very late":** Judy Schaefer, interview with the author, March 7, 2016.

132 **"your life truly didn't begin":** Ibid.

132 **median age of first marriage:** Rebecca Traister, *All the Single Ladies: Unmarried Women and the Rise of an Independent Nation* (New York: Simon & Schuster, 2016).

132 **more single women than married women:** Mark Mather and Diana Lavery, "In U.S., Proportion Married at Lowest Recorded Levels," Population Reference Bureau, September 2010, http://www.prb.org/Publications/Articles/2010/usmarriagedecline.aspx.

132 **to be the norm:** Ibid.

132 **"Young women today no longer have to wonder":** Traister, *All the Single Ladies.*

132 **when women entered the paid labor market:** Eric Klinenberg, interview with the author, August 18, 2016.

133 **"The key to living alone":** Ibid.

133 **the queer community in the 1980s:** Kath Weston, *Families We Choose: Lesbians, Gays, Kinship* (New York: Columbia University Press, 1997).

133 **never-married city dwellers:** Helen Fielding, *Bridget Jones's Diary* (London: Penguin Books, 1996).

133 **of his friends' support:** Ibid.

134 **tells a lie at work:** *Bridget Jones's Diary,* directed by Sharon Maguire (Santa Monica, CA: Miramax Films, 2001), film.

134 **"isn't just one way to live":** Ashton Applewhite, "An Interview with Helen Fielding," BookBrowse, https://www.bookbrowse.com/author_interviews/full/index.cfm/author_number/236/helen-fielding.

134 **prevalent in pop culture:** *Singles,* directed by Cameron Crowe (Burbank, CA: Warner Bros., 1992), film.

134 **prevalent in pop culture:** *Reality Bites,* directed by Ben Stiller (Universal City, CA: Universal Pictures, 1994), film.

134 **the whims of four friends:** *Seinfeld,* created by Larry David and Jerry Seinfeld, 1989, NBC, television series.

134 **"no hugging, no learning":** Edward Kosner, "No Hugging, No Learning: The 'Seinfeld' Credo," *The Wall Street Journal,* August 12, 2006, https://www.wsj.com/articles/no-hugging-no-learning-the-seinfeld-credo-1471032667.

134 **six black twentysomethings:** *Living Single,* created by Yvette Lee Bowser, 1993, Fox, television series.

135 **six white twentysomethings:** *Friends,* created by David Crane and Marta Kauffman, 1994, NBC, television series.

135 **"The well-hidden secret":** James Poniewozik, "All-Time 100 TV Shows," *Time,* September 6, 2007, http://time.com/collection-post/3101660/friends/.

135 **the emotional center of the story:** Brit Bennett, *The Mothers* (New York: Riverhead Books, 2016).

135 **"friends who are married":** Brit Bennett, interview with the author, June 23, 2017.

135 **"My friends have been there":** Ibid.

136 **kind of care family would:** Hopper, interview.

136 **a girl also living with incurable stage IV cancer:** John Green, *The Fault in Our Stars* (New York: Dutton Books, 2012).

136 **"the same level of commitment":** Hopper, interview.

136 **move in with her:** Ibid.

137 **"glad to be able to be there":** Ibid.

138 **observed her parents' long marriage:** Emily Rapp Black, interview with the author, October 27, 2016.

138 **felt sorry for them:** Ibid.

139 **"I really misunderstood":** Ibid.

139 **"They entered this space of sadness":** Ibid.

140 **our friendships make us bigger than ourselves:** Emily Rapp, "Transformation and Transcendence: The Power of Female Friendship," *The Rumpus,* January 22, 2012, http://therumpus.net/2012/01/transformation-and-transcendence-the-power-of-female-friendship/.

141 **"I liked your boots"**: Carmel, interview with the author, June 29, 2016.

141 **"You were a champion for me"**: Ibid.

142 **let each other exist**: Ibid.

143 **"I moved to the other side of the world"**: Ibid.

143 **"They both had a hand on my shoulder"**: Ibid.

143 **introduced to the world by Leslie Knope**: *Parks and Recreation*, created by Greg Daniels and Michael Schur, 2009, NBC, television series.

144 **"There are a lot of writers"**: Michael Schur, interview with the author, September 7, 2016.

144 **"What's Galentine's Day?"**: "Galentine's Day," *Parks and Recreation*, season 2, episode 6, aired February 11, 2010.

144 **"get your best gals together"**: Maggy van Eijk, "23 Reasons You Need to Celebrate Galentine's Day This Year," BuzzFeed, February 2, 2015, https://www.buzzfeed.com/maggyvaneijk/breasties-before -testes?utm_term=.ou6vqLG8o#.bl9rEgYZy.

145 **hosts an elaborate Galentine's party**: Hopper, interview.

145 **the day *before* Valentine's Day**: *Parks and Recreation*.

145 **The holidays were distinct on purpose**: Schur, interview.

146 **the friendship between Knope and Ann Perkins**: *Parks and Recreation*.

146 **"was different at that time"**: Schur, interview.

147 **her best bizarre compliments**: *Parks and Recreation*.

147 **"Leslie's fundamental belief"**: Schur, interview.

147 **always a brunch during a workday**: *Parks and Recreation*.

148 **"Galentine's Day is very bright"**: Schur, interview.

148 **a bag with a bouquet of hand-crocheted flower pens**: *Parks and Recreation*, season 2, episode 6, aired February 11, 2010.

148 **Knope sleeps only four hours a night**: Schur, interview.

148 **"Uteruses Before Duderuses"**: *Parks and Recreation*, season 2, episode 2, aired September 24, 2009.

149 **"I'm very proud"**: Schur, interview.

CHAPTER 5:
OUR BFFS, PEOPLE, AND SOULMATES

150 **"You are my best friend!":** *Broad City,* created by Ilana Glazer and Abbi Jacobson, 2014, Comedy Central, television series.

152 **her best friend, Julia, died in a car accident:** Stephie Grob Plante, interview with the author, July 7, 2016.

152 **"I don't have any memories":** Ibid.

153 **"She'd drop everything":** Ibid.

153 **"you lost your mother":** Ibid.

153 **"'Best friend' gets thrown around":** Ibid.

153 **another *F* for an extra "forever":** Stephie Grob Plante, "This Is a Story About Loss," *Racked,* October 20, 2015, http://www.racked .com/2015/10/20/9487775/unclaimed-baggage-center.

154 **"it's the most serious joke":** Grob Plante, interview.

154 **"I'll just tell Jules about my day":** Ibid.

155 **her national debut:** *The Oprah Winfrey Show,* created by Oprah Winfrey, 1986, syndicated, talk show.

155 **putting on a Wonderbra:** "My Favorite Moments with Oprah and Gayle," YouTube video, posted by "jonluvsmaddy," April 21, 2011, https://www.youtube.com/watch?v=9LxKQLbfKdw&t=89s.

156 **"This is so touching":** *The Oprah Winfrey Show,* February 4, 1994.

156 **"She is the mother I never had":** "Oprah on Her Friendship with Gayle," YouTube video, posted by "Palmetto Peaches," March 24, 2016, https://www.youtube.com/watch?v=4vWegVQYMkQ.

157 **"I feel I'm in her light":** Kenneth Best, "Q&A/Gayle King; On Television, for News and Talk, Too," *The New York Times,* March 29, 1998, http://www.nytimes.com/1998/03/29/nyregion/q-a-gayle-king -on-television-for-news-and-talk-too.html.

157 **best friends were on television:** *I Love Lucy,* written by Jess Oppenheimer, 1951, CBS, television series; *Laverne & Shirley,* created by Garry Marshall, Lowell Ganz, and Mark Rothman, 1976, ABC, television series; *Kate & Allie,* created by Sherry Coben, 1984, CBS, television series.

157 **shows about single professional women:** *Murphy Brown,* created by Diana English, 1988, CBS, television series; *Ally McBeal,* created by David E. Kelley, 1997, Fox, television series.

157 **great modern portrayal of female best friends:** *Grey's Anatomy,* created by Shonda Rhimes, 2005, ABC, television series.

157 **"the secret core of Grey's":** Mark Perigard, interview with the author, September 25, 2017.

158 **"people like to think":** Sandra Gonzalez, "Sandra Oh, 'Grey's' creator Shonda Rhimes Say Goodbye to Cristina," *Entertainment Weekly,* May 15, 2014, http://ew.com/article/2014/05/15/sandra-oh -greys-anatomy-cristina-farewell/.

158 **"There was a lot going on":** Michael Schur, interview with the author, September 7, 2016.

159 **she was her "person":** *Grey's Anatomy,* season 2, episode, 1, "Rain-drops Keep Falling on My Head," aired September 25, 2005.

159 **the moment was going to be so significant:** Gonzalez, "Sandra Oh."

160 **her best friends aren't extraneous:** Aminatou Sow, interview with the author, October 28, 2016.

160 **"My emergency contact is a friend":** Ibid.

160 **starts at a new company:** Ibid.

161 **"not very heteronormative is really insane":** Ibid.

161 **Kim Kardashian was:** Carlos Greer, "Kim Kardashian: I'm Marry-ing My Best Friend," *People,* October 28, 2013, http://people.com /celebrity/kim-kardashian-engaged-to-kanye-west-im-marrying -my-best-friend-she-says/.

161 **"More and more people":** Stephanie Coontz, interview with the author, December 19, 2016.

161 **The jeweler Zales:** Gabriella Paiella, "Marrying Your Best Friend Is a Cliche, but a Good One for Women," *The Guardian,* December 21, 2015, https://www.theguardian.com/lifeandstyle/2015/dec/21/ marrying-your-best-friend-is-a-cliche-but-a-good-one-for-women.

161 **the concept of marrying your best friend:** Coontz, interview.

162 **keep desire high in long-term relationships:** Esther Perel, "The Secret to Desire in a Long-Term Relationship," TED video, filmed

February 14, 2013, https://www.ted.com/talks/esther_perel_the
_secret_to_desire_in_a_long_term_relationship.

162 **"He was my husband":** Judy Schaefer, interview with the author,
March 7, 2016.

162 **it's uniquely American:** Guy Raz and Esther Perel, "Are We Asking Too Much of Our Spouses?" *TED Radio Hour,* NPR, April 25,
2014, http://www.npr.org/templates/transcript/transcript.php?story
Id=301825600.

163 **If something good or bad happens:** Marianne Kirby, interview
with the author, September 19, 2016.

163 **"They're all so important":** Ibid.

163 **"to be happy and functional":** Ibid.

164 **"We're really aware":** Keeley Tillotson, interview with the author, July 18, 2016.

164 **"We'll milk it":** Erika Welsh, interview with the author, July 18,
2016.

164 **they dropped out of school:** Keeley Tillotson and Erika Welsh,
interview with the author, July 18, 2016.

165 **"It wouldn't have worked":** Welsh, interview.

165 **"It was bordering on unhealthy":** Tillotson, interview.

165 **"We had no other friends":** Welsh, interview.

165 **"credit-card debt together":** Alyson Shontell, "How 2 Roommates Got Shot Down by Hundreds of Startup Investors and
Racked Up Credit-Card Debt—but Built a Newsletter Empire Anyway," *Business Insider,* April 21, 2017, http://www.businessinsider
.com/how-carly-zakin-danielle-weisberg-founded-theskimm
-podcast-interview-2017-4.

165 **"the scariest day of our life":** Ibid.

166 **"This was everything":** Ibid.

166 **"We were feeding off":** Lydia Dishman, "TheSkimm Founders on
What It's Like to Start a Business with Your BFF," *Fast Company,*
April 3, 2017, https://www.fastcompany.com/3069292/theskimm
-founders-on-what-its-like-to-start-a-business-with-your-bff.

166 **"No one thing is going to break us up":** Tillotson, interview.

166 **"You have to be careful":** Heather Cocks, interview with the author, August 10, 2016.

167 *"I need to see her face"*: Ibid.

167 **moving in with her childhood best friend:** *Best Friends Forever,* created by Lennon Parham and Jessica St. Clair, 2012, NBC, television series.

167 **both studying sketch comedy:** Lennon Parham and Jessica St. Clair, interview with the author, September 16, 2016.

167 **"had ever made me laugh that hard":** Jessica St. Clair, interview with the author, September 16, 2016.

168 **"We were like,** *This is forever"*: Lennon Parham, interview with the author, September 16, 2016.

168 **"the world sort of melts away":** St. Clair, interview.

168 **"the best portrayal of female friendship":** Julie Beck, *"Playing House*: Finally, a TV Show Gets Female Friendships Right," *The Atlantic,* April 28, 2014, https://www.theatlantic.com/entertainment /archive/2014/04/playing-house-finally-a-tv-show-gets-female -friendships-right/361308/.

169 **"It was sort of bananas":** St. Clair, interview.

169 **another series about best friends:** *Broad City,* created by Ilana Glazer and Abbi Jacobson, 2014, Comedy Central, television series.

169 **averaged 1.2 million viewers:** Philiana Ng, "Comedy Central Renews 'Broad City' for Second Season," *The Hollywood Reporter,* February 24, 2014, http://www.hollywoodreporter.com/live-feed/broad -city-renewed-season-2-683083.

169 **got kicked off a Southwest Airlines flight:** Ali Vingiano, "This College Student Was Kicked off a Plane for Wearing a 'Broad City' T-Shirt," BuzzFeed, March 24, 2015, https://www.buzzfeed.com /alisonvingiano/southwest-broad-city-shirt?utm_term=.qjw 7z5MDG#.obKOlykar.

169 **"we just started to get a response":** Joe Berkowitz, "How the Creators of 'Broad City' Turned Their Web Series into a TV Show," *Fast Company,* February 5, 2014, https://www.fastcompany.com /3025672/how-the-creators-of-broad-city-turned-their-web-series -into-a-tv-show.

169 **"I don't get why we'd watch this":** Nick Paumgarten, "Id Girls," *The New Yorker,* June 23, 2014, http://www.newyorker.com/maga zine/2014/06/23/id-girls.

170 **Comedy Central ordered ten episodes:** Jesse David Fox, "Comedy Central Orders Ten Episodes of Broad City," *Vulture*, March 13, 2013, http://www.vulture.com/2013/03/comedy-central-orders-ten-episodes-of-broad-city.html.

170 **an unpretentious portrait of a friendship between women:** Paumgarten, "Id Girls."

170 **"They're the couple, they're the two that you have to care about":** Ted Simmons, "New York Comedy Fest: Amy Poehler Talks 'Broad City' Roots and Weirdly Specific 'Street-Level Feel'," *The Hollywood Reporter*, November 10, 2014, http://www.hollywoodreporter.com/news/new-york-comedy-fest-2014-747925.

171 **"my focal point":** *Broad City*, season 2, episode 2, "Mochalatta Chills," aired January 21, 2015.

171 **"this show on the road":** Parham, interview.

171 **"Two Ladies and a Baby":** St. Clair, interview.

172 **"best friends in real life":** Parham, interview.

172 **"you can fucking do anything":** St. Clair, interview.

172 **quits her job and moves in with her:** *Playing House*, created by Lennon Parham and Jessica St. Clair, 2014, USA Network, television series.

172 **"It is a fantasy, right?":** Parham, interview.

172 **"caring too much for each other":** Ibid.

173 **diagnosed with breast cancer:** St. Clair, interview.

173 **"Let's not fuck around":** Parham, interview.

175 **"if Molly and Issa have chemistry":** Jenna Wortham, "The Misadventures of Issa Rae," *The New York Times*, August 4, 2015, https://www.nytimes.com/2015/08/09/magazine/the-misadventures-of-issa-rae.html.

175 **melodramatic, manipulative relationships:** *The Real Housewives*, 2006, Bravo, reality show franchise; *Love & Hip-Hop*, 2001, VH1, reality show franchise; *Flavor of Love*, created by Cris Abrego and Mark Cronin, 2006, VH1, reality television show.

175 **act like she and her real-life friends did:** *Insecure*, created by Issa Rae and Larry Wilmore, 2016, HBO, television series.

175 **"I constantly have to get it together":** Morgan Jerkins, "Issa Rae Talks *Insecure*, Sex Scenes, and Black Female Friendship,"

Cosmopolitan, July 24, 2017, http://www.cosmopolitan.com/enter
tainment/tv/a10347648/issa-rae-insecure-season-2-interview/.

CHAPTER 6:
STRENGTH IN NUMBERS

177 **"don't climb the mountain alone":** Sheila Marikar, "How to
Make an American Fashion Brand (No Sewing Required!)," *The
New York Times,* August 26, 2017, https://www.nytimes.com/2017
/08/26/fashion/lpa-los-angeles-lara-pia-arrobio.html?_r=1.

180 **"One of the things always mentioned":** Karen McCullah, interview with the author, May 4, 2017.

180 **"I had some male producer say":** Matt Donnelly and Beatrice Verhoeven, "'Ghostbusters' Director Paul Feig Told to Expect 'Catfights' Working with Female Leads," *The Wrap,* June 4, 2016, http://
www.thewrap.com/paul-feig-sexist-male-producer-said-expect
-catfights-on-all-female-ghostbusters/.

180 **"Not in the slightest":** Beatrice Verhoeven, "'Ocean's 8' Star Sarah
Paulson Talks All-Female Reboot in a Post-'Ghostbusters' World,"
The Wrap, December 13, 2016, http://www.thewrap.com/oceans-8
-sarah-paulson-female-cast-ghostbusters/.

181 **surprise appearances at each other's gigs:** James Wolcott, "When
They Were Kings," *Vanity Fair,* May 1997, https://www.vanityfair
.com/news/1997/05/rat-pack-vegas.

181 **the "Pussy Posse":** Nancy Jo Sales, "Leo, Prince of the City," *New
York,* June 22, 1988, http://nymag.com/nymetro/movies/features/
2793/.

181 **the good time the guys were having playing pranks:** Mike Spi-
nelli, "Joke Bumper Sticker Makes Dick of Pitt," Jalopnik, November 4, 2004, http://jalopnik.com/119623/joke-bumper-sticker-makes
-dick-of-pitt.

181 **she lives with 374 other women:** Sarah Berkes, interview with the
author, April 27, 2017.

181 **"I direct that the said apartments":** "Our Mission," Webster
Apartments, http://www.websterapartments.org/about-us/.

182 *"Is it really catty?":* Berkes, interview.

182 **"men couldn't get at them and deceive them"**: Hilary Stout, "Where the Boys Aren't," *The New York Times,* November 4, 2009, http://www.nytimes.com/2009/11/05/fashion/05webster.html.

182 **"I was used to living with all girls"**: Berkes, interview.

182 **"beau parlors"**: Stout, "Where the Boys Aren't."

183 **"Yo, I'm new"**: Berkes, interview.

184 **"Everyone thinks we're cloistered nuns"**: Ibid.

184 **to always be good girls**: Anne Helen Petersen, "Jennifer Garner's Good-Girl Image Has Become Her Business," BuzzFeed, July 14, 2017, https://www.buzzfeed.com/annehelenpetersen/jennifer-garners-good-girl-image-has-become-her-business?utm_term=.rtg0nXxap#.al8O2Z3aW.

185 *apologizing* **for her expression**: Liz Clarke, "Gabby Douglas, Her Olympics Over, Tearfully Responds to Social Media Critics," *The Washington Post,* August 14, 2016, https://www.washingtonpost.com/sports/olympics/gabby-douglas-her-olympics-over-tearfully-responds-to-social-media-critics/2016/08/14/512cfee8-6219-11e6-8b27-bb8ba39497a2_story.html?utm_term=.2dbe9554763a.

185 **about dysfunctional friendships**: *Girls,* created by Lena Dunham, 2012, HBO, television series.

186 **"you have so much to say"**: Ibid.

187 **"It's hard and lonely at the top"**: Rebecca Johnson, "Why Serena Williams Is Best Friends with Her Fiercest Competitor," *Vogue,* March 21, 2015, http://www.vogue.com/article/serena-williams-april-cover-caroline-wozniacki.

187 **tripped during the first round of the five-thousand-meter race**: Madison Malone Kircher, "Tripped-Up Olympic Runners Finish Race Together in Apparent Attempt to Make Me Weep Uncontrollably at My Desk," *New York,* August 16, 2016, http://nymag.com/selectall/2016/08/olympians-helping-each-other-finish-a-race-are-making-me-feel-things.html.

187 **"She is my story"**: Martin Rogers, "A Fall in the 5,000 Delivers an Uplifting Moment," *USA Today,* August 16, 2016, https://www.usatoday.com/story/sports/olympics/rio-2016/2016/08/16/abbey-dagostino-falls-but-finishes-5000-on-injured-leg/88821348/.

187 **in the pool at age eight:** Kim Vandenberg, interview with the author, August 12, 2016.

188 **"I'm not going to not beat someone":** Ibid.

188 **"Every memory I had in the pool was with her":** Ibid.

189 **three workouts a day:** Ibid.

190 **when #squadgoals was at its most popular:** Matt Stopera, "Please, Everyone, Stop Saying 'Squad Goals,'" BuzzFeed, December 1, 2015, https://www.buzzfeed.com/mjs538/please-everyone-stop -saying-squad-goals?utm_term=.tjdKQ1gqp#.xvnzaJPYx.

190 **"it's a tier":** *The Mindy Project,* created by Mindy Kaling, 2012, Fox, television series.

191 **"We want to be the new generation":** Vanessa Craft, "Gigi Hadid on Changing the Modelling Industry, Social Media, and #Squad-goals," *Elle Canada,* September 29, 2015, http://www.ellecanada .com/culture/celebrity/article/exclusive-gigi-hadid-on-changing -the-modelling-industry-social-media-and-squadgoals.

191 **without mentioning her:** Katy Waldman, "Taylor Swift, Waka Flocka, and the Roots of #Squad," *Slate,* July 29, 2015, http://www .slate.com/blogs/lexicon_valley/2015/07/29/taylor_swift_waka _flocka_and_squadgoals_how_squad_went_from_underdogs _to.html.

192 **"It was a public service announcement":** Jon Caramanica, "Review: On Taylor Swift's '1989' Tour, the Underdog Emerges as Cool Kid," *The New York Times,* May 21, 2015, https://www.ny times.com/2015/05/22/arts/music/review-taylor-swift-1989-tour .html?_r=0.

192 **"When you're not boyfriend-shopping":** Josh Eells, "The Reinvention of Taylor Swift," *Rolling Stone,* September 8, 2014, http:// www.rollingstone.com/music/features/taylor-swift-1989-cover -story-20140908.

192 **the Fourth of July at Swift's beach house:** Sarah Lindig, "Taylor Swift's Epic 4th of July Weekend Continues," *Harper's Bazaar,* July 5, 2015, http://www.harpersbazaar.com/celebrity/latest/a11395/taylor -swift-4th-of-july-party/.

192 **it seems too uniformly cast to be inspiring:** Kara Brown, "Let's Find Taylor Swift a Black Friend," Jezebel, December 3, 2014,

http://jezebel.com/lets-find-taylor-swift-a-black-friend
-1665567775.

193 **"not every girl is going to fit into this":** Elaine Welteroth, interview with the author, August 19, 2016.

193 **unafraid to test and fight about their friendships:** *Bridesmaids*, directed by Paul Feig (Universal City, CA: Universal Pictures, 2011), film.

194 **"wanted it to resonate emotionally":** Amy Dawes, "Sketching Out the Script for 'Bridesmaids,'" *Los Angeles Times*, February 9, 2012, http://articles.latimes.com/2012/feb/09/news/la-en-mumolo -20120209.

194 **destroying an enormous heart-shaped cookie:** *Bridesmaids*.

194 **"I think it's a slightly pandering idea":** Joe Berkowitz, "'Bridesmaids' and 'The Heat' Director Paul Feig on How to Make Female-Driven Comedies Everybody Wants to See," *Fast Company*, October 17, 2013, https://www.fastcompany.com/3020072/bridesmaids-and -the-heat-director-paul-feig-on-how-to-make-female-driven -comedies-everybody-.

195 **a female a cappella group:** *Pitch Perfect*, screenplay by Kay Cannon (Universal City, CA: Universal Pictures, 2012), film.

195 **"Who made that up?":** Kay Cannon, interview with the author, January 20, 2017.

195 **wanted to see more romance:** Ibid.

196 **"The Trebles don't respect us":** *Pitch Perfect*.

196 **"I treated it like a sports movie":** Cannon, interview.

196 **The two were introduced:** Yvonne Villarreal, "Nicole Kidman and Reese Witherspoon on Bringing the Female-Driven 'Big Little Lies' to Life," *Los Angeles Times*, February 16, 2017, http://www.la times.com/entertainment/tv/la-et-st-big-little-lies-feature -20170216-story.html.

196 **a mystery about a murder in a beach town:** Liane Moriarty, *Big Little Lies* (New York: G. P. Putnam's Sons, 2014).

197 **"that was the beginning of it":** Jennifer Drysdale, "Exclusive: Nicole Kidman Reveals Daughters Are Friends with Her 'Big Little Lies' Kids: They're 'at My House!,'" *Entertainment Tonight*, September 17, 2017, http://www.etonline.com/exclusive-nicole-kidman

-reveals-daughters-are-friends-her-big-little-lies-kids-theyre
-my-house.

197 **"It was kind of amazing to feel the interest"**: Patricia Garcia,
"Nicole Kidman on Big Little Lies, Those Therapy Scenes, and
Coming Home Covered in Bruises," *Vogue*, March 27, 2017, https://
www.vogue.com/article/nicole-kidman-interview-big-little-lies
-celeste.

197 **Red Vines candy and brown lipstick:** Isaac Oliver, "Reese Witherspoon and Laura Dern, Wildly Close," *The New York Times*,
March 24, 2017, https://www.nytimes.com/2017/03/24/arts/reese
-witherspoon-laura-dern.html?_r=0.

197 **"We couldn't get enough":** Patricia Garcia, "Reese Witherspoon
on Who She Initially Wanted to Play on *Big Little Lies*—and What
She Thinks about Those Critics who Dismiss the Show as Just Another Soap Opera," *Vogue*, March 29, 2017, https://www.vogue
.com/article/reese-witherspoon-big-little-lies-madeline
-mackenzie.

198 **"a friendship that then created opportunities":** "Big Little Lies
Wins Outstanding Limited Series at the 69th Emmy Awards," You-
Tube video, posted by "CBS," September 17, 2017, https://www
.youtube.com/watch?v=w0-g2p3vrme.

198 **a good friend of Clinton's:** Linda Bloodworth Thomason, interview with the author, October 19, 2016.

199 **"Well, it's exciting":** Ibid.

200 **"in her daughter's spine":** Ibid.

200 **declined to call herself a feminist:** Marisa Meltzer, "Who Is a
Feminist Now?" *The New York Times,* May 21, 2014, https://www
.nytimes.com/2014/05/22/fashion/who-is-a-feminist-now.html.

200 **"Grind it out":** Welteroth, interview.

200 **mostly about personal and professional advancement:** Jessica
Testa, "The Last Girlbosses," BuzzFeed, April 20, 2017, https://
www.buzzfeed.com/jtes/the-last-girlbosses?utm_term=.tyBw
P3RaYM#.ulY9Mv54PL.

201 **in a Facebook post:** Amanda Hess, "How a Fractious Women's
Movement Came to Lead the Left," *The New York Times Magazine,*
February 7, 2017, https://www.nytimes.com/2017/02/07/magazine/

how-a-fractious-womens-movement-came-to-lead-the-left.html? mcubz=2&_r=0.

202 **estimated to be between 3.2 million and 5.2 million:** Erica Chenoweth and Jeremy Pressman, "This Is What We Learned by Counting the Women's Marches," *The Washington Post*, February 7, 2017, https://www.washingtonpost.com/news/monkey-cage/wp /2017/02/07/this-is-what-we-learned-by-counting-the-womens -marches/?utm_term=.3bdcb83017fd.

202 **carrying signs that said:** Julia Reinstein, "61 of the Greatest Signs from Women's Marches Around the Country," BuzzFeed, January 21, 2017, https://www.buzzfeed.com/juliareinstein/best-womens -march-signs?utm_term=.wp3wm8Y9R#.wj2opqD9e.

202 **there is division:** Jia Tolentino, "The Case Against Contemporary Feminism," *The New Yorker*, February 8, 2017, http://www.new yorker.com/books/page-turner/the-case-against-contemporary -feminism.

202 **What contributes to our individual selves beyond our sex:** Farah Stockman, "Women's March on Washington Opens Contentious Dialogues About Race," *The New York Times*, January 9, 2017, https:// www.nytimes.com/2017/01/09/us/womens-march-on-washington -opens-contentious-dialogues-about-race.html?_r=0.

203 **"there's a double whammy":** Welteroth, interview.

203 **have friends who are of the same race:** *Scandal*, created by Shonda Rhimes, 2012, ABC, television series; *The Mindy Project*; *Modern Family*, created by Christopher Lloyd and Steven Levitan, 2009, ABC, television series.

203 **"They have mostly white friendships":** Nancy Wang Yuen, interview with the author, July 19, 2017.

204 **starting to show more of them:** *Insecure*.

204 **real-seeming black women:** *Girlfriends*, created by Mara Brock Akil, 2000, UPN, television series.

204 **"*Girlfriends* doesn't get the credit it deserves":** Angelica Jade Bastién, "NYT Recommendation: Girlfriends," *The New York Times*, https://www.nytimes.com/watching/recommendations/watch ing-tv-girlfriends?mcubz=2.

204 **casts of black characters:** Dara T. Mathis, "Was UPN Black America's Last Hope for a Black Sitcom-Friendly Broadcast Television Network?" IndieWire, November 14, 2014, http://www.indiewire.com/2014/11/was-upn-black-americas-last-hope-for-a-black-sitcom-friendly-broadcast-television-network-157147/.

204 **"Guys, don't you understand the money":** Rawiya Kameir, "How Mara Brock Akil Plans to Save TV," *The Fader,* April 22, 2016, http://www.thefader.com/2016/04/22/mara-brock-akil-interview-warner-bros.

205 **mostly Asian American women:** *The Joy Luck Club,* screenplay by Amy Tan and Ronald Bass (Burbank, CA: Buena Vista Pictures, 1993), film.

205 **"Handsomely brought to the screen":** Janet Maslin, "Review/Film: The Joy Luck Club; Intimate Generational Lessons, Available to All," *The New York Times,* September 8, 1993, http://www.nytimes.com/movie/review?res=9F0CE1DA1031F93BA3575AC0A965958260.

205 **a financial success:** Susan Cheng, "Why Hollywood Bet on 'The Joy Luck Club,'" BuzzFeed, June 6, 2017, https://www.buzzfeed.com/susancheng/why-hollywood-bet-on-athe-joy-luck-cluba?utm_term=.fq1J908oK#.nrBVJDKM5.

206 **"Friends are the people":** *Waiting to Exhale,* directed by Forest Whitaker (Los Angeles, CA: 20th Century Fox, 1995), film.

206 **"part entertainment, part social phenomenon":** Elaine Dutka, "'Waiting' to Start a Trend?: Studios Are Anxious to See How Upcoming Black Films Will Fare," *Los Angeles Times,* January 9, 1996, http://articles.latimes.com/1996-01-09/entertainment/ca-22497_1_black-middle.

206 **"in spite of fractured relationships":** Allison P. Davis, "*Waiting to Exhale* Has Aged as Well as Angela Bassett," *The Cut,* December 23, 2015, https://www.thecut.com/2015/12/20-years-later-waiting-to-exhale-still-rules.html.

206 **behave badly in New Orleans:** *Girls Trip,* directed by Malcolm D. Lee (Universal City, CA: Universal Pictures, 2017), film.

206 **"black women being carefree":** Arlene Washington, "'Girls Trip' Stars Celebrate Sisterhood at L.A. Premiere," *The Hollywood Re-*

porter, July 14, 2017, http://www.hollywoodreporter.com/news /girls-trip-stars-celebrate-sisterhood-at-la-premiere-1021169.

207 **the "Flossy Posse":** *Girls Trip.*

207 **"I love how soft they are with each other":** Ashley Lee, "'Girls Trip' Director on Black Girl Magic, Tiffany Haddish and Future 'Best Man' Movies," *The Hollywood Reporter,* July 18, 2017, http:// www.hollywoodreporter.com/news/girls-trip-director-black-girl -magic-tiffany-haddish-future-best-man-movies-1021898.

207 **Washington, DC, crisis fixer:** *Scandal,* created by Shonda Rhimes, 2012, ABC, television series.

208 **"a onetime thing":** Ruthie, interview with the author, April 13, 2017.

208 **"sometimes we meet and don't watch *Scandal*":** Amanda, interview with the author, April 13, 2017.

209 **"I didn't get suckered into this":** Ibid.

210 **"With most groups":** Ruthie, interview.

211 **pregnant with her first child:** Elizabeth Spiridakis Olson, interview with the author, July 20, 2016.

211 **"a funny environment of mom real talk":** Ibid.

212 **"You need a safe space":** Ibid.

CONCLUSION:
HOW OUR FRIENDSHIPS END, CHANGE, AND ENDURE

213 **"I'm glad I came with you":** *Thelma & Louise,* Written by Callie Khouri (Beverly Hills, CA: Metro-Goldwyn-Mayer, 1991), film.

214 **"a very talented bungee-jumping expert":** Amy Poehler, *Yes Please* (New York: HarperCollins Publishers, 2014).

214 **"That's the love of my life right there":** Kristen Caires, "Michelle Williams Says BFF Busy Philipps Is 'Proof That the Love of Your Life Does Not Have to Be a Man!'" *People,* December 19, 2016, http://people.com/movies/michelle-williams-busy-philipps -manchester-by-the-sea/.

214 **part of the lyrics:** Jason Isbell, "Cover Me Up," on *Southeastern,* Southeastern Records, 2013.

215 **"she wasn't a proper young lady":** Sharon Marcus, interview with the author, December 13, 2016.

215 **"I think they mostly didn't care":** Ibid.

216 **"to sit at her feet like a dog":** Sharon Marcus, *Between Women: Friendship, Desire, and Marriage in Victorian England* (Princeton, NJ: Princeton University Press, 2007).

216 **"my new and most interesting charge":** Ibid.

217 **"as happy and independent as birds":** Louisa May Alcott, *An Old-Fashioned Girl* (Heraklion Press, 2013).

217 **"unmarried by every implication of her being":** Henry James, *The Bostonians* (Adrien Devret, 2017).

217 **two best friends in their twenties in Chicago:** *Brown Girls*, written by Fatimah Asghar, OpenTV, web series.

218 **"are not caricatures":** Britt Julious, "Why These Women Are Bringing *Brown Girls* to Television," *Elle*, June 5, 2017, http://www.elle.com/culture/movies-tv/news/a45725/brown-girls-hbo-tv-series-development/.

218 **nominated for an Emmy:** Dee Lockett, "*Brown Girls* Is Now an Emmy-Nominated Show Well Ahead of Its HBO Debut," *Vulture.com*, June 13, 2017, http://www.vulture.com/2017/07/brown-girls-emmy-nominated-well-ahead-of-its-hbo-debut.html.

218 **"people want shows like this":** Hannah Giorgis, "'Brown Girls' Is the Future of Television," Ringer, February 22, 2017, https://www.theringer.com/2017/2/22/16036334/brown-girls-open-tv-fatimah-asghar-sam-bailey-web-series-6e44b80cb8ad.

218 **she was moving:** Alexandra, interview with the author, February 14, 2017.

219 **wanted to marry and have children:** Ibid.

219 **"I would have done it with her":** Ibid.

220 **"She had this escape plan":** Ibid.

220 **she won't automatically suggest Melissa join her:** Ibid.

222 **"it would have been an adventure":** Susanna Fogel, interview with the author, March 7, 2017.

222 **"We formed these rituals":** Ibid.

223 **being the only straight girl:** Ibid.

223 **"you're supposed to be one hundred percent happy":** Ibid.

224 **"I want to tell my best friend about it":** Ibid.

224 **"lets friendships drift apart":** Shasta Nelson, interview with the author, July 13, 2016.

224 **"processing our transition together":** Fogel, interview.

224 **a routine a lot like Susanna and Joni's once was:** *Life Partners,* directed by Susanna Fogel (New York: Magnolia Pictures, 2014), film.

225 **"those in-jokes about my life":** Fogel, interview.

225 **"But I needed you":** Ibid.

226 **"you stop needing that":** *Life Partners.*

226 **"have that much in common":** Fogel, interview.

227 **she felt lonely:** Carla Bruce-Eddings, interview with the author, July 11, 2017.

227 **had a community like that before:** Ibid.

227 **"I'm so glad you started this group":** Ibid.

228 **"we're sharing this journey":** Ibid.

228 **getting married and having children:** Carly de Castro and Stephanie Danler, interview with the author, February 27, 2017.

228 **isolated in the apartment:** Ibid.

229 *"You can't not respond to me":* Carly de Castro, interview with the author, February 27, 2017.

229 **"really communicate":** Ibid.

229 **"Everything just shifted":** Stephanie Danler, interview with the author, February 27, 2017.

229 **"We're going to do this":** de Castro, interview.

230 **"felt like it was happening to me":** Danler, interview.

230 **weeks sleeping on Carly's couch:** Ibid.

230 **"not a lot of pettiness":** de Castro, interview.

230 **"this profound understanding":** Danler, interview.

230 **"Playdates are more important than you realize":** Laurie Simmons, "The Lenny Interview: Molly Ringwald," *Lenny Letter,* June 17, 2016, http://www.lennyletter.com/work/interviews/a438/the-iconic-actress-on-being-your-former-teenage-crush/.

231 **to write computing code:** Sara Chipps and Brooke Moreland, interview with the author, August 18, 2016.

231 **"Signaling affection for your friends":** Sara Chipps, interview with the author, August 18, 2016.

233 **most of her friends are married and moms:** Julia Chang, interview with the author, July 9, 2016.

233 **"the friends I grow old with":** Ibid.

233 **"many people you can say that about":** Ibid.

SELECTED BIBLIOGRAPHY

Abbott, Megan. *Dare Me*. Reagan Arthur Books, 2012.

Alcott, Louisa May. *An Old-Fashioned Girl*. Heraklion Press, 2013.

Bechdel, Alison. *The Essential Dykes to Watch Out For*. Boston: Houghton Mifflin Harcourt, 2008.

Blume, Judy. *Summer Sisters*. New York: Delacorte Books, 1998.

Classen, Albrecht, and Sandidge, Marilyn. *Friendship in the Middle Ages and the Early Modern Age*. Berlin: De Gruyter, 2011.

Coontz, Stephanie. *Marriage, a History: How Love Conquered Marriage*. New York: Penguin Books, 2006.

Douglas, Susan J. *Where the Girls Are: Growing Up Female with the Mass Media*. New York: Three Rivers Press, 1995.

Faludi, Susan. *Backlash: The Undeclared War Against American Women*. New York: Broadway Books, 2009.

Flynn, Gillian. *Gone Girl*. New York: Crown Publishing Group, 2012.

James, Henry. *The Bostonians*. Adrien Devret, 2017.

Klam, Julie. *Friendkeeping: A Field Guide to the People You Love, Hate, and Can't Live Without*. New York: Riverhead Books, 2012.

Klinenberg, Eric. *Going Solo: The Extraordinary Rise and Surprising Appeal of Living Alone*. New York: Penguin Books, 2013.

Marcus, Sharon. *Between Women: Friendship, Desire, and Marriage in Victorian England*. Princeton, NJ: Princeton University Press, 2007.

Mooney, Catherine. *Gendered Voices: Medieval Saints and Their Interpreters*. Philadelphia: University of Pennsylvania Press, 1999.

Nehamas, Alexander. *On Friendship*. New York: Basic Books, 2016.

Nelson, Shasta. *Frientimacy: How to Deepen Friendships for Lifelong Health and Happiness*. Berkeley, CA: Seal Press, 2016.

Perel, Esther. *Mating in Captivity: Unlocking Erotic Intelligence*. New York: HarperCollins e-books, 2009.

Pipher, Mary. *Reviving Ophelia: Saving the Selves of Adolescent Girls*. New York: Riverhead Books, 2005.

Plath, Sylvia. *The Bell Jar*. New York: Harper Perennial Modern Classics, 2013.

Poehler, Amy. *Yes Please*. New York: HarperCollins Publishers, 2014.

Rapkin, Mickey. *Pitch Perfect: The Quest for Collegiate A Cappella Glory*. New York: Avery, 2008.

Reardon, Joan. *As Always, Julia: The Letters of Julia Child and Avis DeVoto*. New York: Houghton Mifflin Harcourt, 2010.

Sales, Nancy Jo. *American Girls: Social Media and the Secret Lives of Teenagers*. New York: Knopf, 2016.

Simmons, Rachel. *Odd Girl Out: The Hidden Culture of Aggression in Girls*. San Diego, CA: Harcourt, 2002.

Selected Bibliography

Traister, Rebecca. *All the Single Ladies: Unmarried Women and the Rise of an Independent Nation*. New York: Simon & Schuster, 2016.

Weston, Kath. *Families We Choose: Lesbians, Gays, Kinship*. New York: Columbia University Press, 1997.

Wiseman, Rosalind. *Queen Bees and Wannabes: Helping Your Daughter Survive Cliques, Gossip, Boyfriends, and Other Realities of Adolescence*. New York: Three Rivers Press, 2002.

Yanagihara, Hanya. *A Little Life*. New York: Doubleday, 2015.

ACKNOWLEDGMENTS

I n what felt like an instant, Allison Hunter understood my vague thoughts about friendship, turned them into a book idea, *and* became my friend.

Maya Ziv's editing skill, energy, and enthusiasm floor me. She is a true friend, who was right to push me to make this story more personal, and the genius title is all hers.

My friend Andrea Woo is barely mentioned in the book and yet is on every page. She makes everything better.

Chris Strauss made sure I got to write this book and never stopped telling me it was important. I am very lucky to know him.

I don't know what I'd do without the women I'd call if I needed to hide a body: Erica Cerulo, Julia Chang, Stephanie Clifford, Amanda Dobbins, Valerie Johnson, Claire Mazur, Marisa Meltzer, Andrea Oliveri, Ellie Slack, Nicole Vecchiarelli, Carmel Melouney, and Kim Warner. This book is built on their awesomeness.

Thank you to Ruthie Baron for sitting for the interview.

My only regret about writing a book about how incredible it is to be best friends with her is that everyone who reads it will want to be best friends with her, too.

My male friends mean just as much to me. Thank you to Albert Chen, Nien Lam, Hoa Mai, and Yaran Noti for advising me on absolutely everything. Matthew Collins-Gibson keeps me strong in so many ways, and every sappy thing I have to say about lifelong friends goes for him, too.

I've seen Julien du Castel as exceptional since I met him two decades ago and continue to be inspired by him today. That he believes in me just as much is overwhelming.

Thank you to my brother, Jarrett Schaefer, who was the first person to tell me to write about what was important to me, and to my dad, Phil Schaefer, who let me read stacks of books at football games instead of watching what was happening on the field and is the hardest working unpaid publicist I know.

Finally, my mom, Judy Schaefer, has shown me how to find joy in anything. There's no one like her.

ABOUT THE AUTHOR

Kayleen Schaefer is a journalist and author of the best-selling Kindle Single memoir *Fade Out*. Her work has appeared in *The New York Times*, *Vogue*, *The New Yorker*, *Vanity Fair*, and many other publications. She currently lives in New York City, and *Text Me When You Get Home* is her first book.